UNHEARD
WORDS

UNHEARD WORDS

*Women and Literature
in Africa, the Arab World, Asia,
the Caribbean and Latin America*

Edited by
MINEKE SCHIPPER

Translated from the Dutch by
BARBARA POTTER FASTING

Allison & Busby
LONDON · NEW YORK

1985

This edition first published in Great Britain 1985 by
Allison & Busby Limited
6a Noel Street, London W1V 3RB
Distributed in the USA by
Schocken Books Inc.
62 Cooper Square, New York, NY 10003

Copyright © 1984 Het Wereldvenster/Unieboek, Weesp,
Netherlands
Original title: *Ongehoorde Woorden*
This translation copyright © Barbara Potter Fasting 1985

British Library Cataloguing in Publication Data

Unheard words: women and literature in Africa,
    the Arab world, Asia, the Caribbean and
    Latin America.
    1. Literature — Women authors — History
    and criticism
    I. Schipper, Mineke   II. Fasting, Barbara
    Potter   III. Ongehoorde, Woorden. *English*
    809'.89287   PN471

ISBN 0-85031-639-1

Set in Palatino by Ann Buchan (Typesetters) Ltd
Walton-on-Thames, Surrey

Printed and bound in Great Britain by
Richard Clay (The Chaucer Press) Ltd
Bungay, Suffolk

For the English translation of this book a grant was given by the Netherlands
Minister of Development Co-operation.

Contents

FOREWORD

A subject as broad as women and literature, and an approach which covers such a wide variety of areas, must be presented with due modesty. The range of this volume does not permit an in-depth study of the subject. The authors were fully aware of these limitations and were continually obliged to pare down their contributions in order to keep within the allotted number of pages. The book is intended as an introduction to a subject on which much more could be said. To my knowledge there are no English or French works which deal with the subject on an "intercontinental" scale, and it is rare to find publications on women and literature outside Europe which cover even one country, region or culture.

The essays themselves need no explanation, but I would like to include a word about the arrangement of the various pieces. In two cases (the Arab world and Asia) more than one author was asked to contribute to the study of an area. French-language North African literature has been included as a separate section, in addition to the literature of the Arab East and that of North Africa. The enormous continent of Asia has also been divided into two parts, i.e. Southern Asia and South-east Asia. In addition to the list of publications which follows each essay, a short list of titles has been included at the back of the book, for anyone requiring more information on a particular area or some special aspect of the subject. I would like to take this opportunity to thank all those who collaborated on this book; it was a pleasure to work with them.

Each chapter opens with a series of proverbs about women from that particular region. Through the years I have come to realize what an important part proverbs play in conversation all over Africa, particularly in rural areas, where they are widespread. We found that this is also the case in the other areas studied. Anthropologists believe that you can get to know people better by studying their proverbs, as they present in compact form a view of life as well as a way of thinking and reasoning and perceiving. The proverbs which appear here are representative of a great many different countries and were collected by a great many people, to whom I am truly grateful. Their names and the sources appear after the proverbs in each individual section.

In spite of the differences in geographical origin, there are a number of views on women which are common to all these proverbs. First, sons are more important than daughters. Second, women are easily replaced, but mothers are unique. A third lesson to be gained from these proverbs is that a man should know more than his wife and be better at everything than she is. The Sena of East Africa warn their menfolk: "Never marry a woman with bigger feet than your own." But what of our modern world, where so many women's feet are just starting to grow?

The interviews are all quite different and yet there are points of reference, and interrelated themes. They show us something of the practical potential as well as the problems of the woman writer trying to communicate with readers from her own or a different culture or both, men and women with differing norms and expectations. She could not possibly meet the needs of all these readers, even if she should wish to.

I am extremely grateful to the women writers who contributed to this book: Miriam Tlali, Etel Adnan, Nabaneeta Deb-Sen, Astrid Roemer and Cristina Peri Rossi. It is to them and to their sisters in Africa, the Arab world, Asia, the Caribbean and Latin America that this book is dedicated.

M.S.

INTRODUCTION

MINEKE SCHIPPER

Women and Development

Within every cultural context human conduct is determined by norms. Those who flout the rules risk the sanctions of the community to which they belong, where the ruling group dictates standard images and ideas concerning itself and others, in order to legitimize existing relationships.

Reports and statistics from such organizations as the United Nations and the International Labour Organization show that women, who make up half the world's population, account for almost two-thirds of the total working hours, while roughly one-hundredth of the world's wealth and property is in their hands (Bisilliat and Fiéloux 1983:7). Moreover, their freedom and potential are often limited not only by material problems but also by sets of rules which they must accept simply because they are women. Despite differences in culture, religion and social structure, women in Africa, Asia, the Caribbean and Latin America are faced with comparable difficulties. All are forced to grapple with a repressive system of rules. Besides their reproductive function, most women have in common that they are expected to perform domestic duties even when they also work outside the home. Statistically, housework does not count as "work". Another problem which women in the various areas share is their lack of economic, social and political power. This is due to the fact that in the context of existing values, women are assigned a separate place, outside the realm of power, on the basis of ideologies which have proved effective in the past:

> Women are the victims of a continual reversal of values; those concerned exclusively with women are seen as negative. Biologically pregnancy sets them apart, while ethically their uncleanness isolates them from the world. Metaphysically their very being is culpable and the major religions provide for their condemnation, in Christianity through original sin and in

9

Hinduism through reincarnation in the body of a woman, as
punishment for a sinful life. Through the ages women have been
subjected to constant and multifarious indoctrination. They have
had no choice but to accept those cultural models which to a large
extent determine their lives. (Bisilliat and Fiéloux 1983:92)

Women have always played a vital role in the struggles to
liberate their country. They were involved in the conflicts
which led to the independence of such countries as Algeria,
Zimbabwe and Mozambique, and the resistance to dictatorships in Chile, Uruguay and El Salvador. Women in
resistance movements have often had to work twice as hard to
overcome the prejudices of their male comrades and prove
they were the equal of men. Once independence is achieved,
however, men often prefer to return to "normal"; they take up
the old role patterns and the double standard again goes into
operation. This phenomenon will no doubt be familiar to
Western women who were part of the resistance movement
during the Second World War. It reveals a painful contrast
between principles of freedom and equality and the docile
acceptance of traditional female submission (cf. Davies 1983).

An important facet of the male-female discussion is
whether or not Western feminism ought to be rejected. A
variety of reasons for doing so have been put forward by,
among others, the Left in Latin America. The main arguments
are of an economic nature, the social aspects of the question
being either passed over or ignored completely. The Western
women's movement is seen as a huge, unwieldy North
American institution, an offshoot of "US imperialism". The
same is largely true in Africa and Asia where, under the motto
"first things first", emancipation is regularly passed off as a
low-priority item, born of Western influence. It is "not a
problem here". The question is, of course, for whom it is "not
a problem". Women everywhere are asking this question with
ever-increasing urgency.

There are naturally many different views on the kind of
liberation that women ought to be aiming for, depending on

their social and cultural background and educational opportunities. The Ghanaian writer Efua Sutherland told me that during a trip through the United States she heard of a project initiated by wealthy lesbians, who wanted to set up an institute in Accra for the benefit of lesbians in Ghana. Efua could not help wondering why they had not chosen to devote their efforts to more primary needs, such as good drinking water and cooking facilities, in a country where women have to walk miles a day for their water and firewood. This was just one more proof of the fact that Western aid is often patterned on Western needs, instead of being based on knowledge of the needs and requirements of the recipient countries themselves.

This view is shared by the Bolivian Domitila Barrios de Chungara. In her opening speech at the Mexico Conference on the United Nations Women's Decade, she said she saw both machismo and feminism as "imperialist weapons". This decade is now drawing to a close and on balance it has probably not achieved a great deal. Moreover, after ten years people may be tempted to think that "the problem" has received enough attention and that the parties concerned ought to be satisfied.

Perhaps the most important result is that on the international front women can no longer be ignored, provided they continue to remind the other sex of their presence. But that is not the only benefit to arise from the Women's Decade. In spite of the continuing North-South contrasts and conflicts, women in South and North have discovered each other. They have begun to recognize each other's problems and that recognition provides a basis for future solidarity. Truly no small victory.

Women and Literature

This mutual recognition cannot always take place on a personal level, and thus it is fortunate that there is such a thing as literature. This book is about women and literature in Third World countries. Most experts on the problems of developing countries continue to view culture, and more particularly literature, as luxury items. For the benefit of those who believe that culture is unimportant, I would like to quote Ernesto Cardenal of Nicaragua. In an interview with a Dutch weekly he maintained that hunger for culture is just as vital a human need as hunger for food:

> If we were to provide people with food and medicine only, we would be treating them like animals. Food is important, health is important, but both are meaningless if we cannot live as people, as human beings.

Culture is a necessity of life, and any development policy which is not rooted in the culture of a people will bear no fruit. From what has been said previously about the position of women throughout the world, it is clear that most of them never achieve real human life, at least not in the sense that Cardenal uses the term. Every day they must fight for (material) survival, and that struggle leaves very little time for social and cultural activities. The daily fight to survive is no less a fact of life for men, but in the words of Miriam Tlali (p. 60), ''Women have so much less time, because they have to run the house in addition to holding down a job. It is very rare for a black man to help with domestic chores.''

As long as this type of work is not shared, women will be unable to catch up, unable to make up for their lack of opportunity in the past. Because of these household tasks girls are often taken out of school, when the mother is ill or absent. They receive less schooling and the level of illiteracy among girls is considerably higher.

In this light it is not surprising that there are more men writing than women, notably in many developing countries. The essays and interviews in this volume make it abundantly clear that in addition to those problems of a material and political nature which are common to all, women writers are faced with a number of additional obstacles. The Indian writer Nabaneeta Deb-Sen, for instance, tells of the self-censorship which she exercises before submitting her work for publication. She is fearful of possible consequences if she should violate existing norms (cf. p. 163). Even more so than in the West, the woman writer in India runs the risk of being identified with the characters she portrays in her books. If her characters overstep the bounds, then the writer too has "gone too far". She may find that she is personally censured for the happenings described in her book, while her male counterpart who shocks his readers may easily find himself rewarded with a *succès de scandale* and a spot on the best-seller list.

Growing numbers of women writers have had the courage to defy existing rules and taboos and to build a life — and a literary career — of their own. The Lebanese Etel Adnan and the Surinamese Astrid Roemer, who were interviewed for this book, are two such women. But often the price is high, and only a woman who is strong-willed and independent will be able to resist the pressures of the world around her.

Within oral literature women have always played an important role as narrators. In some cultures, in certain areas of Africa for instance, older women are considered the best storytellers. In the Arab world and in Asia too, women play an important part in the oral tradition.

In some cultures poetry is considered a "feminine" genre, and there is a special kind of poetry which women are free to take up without fear of reprisals. This poetry is considered suitable for the "emotional outpourings of a sweet young thing", as Nabaneeta Deb-Sen put it (cf. p. 161). She added that writing essays, on the other hand is seen as typically male occupation, and that in India men are inclined to react with hostility to critical work by women essayists.

Cristina Peri Rossi says that the same thing is true in Latin America: the world is for men and emotions are for women. The word "poetess" has in itself an unfavourable connotation, in a context in which men poets and women poets are seen to belong to two quite different categories. At a dinner in honour of a powerful politician, for instance, a poetess demurely "recites" a few "verses", and her charm and beauty are at least as important as her poetry. Real poetry is written by men only, and "poetesses" have no part in it. (cf. p. 257f.).

Women who do not keep to their "own territory" find themselves in difficulty, and this is even more true for the other genres than for poetry. Essays with a political tenor by women writers are particularly likely to produce hostile reactions, no doubt because these women have broken an unwritten law and are therefore seen to constitute a threat. Politics is, after all, not a woman's domain!

Literary criticism is primarily in the hands of male critics. In Africa and the Caribbean there are few female critics and in Latin America it is only recently that women have gained entry to that exclusive club. And since the critics determine who is and who is not an "important author", the status of a writer depends largely on their assessment. Women authors are often disregarded by the male critics, which means that they are effectively excluded from "official literature". In Africa the work of women is still seldom if ever included in the well-known collections of critical essays. In Asia, we are told, they have to be exceptionally good and often must have an extensive literary career behind them before they are given the attention regularly accorded their male counterparts (cf. p. 160). In Latin America a woman writer gives the critics and her male colleagues a "bad conscience" when she defies existing role patterns and refuses to remain in her "natural place" (p. 261).

As a result of the ambivalent attitude of the critics, who would be only too happy to leave women writers to the feminist critics, African, Arab, Asian and Latin American women writers are much less well-known internationally than their male colleagues. Ana Sebastián, a critic from Argentina, quite rightly observes that the Latin American literary boom which began during the 1960s was largely the work of "energetic propaganda systems, journalists and critics. Women were conspicuous by their absence from that boom. We do not believe that this is because there was no literary production by women during those years, but rather that they

(. . .) were at times the victim of propagandist forgetfulness". And she ends her article in the Meulenhoff Latin America Newsletter (June 1984) as follows: "Much more must be done by women, by writers, by publishers and by the public". This is equally true of the other areas dealt with in this book.

Women, Literature and Literary Theory

In the West a controversy has developed as to whether there is any such thing as feminist literary theory. An extremely lucid article on the subject by Mieke Bal appeared in a Dutch journal in 1981. She does not believe in feminist methods and I agree with her. Scientific methods are, or ought to be, general, well-founded, systematic, relevant, accessible and verifiable. Such methods do, of course, lend themselves to research undertaken from a feminist approach which asks other questions and formulates and studies existing questions in new ways. During a lecture for the Utrecht Summer School of Critical Semiotics in June 1984, Mieke Bal presented an extended model which makes it possible to analyse the power balance concealed within a text, by which readers can easily be manipulated. It is obvious that in the process of communication between author and reader the text operates as a "message", a message which is at least in part ideologically determined. Texts report on events, in the broadest sense of the word. This reporting is not neutral, and it is important for the reader to recognize any ideological presuppositions that may underlie the text. There are three main questions which are fundamental to this approach: *Who is speaking?*, *Who is seeing?* and *Who is acting?* These three questions can be amended in two different ways.

First they can be put into the negative: who is *not* speaking? Who has *no* right to speak? Who does *not* see? Whose view is *not* expressed? Who does *not* act? Who has been deprived of the right to act? Who is powerless to act, to take the initiative; who is forced to submit to the acts of others?

A second elaboration of the original questions is focused on

15

the object of the three basic activities. What is the speaker saying? What kind of action is he taking? What does he consider worth including in his story? And again, what is not included? What kind of opinion is expressed and to what extent is it consistent with other opinions expressed? What are the characters doing? Are they acting alone or together? (cf. also Bal 1985.)

Questions like these make it possible to gain a better insight into the meaning of a text. They can help explain how power and other interests operate in language and literature. I have referred to this approach extensively here because I believe it is not only suited to the study of ideological aspects of the relationship between men and women. These same questions are also relevant to the analysis of literary texts (and of literary criticism) with a view to uncovering other relationships based on power. I am thinking here primarily of the intercultural and political North-South oppositions of interest as expressed in texts, and the effect which these can have on readers from various cultural backgrounds. And then there are the texts in which the male/female and the North/South oppositions both play a role. On the basis of the questions formulated above we can discover to what extent Indians, Africans and Asians speak, think and act in the works of colonial Western writers, and whether as characters they are reduced to passive objects or relegated to the background. It is likewise possible to discover whether — no doubt as a reaction — the reverse is the case in literary works by Latin Americans, Africans, Arabs, and Asians. It is possible to determine not only what roles female characters are assigned in the work of male authors in both colonial and postcolonial literature, but also what roles men play in the work of women writers.

A critical and above all self-critical attitude is indispensable in scientific research, not least for the unsuspecting Western literary researcher venturing into the field of inter-cultural studies. The legacy of Eurocentrism is still with us. I do not believe we should re-open the discussion on whether the "other" is indeed capable of studying "us", irrespective of whether the "other" is a man or someone from a different culture and whether "we" are women, or someone from this or another culture. This discussion centres on the question of whether other methods are needed in order to study the aforementioned texts. In my opinion the answer is no. This question has been repeatedly raised in feminist circles by radicals who totally reject the male perspective; in their view the insurmountable viricentrism in texts and criticism makes it impossible for the "other" to study "our" texts.

I would like to recommend frankness and a critical approach to subjectivity, which will be better guidelines for the researcher than the petty protectionist regulations laid down by members of one group to the exclusion of another. I believe that it is the result — the literary text, the critical or scientific work — that ought to be studied in detail.

The tools forged by literary theorists must of course be continually tested to see if they have retained their usefulness, and, if necessary, adjusted to new developments in the field. For their part, the theorists must be willing to acquaint themselves with the results which certain methods have produced in the course of the (intercultural) study of literature in various parts of the world. In such a climate Eurocentrism will wane and literary theory will at last be on the way to becoming universal. I hope that this book will play a modest role in stimulating further research into the literatures of Africa, the Arab world, Asia, the Caribbean and Latin America, and in particular the place reserved within those literatures for the writings of women.

REFERENCES

Bal, Mieke, 1985, *Femmes imaginaires. L'ancien testament au risque d'une narratologie*, Utrecht, HES/Montreal, HMH.
Bisilliat, Jeanne, and Michèle Fiéloux, 1983, *Femmes du Tiers Monde*, Paris, Le Sycomore.

Davies, Miranda (ed.), 1983, *Third World, Second Sex. Women's Struggles and National Liberation*, London, Zed Press.

Schipper, Mineke, 1984, "Eurocentrism and Criticism: Reflections on the Study of Literature in Past and Present", in: *World Literature Written in English*, vol. 24, no. 1, pp. 16-27.

Sebastián, Ana, 1984, "A Lack: Women's Literature in Latin America" (in Dutch), in: *Meulenhoff Latijns-Amerika Krant*, June, pp. 20-1.

I. AFRICA

(*Foto*: **Jan Stegeman**)

PROVERBS

1. Women have no mouth. (Beti, Cameroon)
2. The woman is a spring in which all calabashes break. (Cameroon)
3. Beat your wife regularly. If you do not know why, she will know why. (West Africa, possibly of Arab origin)
4. The intelligence of a woman is the intelligence of a child. (West Africa)
5. A woman is like a path: don't try to find out who has walked on it or who will walk on it. (Wolof, Senegal)
6. Love your wife, but do not trust her. (Wolof, Senegal)
7. A woman who has given birth to twins is not afraid of a big penis. (Baoulé, Ivory Coast)
8. A woman who has not been married twice cannot know perfect marriage. (Yoruba, Nigeria)
9. Not even God is ripe enough to catch a woman in love. (Yoruba, Nigeria)
10. Take a woman for what she is: a sister of the devil. (Yoruba, Benin)
11. No fetish so feared as a woman. (Yoruba, Benin)
12. Woman is the only being for whom a shrine should be made. (Yoruba, Benin)
13. If in times of drought a woman comes and tells you she has found a well, don't listen to her. (Watshi/Ewe, Benin/Togo)
14. To take one's own life for a woman is to give one's life for wind. (Fon, Benin)
15. Woman is the source of all evil. Only our soul will save us from the harm she does. (Fon, Benin)
16. Much patience is needed to bear the vicissitudes of life; more is needed to live with a woman. (Hausa, Nigeria)
17. Don't ridicule a thin mother-in-law. (Ewe, Togo)
18. Woman is like a shadow: if you go to hern she runs away; if you leave her, she'll follow you. (Luba, Zaïre)
19. Do not sleep on [trust] a woman who lightens her skin. (Lingala, Zaïre)
20. To eat with a woman is to eat with a witch. (Lingala, Zaïre)

PROVERBS

21. Woman is like the skin of the small antelope: only one person
    can sit on it. (Luba, Zaïre)
22. To have one wife is to be one-eyed. (Luba, Zaïre)
23. If you marry two, you'll die all the younger. (Luba, Zaïre)
24. Women sow discord. (Luba, Zaïre)
25. The pipe is right, the tobacco is wrong [pipe = man, tobacco =
    woman]. (Luba, Zaïre)
26. Married women are like elephant tusks: don't touch them.
    (Kenya)
27. No man is a hero in his wife's eyes. (Swahili, East Africa)
28. A child that does not cry dies on his mother's back [please say
    what you have to say]. (Zulu, South Africa)
29. Mother is God number two. (Chewa, Malawi)
30. Never marry a woman with bigger feet than your own. (Sena,
    Malawi/Mozambique)

ACKNOWLEDGEMENTS

Irène d'Almeida, Benin (3, 4 and 5); *Edris Maquard*, Senegal (6); *Biodun Jeyifo*, Nigeria (8 and 9); *Soulé M. A. Issiaka*, Benin (10-16); *Eliasabeth Mboyi*, Zaïre (18 and 19); *Clémentine Nzuji*, Zaïre (21-5); *M. Schoffeleers*, the Netherlands (29); numbers 2, 7 and 20 were heard and recorded by the editor; the remaining proverbs came from the following works:

J. F. Vincent, 1976, *Traditions et transitions: Entretiens avec des femmes beti du Sud-Cameroun*, Paris, ORSTOM, Berger/Levrault (1).

Jean Cauvin, 1981, *Comprendre les proverbes*, Issy-les-Moulineaux, Editions Saint-Paul (17).

Ruprecht Paqué (Hrsg.), 1976, *Auch schwarze Kühe geben weisse Milch*, Mainz, Matthias Grünewald-Verlag (26).

L. Kaligula and A.Y. Lodhi, 1980, *More Swahili Proverbs*, Uppsala, Scandinavian Institute of African Studies (27).

C. L. Sibsiso Nyembezi, 1963, *Zulu Proverbs*, Witwatersrand University Press (28).

Ruth Finnegan, 1970, *Oral Literature in Africa*, Oxford, at the Clarendon Press (30).

WOMEN AND LITERATURE IN AFRICA

MINEKE SCHIPPER

Illiteracy in Africa is four times as high among women as among men, and the higher the level of education, the lower the percentage of girls. Thus it is not surprising that most African literature is the work of male authors, and that the majority of literary critics are men.

Female anthropologists have sometimes tended to idealize the position of women in pre-colonial society, maintaining that men and women were equal before the coming of the Europeans, and that inequality was the result of capitalist exploitation by Westerners (e.g. Leacock 1979). African (oral) literature offers no confirmation of such wishful thinking — which does not mean that the reverse is true, and that the position of women in Africa is significantly better as a result of contact with the Western world. There is just as little evidence to support this view, at least in the written literature of Africa.

As for the oral tradition, it is often impossible to say whether a certain story or song was made up by a man or a woman. But after carefully examining recorded texts, one does begin to wonder to what extent a certain myth, story, proverb or song is intended to favour or prejudice certain interests within a society.

Africa's written literature began to develop during colonial times, and this has undoubtedly influenced the way in which men and women are depicted within that literature. This is true not only of African literature itself but also of works by European authors set in colonial Africa. Having seen that up until now most African literature and criticism has been the work of male authors, we naturally wonder if this fact has made a difference. Has this "male legacy" perceptibly influenced African literature? What difference has it made to the image of women which, like all ideas and concepts, is formed in part by literature?

In this article we will be taking a closer look at the following topics: *oral literature,* because of the prominent role it continues to play in Africa; *the colonial legacy; developments since the 1960s,* when so many African countries obtained their independence; *the first women writers* and finally, *literary criticism.*

Generally speaking, literary history is characterized not only by the continuation of existing literary traditions, but also by a reaction to those traditions. This is equally true of that portion of African literature which is the work of female authors. Their writings are influenced by a cultural and social heritage, even though they may resist that influence.

Oral Literature: Myths and Stories

The story of Genesis tells us in great detail how first man was created and then woman, how she was "taken from him" and is thus part of him. Numerous passages in the Bible have been seen as a confirmation of the superiority of man to woman.

Similar patriarchal culture patterns are to be found in Islam. The Koran says, for example: "Men are the managers of the affairs of women for that Allah has preferred in bounty one of them over the other" (Sura 4:34).

Myths are assumed to be true; the dogmas and pronouncements which they contain are not to be questioned within the community to which they belong. In fact, of course, myths have often been modified and manipulated by those in power to serve their own aims. Myths confirm and explain how man created order out of chaos, and how, by means of culture, he succeeded in imposing his will on nature. In mythology there are two main senses in which woman and nature have been associated, one positive and one negative. On the one hand she is the life-giving mother figure and on the other the terrifying dangerous witch who must be subjugated, or at least restricted by codes and norms.

A number of African myths explain how the existing hierarchy was created, and how it has been ever since — right from the beginning. In myths dealing with creation and origin woman has often been relegated to a secondary role. In those stories where man and woman are not created or placed on earth simultaneously, the woman rarely appears first. Once in a while she is created "by accident", as in the Saramo myth from Tanzania:

> Long ago there were no women. There were only two men who lived on honey. One of the men climbed into a tree. There was honey in the tree and he wanted to get it out with his axe. The sharp blade of the axe fell down and hit the other man who was lying on his back asleep. The axe fell onto his penis and cut it off. What was left was a bleeding wound, like women have.
> His companion climbed down and asked, "What is that?"
> "The axe cut it off," he replied. . . .
> Ever since that day women lose blood, just like that first woman.
> (Schipper 1980: 103)

Here woman is portrayed as a mutilated man. Among the Fang of Gabon man is created by God, but it is man who shapes woman from a piece of wood. According to another Fang myth, she was made out of one of man's toes.

Where the myths relate the story of original sin and the fall, or some other primeval fault through which the peace and tranquillity of paradise is destroyed, or man is driven out of Eden, the woman is often portrayed as the guilty party. Among the Tutsi of Rwanda, it is the woman who speaks out of turn, betraying the secret of Imana, the Supreme Being; her children are driven out of paradise and relegated to earth. In the Hungwe myth (Zimbabwe), Morongo persuades her husband to make love to her against the will of Maori. The Bambara of Mali believe that it was the first woman, Muso Koroni, who destroyed the peace and harmony of paradise. According to the Kulwe of Tanzania a woman is to blame for the hunger and evil in the world, and the fact that human beings must work for a living. She ignored God's command to grind only one grain of wheat which would then multiply. The Bini (Nigeria) believe that the sky receded from earth because of a greedy woman. In the beginning people never had to till the soil, because they were allowed to cut off a piece of the sky and eat it whenever they were hungry. But the sky had warned them not to cut off too much because then they would have to throw it away and he didn't want to end up on the rubbish heap. Everyone was very careful to observe this rule until one day a greedy woman went too far.

> She cut a huge piece of sky and ate as much as she could, but she couldn't finish it. She was frightened and called her husband, but he didn't want any more. She called all the villagers but they couldn't finish it either. In the end she had to throw what was left onto the rubbish heap.
>
> The sky became very angry indeed and rose up high above the earth, far beyond the reach of men. And from then on men have had to work for their living. (Beier 1966: 51)

The story does not tell us what the consequences of this offence were for the woman in question. In myths transgressions often call forth "punishments" which become permanent, such as menstruation, subordination, and the like. Sometimes man and woman commit the offence together, but even then the woman may be punished more severely. For instance in the Ashanti myth (Ghana) which tells how man and woman first came together, against the will of the creator, it is clear from the story that man sinned first. He took the initiative. And yet woman will suffer more than man:

> Here is the punishment for the men: when a man sees a woman whom his heart desires he will have to give her gold, clothes and many other fine things before he can possess her. And here is the punishment for the women: since you also disobeyed, when you see a man whom your heart desires you will have to keep it to yourself in your head! In addition, you will have to pound the fufu and do all the work, before eating it yourself.(. . .) You will be with child nine to ten months and you shall give birth in great pain. (Schipper 1980:101)

There are, however, exceptions to this anti-female rule. The Ekoi of Nigeria say that in the beginning the earth was

25

inhabited exclusively by women. One day Obassi Nsi (God) accidentally killed one of these sisters, and to atone for his offence he told the women they could choose whatever they wanted out of all his possessions. He described everything he owned, but the women refused his fruits and birds and animals. Finally there was only one thing left: man. And they readily agreed to take man

> . . . as compensation for the fellow woman whom they had lost. Thus men became the servants of women, and have to work for them to this day. For, though a woman comes under the influence of her husband upon marriage, yet she is his proprietor and has a right to ask any service, and to expect him to do whatever she chooses. (Ibid: 104)

The Ekoi believe that Obassi Nsi was originally a female god (the earth goddess?). According to the Ekoi man who related the story, "Obassi Nsi must be a woman and our mother, because everyone knows that mothers have the tenderest hearts" (ibid.: 184). Later Obassi Nsi did become a male god, though the myth is still told in its "pro-female" form.

The majority of the creation myths which I have studied, and which come from all parts of Africa, reveal a predominantly negative image of women. The question of who actually made up the myths must remain unanswered. It is clear in any case that women are very often seen as the cause of all the evil in the world. Another moot point is to what degree myths still form the basis of social relationships as they have gradually developed.

Proverbs play a major role in oral cultures. They are the "palm oil with which words are eaten" (Achebe 1958:10). A number of proverbs stress the positive aspects of womanhood, in particular as they refer to maternal functions. But there seem to be far more proverbs which paint a negative picture of womankind. She is seen as a (foolish) child, a witch, a dangerous natural force, a being that devours or castrates men, a temptress who is the undoing of man.

Similar views are to be found in fairy tales and stories of

Africa's oral tradition, as Denise Paulme showed in her book *La mère devorante* (1975). Painstaking research will be necessary before any more definite conclusions can be drawn. Not only the structure of the recorded texts will have to be carefully studied, but also the context and the audience for which they were (or are) intended. It will suffice here to say that both these concepts are to be found in many different kinds of stories: the woman as negative force is contrasted with woman as the gentle virgin or the virtuous maternal character. The positive view of woman is generally associated with her reproductive function; she is the loving and beloved mother who cares for her children and sacrifices herself for them. Both images are well represented in African oral literature. They have become proverbial, not only in the literal sense and not only in literature. . . .

The Colonial Legacy

According to Simone de Beauvoir and many others in the West who are fighting for the rights of (white?) women, there are parallels between the position of women and that of blacks. As she says in *Le deuxième sexe* (1949), both groups are struggling to free themselves from the grip of the white man. He tries to keep them in their place, i.e. the place which he has assigned to them. The white man is generous in his praise of the "good black" who, unconscious of his position, lives out his life in cheerful and childlike resignation. In similar terms he praises the woman who is "truly woman", and by definition childish, vain and irresponsible, the woman who acknowledges him as her master and willingly submits to him.

During an interview in 1974, I asked the Senegalese poet and ex-president Léopold Sédar Senghor to comment on the views expressed by Simone de Beauvoir. He was in complete agreement with her, for "women and blacks are so much more emotional than the insensitive white man who tyrannizes them". Senghor, however, is the exception that proves the rule. He has often been accused of assimilation, and of playing into the hands of the French, and there is no longer much support in Africa for his negritude theory of "Western reason and African emotion". Moreover in the African context it is much more relevant to ask what happens to the black woman who is caught in the crossfire: is she doubly oppressed, by the white man and by her black brother?

This kind of comparison has been made in certain Western feminist circles and sometimes still is, but in Africa it is totally irrelevant. When has a black man ever expressed genuine compassion for white women or affirmed his solidarity with them because they suffer the tragic fate of the oppressed? There is in any case no such analogy to be found in the writings of African male authors. On the contrary, in the eyes of Africans, during the colonial period at any rate, white women were privileged beings more to be envied than pitied, a fact which is stressed in many novels of the period. And this is not surprising, considering the favoured circumstances of the white woman in colonial days. In her domain she wielded the sceptre over one or more black servants. She lived in a fine house with a lovely garden, like Margery Thompson in Ngugi's *A Grain of Wheat* (1967):

> A neatly trimmed hedge of cider shrub surrounded the Thompsons' bungalow. At the entrance, green creepers coiled on a wood stand, massed into an arch at the top. (. . .) The hedge enclosed gardens of flowers: flame lilies, morning glory, sunflowers, bougainvillea. However, it was the gardens of roses that stood out in colour above the others. Mrs Margery Thompson had cultivated red roses, white roses, pink roses — roses of all shades. Now she emerged from this garden of colour and came to the door. She was dressed in thin white trousers and a blouse that seemed suspended from her pointed breasts. (. . .) She was bored by staying in the house alone. Normally she chatted with her houseboy or with her shamba-boy. At times she quarrelled with them and her raised voice could be heard from the road. (p. 34)

Against a colonial background a woman who would have

been of no consequence in Europe, keeping house and caring for her children herself, is often viewed in a strong racial light, as can still be seen in South Africa (see Cock 1980). Many African novels set in the colonial period illustrate this point. The white woman is often described in detail: her appearance, her pale skin, the colour of her hair and eyes, the way she does her hair, her clothes, her make-up, etc. Often her beauty is stressed and only rarely is she presented as ugly. The more unapproachable she is, the more she seems to be idealized and put on a pedestal. In *Une vie de boy* (1956) by the Cameroonian writer Ferdinand Oyono, the servant Toundi describes the beauty of his *Madame*, the wife of his boss, who is the colonial District Officer. She has just arrived from Europe and has not yet been infected with the colonial mentality (which, however, she is quick to adopt). So it is that upon arrival she accidentally shakes hands with him. In his diary Toundi wrote about her:

> She has arrived at last. How pretty she is, how nice! (. . .) She offered me her hand. It was soft, tiny and limp in my big hand that swallowed it up like a precious jewel. Madame went quite red. (. . .)
>
> My happiness has neither day nor night. (. . .) I have held the hand of my queen. I felt that I was really alive. (. . .) My hand belongs to my queen whose hair is the colour of ebony, with eyes that are like the antelope's, whose skin is pink and white as ivory. A shudder ran through my body at the touch of her tiny moist hand, that trembled like a flower dancing in the breeze. (. . .) Her smile is refreshing as a spring of water. Her look is as warm as a ray from the setting sun. It bathes you in a light that warms the depth of the heart. I am afraid . . . afraid of myself. (English translation 1966:55f)

And pretty, well-dressed white women abound in novels set in the colonial period. According to Eldridge Cleaver in *Soul on Ice* (1968), the white woman has come to symbolize freedom for the oppressed black man. And so he dreams of her and places her on a pedestal. Her desirability is due largely to the fact that she is not submissive, as the black woman is or, indeed, as he himself is. One of Cleaver's characters is the old man Lazarus. While in prison — symbol of the oppressed black — he dreams about white women. To Lazarus every white woman is beautiful, even if she's bald and toothless:

> She is like a goddess, a symbol. My love for her is religious and beyond fulfilment. I worship her. (. . .) In my dreams I see white women jumping over a fence like dainty little lambs. And every time one of them jumps over, her hair just catches the breeze and plays out behind her like a mane on a Palomino stallion: blondes, redheads, brunettes, strawberry blondes, dirty blondes, drugstore blondes, platinum blondes — all of them. They are the things in my nightmares. (p. 108)

In *Peau noire, masques blancs* (1952), Frantz Fanon observed that an oppressed black man will often try to "liberate" himself by choosing a woman with lighter skin than his own. Through her love he hopes to become less black, and therefore more free. According to Fanon this freedom can best be achieved through the "fairest" of white women, the blonde with blue eyes. He pointed out that this preference is the result of white criteria imposed upon blacks not only by colonialism but also by Western advertising, magazines and, above all, films.

In spite of her beauty, the white woman in African novels is generally portrayed as a moody and discontented creature. She rarely has a status of her own, has no profession and is dependent on the position of her husband. In a word, she is only "somebody's wife".

She seems to be concerned above all with her outward appearance, her face, her figure, her clothes, her jewelry. Within the small colonial community the women all vie with one other, each eager to be thought the most beautiful. Another popular diversion among white women is finding fault with Africa and the Africans, something at which they are no less proficient than their male counterparts. This appears to be an inexhaustible subject among colonial whites. And there is much to complain about in the damnable country, with its heat and its downpours (that flood the tennis courts), where you can't find a decent hairdresser and you perspire from morning to night. You're surrounded by lazy blacks who lie and steal and stink. "In the morning when I'm met on the veranda by the smell of liquor and filth, then I know the boy is on his way in", says one matron triumphantly in Oyono's *Une vie de boy* (p. 78). Toundi's *Madame* in the same novel is one of those colonial women who starts an affair with another man out of boredom. When it doesn't work out, such characters take out their displeasure on their servants. They have no imagination and no outside interests, which makes them capricious and unpredictable. In fact they fit quite closely the description which Simone de Beauvoir gave of the "truly feminine woman" in *Le deuxième sexe*, the fatuous, frivolous little creature we referred to earlier.

Many novels confirm the negative impression the Western women obviously made in Africa during the colonial period. It was often made worse by the racism and prejudice which these women fostered in themselves and others, in a society which offered fertile grounds for these feelings.

One is struck by the fact that Western women are seldom if ever cast in the role of devoted and loving mothers. They are usually unhappily married due to the unfaithfulness of one or both partners. Relationships between white women and black men, however, are all but unheard of during the colonial era. When they do appear they are often set in a European context. Even then they give rise to considerable difficulties due to the disapproval of outsiders (see Ousmane Socé's *Mirages de Paris*, 1937). The most striking aspect of these affairs is that they invariably end in tragedy, through the death or suicide of one of the partners. It is almost as if the authors are trying to tell us that a society dominated by the white male will not allow anything or anyone to escape his authority.

In colonial times there were practically no African women

31

writers and the literary image reflected above is provided by male writers. How do they see their own sisters? In their novels African girls tend to view white women as dangerous rivals. They are well aware that these women appeal to their men, and that an African who has been to Europe will try to impress his friends with stories of his affairs with white women. Small wonder then that African girls do their best to imitate this ideal and that some try to find a white lover themselves. Turning their backs on tradition, they start wearing close-fitting clothes, even trousers, to show off their figures — shameful practices in the eyes of the older generation. Black girls straighten their hair, wear lipstick and do their best to speak the European language instead of their native tongue. In short, they try to live up to the expectations of the "modern" man, black or white.

The older generation is increasingly troubled by this development, wondering where it will all end: everyone knows that white women are the embodiment of immorality. Traditions and morals can no longer be upheld when girls start identifying with that kind of role pattern. Literature does indeed provide a stereotype image of the "modern" woman, and authors with traditional views are critical of the changing times, not least where women are concerned. The African woman who adopts "Western" dress and asserts her independence proves the undoing of the male character and of society itself. She is the antithesis of the conventional mother, virtuous and devoted. We see here the two extremes of good and evil from oral literature, to which has been added the opposition modern-traditional. Modern motherhood would seem a *contradictio in terminis*.

Cyprian Ekwensi's *Jagua Nana* (1961) illustrates this point. In Lagos Jagua wears seductive clothes, a low-cut transparent blouse "through which her pink brassière could be seen — provocatively — and much more besides" (p. 7). Dressed in a "sheath dress, with painted lips and glossy hair", she goes to the Tropicana Club with her boy friend Freddy. This is how the women there are described:

> All the women wore dresses which were definitely undersize, so that buttocks and breasts jutted grotesquely above the general contours of the bodies. At the same time the midriffs shrunk to suffocation. A dress succeeded if it made men's eyes ogle hungrily in this modern super sex-market. (p. 13)

Everything ends well for Jagua. She returns to her village and becomes a loving mother, so that virtue and tradition triumph over the evils and dangers of modern life.

One of the most famous examples of this opposition is Okot p'Bitek's *Song of Lawino* (1966). The poetry of the late Ugandan writer was inspired by the Acoli verse form. His book was warmly received in East Africa and elsewhere and became one of the best-selling volumes of English-language poetry. It is a dramatic monologue in the form of a long lament, which contrasts two scales of values. The presentation is such that the traditional view, personified by Lawino, wins the reader's sympathy, and not the modern values represented by her husband Ocol and her rival Clementine. Clementine is modern, she uses make-up, lightens her skin and tries to lose weight like a white woman. She impresses Ocol, who has had a Western upbringing and loves city life. When Ocol repudiates Lawino, she pours forth her lament in the presence of her tribe. She idealizes the past and recalls how Ocol has gradually changed. She defends the old African values and denounces the Western influences which have led to the deterioration of society.

The song is full of nostalgic overtones. Okot p'Bitek idealizes African traditions in the East Africa of the sixties, just as the West African negritude poets did in the late thirties.

Clementine wants to look like a Western woman and she indiscriminately copies everything that is considered part of that image. She thinks this will make her more attractive and more interesting, but from a traditional point of view the opposite is true. Modern is equated with shameless. The

Clementines dance like white people dance, close together; they kiss men in public, which shocks Lawino:

> I am completely ignorant
> Of the dances of foreigners
> And I do not like it.
> Holding each other
> Tightly, tightly,
> In public,
> I cannot.
> I am ashamed.
> Dancing without a song
> Dancing silently like wizards.
> Without respect, drunk. . .
>
> If someone tries
> To force me to dance this dance
> I feel like hanging myself
> Feet first! (p. 41)

In the period shortly before and after independence this idealized, nostalgic view of the past was a means of emphasizing the dignity of the African, in the face of the powerful colonial influence which threatened African culture. And yet in the sixties, which ushered in the independence of Africa, that romantic nostalgia for the pre-colonial past displayed by many writers was not very conducive to women's emancipation especially if they get no other choice than the one between being a Lawino or a Clementine.

Developments Since the 1960s

In her book *Emancipation féminine et roman africain* (1980), Arlette Chemain-Degrange analysed the image of African women presented in Francophone African novels. After studying the novels published by male authors up to 1976 — there were as yet none by women writers — she concluded that these authors often take it for granted that women defer to men and to tradition. They maintain that women traditionally had their own place in pre-colonial society. But the same is true of men, and very few of them would today choose to return to the past. As the African proverb says, "the river never returns to its source."

In these novels women are often punished for showing their independence. The possibility that some good, some positive, liberating influence might come of the break with the past is not even considered. The "modern" woman who shows signs of becoming emancipated is often accused of losing her African identity, a charge which is difficult to refute. It is, however, commonly used by literary critics in their discussion of women authors, as we will see shortly.

And yet Arlette Chemain also observes that some male writers she has studied do have quite emancipated views. The Senegalese writer Sembène Ousmane (1960, 1964) is one of them. He is a relentless critic of the inequality of black women and, above all, their resignation to their fate. He pointed out how vital women are to the development of society and to political agitation, as illustrated by the rail strike in *Les bouts de bois de Dieu* (1960). Other novelists worthy of mention in this respect are Henri Lopès (1976) of Congo-Brazzaville and Ahmadou Kourouma (1968) of the Ivory Coast.

The Cameroonian playwright Guillaume Oyono-Mbia is another example. In his own country he has quite a following among young girls, who call him the "champion of the emancipation of African women". His reputation is based on plays like *Trois prétendants, un mari* (1964), in which he pokes fun at the excesses to which the dowry system has led. A daughter is sold off to the highest bidder by her family, and she has no say in the matter whatsoever. He is today one of the most successful playwrights in Africa.

In *The Married Bachelor* (1973) Francis Imbuga also contrasts conservatism and emancipation, in the person of his main characters Denis and Mary. At one point Mary, who occasionally attends women's liberation meetings, tells Denis that she has a child by another man. He promptly throws her out. But he too has a son, and when Mary maintains that that puts them in exactly the same situation, he protests vigorously:

> *Denis:* You are a woman, I am a man. You have once been pregnant. I have not. Do you still believe us to be similar?
>
> *Mary:* But the basic facts are the same.
>
> *Denis:* Basic facts? What do you know about basic facts? The trouble with women is that you listen to the preaching of some Western intellectual, talking about the equality of men and women and you imagine he is right. What you fail to realize is that woman is dangerously handicapped. This calls for more restriction of her physical desires. Women must exercise greater control over themselves if they are to retain their dignity in society. Right now yours, if you had any, has vanished into thin air.
>
> *Mary:* Please, Denis, be kind. You are hurting me. Please.
>
> *Denis:* I am not hurting you. You hurt yourself the moment you allowed a man to share a blanket with you, give you a child and get away with it. (pp. 53f.)

It is indeed not easy for a woman to actually obtain her rights, for most young men will opt for tradition (and discrimination) when it is to their advantage. And when women protest, they are accused of being unduly influenced by the Western women's movements. As if African women aren't capable of deciding for themselves that equality is preferable to a system of rules which appear to be binding on only one of the parties concerned. Many men still claim the same authority that their fathers once wielded in the home, that paternal authority which has been transmitted from generation to generation through the norms and myths of the past. Young men want to marry virgins, but their own conduct is judged by other standards. Women are expected to observe lifelong fidelity but have no right to expect the same of their husbands in return.

In many ways the modern sector of African society is a reflection of Western society. Views on typically "feminine" and typically "masculine" professions that originated in the West are often adopted by African countries. The first women to enter skilled professions were teachers and nurses, and in government and the business world women are not generally considered suited for any position except that of typist, secretary or telephone operator. As we have seen, girls also have much less chance of getting an education, and their schooling is concentrated more on domestic and service sectors than on technical subjects. The fact that the greater part of African literature is the work of male writers is closely bound up with developments in society as a whole.

Reading through the letters to the editor in African newspapers, one is struck by the disapproval heaped upon women who attempt to change their lives and to escape from the oppressive code of conduct dictated by society. This is confirmed by studies on the role of women in a changing society (Obbo 1981; Thadani 1979).

In an interesting article on contemporary theatre the Zaïrean author Ngandu Nkashama (1982) describes the themes which dominate urban theatre in his country. He associates the present crisis in society with the negative attitude towards women who aspire to a greater measure of freedom. In his view the sad state of society as a whole is reflected in the theatre, where women characters are (once again) seen as the source of all today's misery. They are cunning, double-tongued and dabble in all manner of evil. They are pitifully narrow-minded, have an inordinate love of luxury and are inclined to back-biting and iniquity of all kinds. Ngandu notes in his essay that the tendency to blame women for all the ills of society is closely connected with the disintegration of the family. Against the often violent background of the new cities, these plays imply that women are to blame for the death and loneliness of the cities. They are the symbol of death in the form of abortion and infanticide; they have rejected traditional values and the voice of their ancestors; they paint their faces, masking them with makeup and making themselves unrecognizable. This is the ultimate negation of their identity.

According to Ngandu, feminism is associated with ancient images of women gravediggers, societies of witches who eat their own children. "In the professional theatre of the eighties one finds such negative female characters as the 'barren woman' who is subjected to horrible torture, the 'fallen woman' and the 'incestuous girl' " (p. 67f). Thus, women characters are blamed for all that goes amiss in society: the destruction of cultural identity, the social and economic callousness, the disintegration of family life in the cities, where human relationships are lost or sacrificed.

Ngandu believes that men put the blame on women partly because they feel lost in a society which has humiliated them and written them off. He does not see this as anti-feminism, but rather as the projection of an immense social drama on to the image of women. They are burdened with the anger of a society which cannot accept its own situation (ibid.).

One may still ask why it is that the woman must be made sole scapegoat for all that has gone wrong. Is it because her position has always been vulnerable, making her even more "victimized" than man? Or is it because the male perspective prevents him from blaming man for what went wrong — even partly? In actual fact women have very little influence in the cities and play only a "marginal role in the modern sector" (Thadani 1976:81). Moreover there is not a single woman writer among the playwrights whom Ngandu discusses in his book. One wonders whether there *are* any female playwrights in Zaïre, which in itself gives pause for thought.

In African written literature as a whole women clearly do not yet have an equal voice. Not only are there very few women playwrights and poets, but novels too are largely the domain of men. This has resulted in a fairly one-sided view, especially in the city novels, in which non-traditional women are commonly seen as a source of perdition and of menace to society.

In her study of the image of women in the Kenyan novel, Eleanor Wachtel comes to the conclusion that "modern" women are regularly associated with the dangers of city life, such as alcohol, violence, seduction and prostitution. They are depicted as contemptible parasites, and contrasted with the ideal of the traditional mother image. From there it is only one step to the stereotype antipoles of the mother and the whore. In Wachtel's view this device is common in contemporary Kenyan novels because they are written largely by men. This is true, she added, not only of Kenya, but of almost every Third World country:

> Their central characters are preponderantly males. Further, the male viewpoint is underlined not only by the many characterizations of young men, but by the literary device of the first person protagonist. (. . .) This is quite natural to the relatively inexperienced author who would tend to be somewhat autobiographical anyway. At the same time, however, it is also more intimate, personal, and hence more explicitly male in outlook and tone.(. . .) This device creates a rapport between author and reader and enlists the latter's sympathy. It does not allow for another point of view.(. . .) Women are necessarily "the other". (Wachtel 1977:42)

Wachtel believes that the male perspective of writers accurately reflects the actual state of society in a country like Kenya. In literature, as in society, men are the primary decision-makers.

Obviously the best way to counter a one-sided view is to provide a new and different image, seen from a different perspective. There are male writers, some of whom we have already mentioned, who have contributed to this new perspective. But it is above all the women who must take up their pens and give expression to their ideas and experiences in a new African literature. Their "reality" is necessary to complete (and where necessary correct) the present male-dominated perspective. This was one of the conclusions reached by a number of African women writers themselves during a conference on women and literature in Africa, held in Mainz in 1982.

Women Writers — Mother Africa on a Pedestal?

Women narrators and poets — in West Africa they are known as *griotes* — have played an important role in the oral literature of Africa. Writers sometimes take pains to mention in interviews, or in the foreword to a book, that they owe much of their talent and inspiration to their mothers, who used to tell stories or sing songs for them when they were young. This is certainly true of the Senegalese writer Birago Diop, whose stories of Amadou Koumba (1947) have long been extremely popular.

Women writers have been slow to come forward and even now they are relatively few in number. And yet there are too many to study here in detail. So instead of giving an exhaustive but unilluminating list of authors who are almost unknown internationally, I shall discuss briefly the work of just a few of these writers. Anyone who requires additional information may consult the list of references and further reading.

Very few women have published their poetry in book form, and those who have are still more or less unknown. There is Annette Mbaye d'Erneville of Senegal and on the other side of the continent Micere Githae Mugo of Kenya. Her small volume *Daughter of my People, Sing* (1976) is a collection of unpretentious, simply-structured poems which hark back to the oral tradition. The commercial edition of her dissertation *Visions of Africa* (1978) is much more widely known, as is *The Trial of Dedan Kimathi* (1976), the play which she co-authored with her colleague and fellow Kenyan Ngugi wa Thiong'o. Clémentine Nzuji of Zaïre has published quite a few small volumes, but her extremely personal poetry has limited appeal and its popularity is confined to a comparatively small group of admirers within Zaïre itself. Through the African National Congress, the liberation movement of South Africa, a volume of militant poetry by women members has been published under the title *Malibongwe, ANC Women: Poetry is Also Their Weapon* (edited by Sono Molefe). The poems are about suffering, resistance and the yearning of black people for freedom. Solidarity among comrades — male and female — plays an important part in the poems, for "the liberation of men, women and children, victims of the apartheid regime, is at stake". It goes without saying that that struggle must take precedence, though this does not mean that equality between men and women is already a fact.

In the case of drama, too, I would like to limit the discussion to a few prominent writers. In addition to Ama Ata Aidoo (Ghana) and Rebecca Njau (Kenya), whose plays will come under discussion, I would like to mention Werewere Liking (1979, 1980) of Cameroon. Liking, whose work can be described as combative, published a *chant-roman* (song-novel) called *Elle sera de jaspe et de corail* (1983) and somewhat provocatively subtitled "diary of a manhater". During an interview with *Jeune Afrique* (22 June), Liking said she found men "disappointing rather than convincing", but maintained that this is only possible because women are satisfied to be "mediocre". She found it "sad that relations between the sexes seem to be limited to sex". In addition to poetry, this outspoken writer previously published a number of plays in which she made use of the wealth of theatrical tradition to be found in African culture. The actors as well as the spectators are confronted with the mythical themes upon which her plays are based. Liking herself defines her work as "ritual theatre", in which each individual is prompted to go to the core of his own existence, in order to search out in his own soul the cause of all that has gone wrong in the community to which he belongs. Liking has drawn much of her inspiration from the study of her own people, the Bassa of Cameroon. The male-female confrontation is given little or no emphasis in her plays.

The African women writers who are best known in their own country and abroad are novelists and short story writers. The first African woman writer to gain international recognition was Flora Nwapa. Her first novel, *Efuru* (1966), was unique in that it provided a female view of the world of Eastern Nigeria, which a number of male writers, notably Chinua Achebe, had previously described in their novels. Efuru, the heroine of the book, is rich and beautiful, but not happy. Her first child dies, her husband leaves her and later she leaves her second husband. Efuru is intelligent, independent and capable of managing her own life. But childlessness is a disgrace, a "curse and a failure". A daughter-in-law without children is worthless. "She may be beautiful, but we cannot eat beauty. She may be rich, but we cannot send money on an errand" (p. 205). Efuru remains childless because, as we are told, she has been singled out by the water goddess to be her companion. This causes gossip and her narrow-minded and superstitious neighbours do not come off well in the book. Flora Nwapa's second novel *Idu* (1970) is about a woman's struggle to retain some measure of independence. Again the heroine finds herself in an uncommon situation, but this time she takes her fate into her own hands, instead of leaving everything to a goddess or "the others". Defying tradition, Idu refuses to marry her dead husband's brother, preferring to join her husband in the hereafter. Nwapa's volume of stories *This is Lagos* (1971) deals with a number of themes, and again there is a prominent role for the woman victimized by convention or by the rapidly changing, crowded and chaotic world of the Nigerian capital.

The Ghanaian Ama Ata Aidoo has written not only stories but a number of plays as well. One of them, *Anowa* (1970), is based on a familiar story from the oral tradition. A wilful young beauty refuses all the marriage partners proposed by her parents because she wants a man of her own choice. Later it becomes clear that she is married to a devil. The moral of the story is of course that a woman must conform to the rules, otherwise she will come to a bad end.

Ama Ata Aidoo chose to situate the old familiar tale in a nineteenth-century context. Against her parents' will Anowa marries a trader in hides who has become rich by exploiting his slaves. Anowa's mother represents the conventional feminine code of conduct and her ideals contrast sharply with those of her headstrong daughter:

> I want my child
> To be a human woman
> Marry a man
> Tend a farm
> And be happy to see her
> Peppers and onions grow.
> A woman like her
> Should bear children
> Many children,
> So she can afford to have
> One or two die.
> Should she not take
> Her place at meetings
> Among the men and women of the clan
> And sit on my chair when
> I am gone? (p. 12)

Anowa proves to be just as stubborn a wife as she was a daughter. She is against the principle of slave labour and in the end she is proved right. It is against the will of the gods, and they punish her and her husband with childlessness. Anowa is unhappy because her status prevents her from working. The play ends in a double suicide: Anowa drowns herself and her husband Kofi shoots himself. Aidoo's themes broach relevant social questions, the language is impressive and the role of Anowa is completely credible.

Aidoo's short stories too are dramatically sound, due in part to the extensive use of dialogue, and several of them have been successfully adapted as radio plays. In her sole novel, *Our Sister Killjoy* (1977), she relates her experiences in Europe, as so many Africans have done of late. "Been-tos" is the name given to people who have been to the metropolis. As a been-to she observes the strange ways of the Westerners and their reactions to Africans. The heroine Sissy records her impressions of life as a grant student in Germany and she is not sparing in her criticism of that curious culture. European readers will find the views of the African been-tos on Western society most enlightening. There are many ways of looking at that society, most of them quite different from the Westerner's own perspective. In a letter to her brother, Sissy describes her experiences in Europe:

> I have been to a cold strange land where dogs and cats eat better than many many children;
> Where men would sit at table and eat with animals, and yet would rather die than shake the hands of other men.
> Where women who say they have no time to bear children and spoil their lives would sit for many hours and feed baby dogs delicate food with spoons, and make coats to cover the hairy animals from the same cloth they wear, as sisters and brothers and friends in our village would do on festive occasions. My brother, I have been to a land where they treat animals like human beings and some human beings like animals. (p. 99)

The Nigerian Buchi Emecheta is also a been-to. She has lived in England for many years, since the 1960s, although she has been back to Nigeria on several occasions. She has written a number of novels about the vicissitudes of her life, first as a married woman, later on her own, but always with several children whom she ultimately raised singlehandedly. When she first came to London she was a housewife, but later she found a job, went to university and began writing. Her husband destroyed her first manuscript because he could not bear the idea that his wife was thinking and acting for herself and concerning herself with matters that were foreign to him. She describes their relationship in her autobiographical novel *Second-Class Citizen* (1974), and in an interview commented on the character of Francis:

> Much of what the husband Francis does in this book is not condoned, but rather made understandable by a knowledge of his background. Women have asked me why I didn't portray this character even more scathingly, but I understand why he reacted

the way he did. He had been spoiled by his mother in Nigeria, and he was helpless in the hard-boiled atmosphere of English society, where he was without the support of his family (Emecheta 1983).

Buchi Emecheta has several novels and children's books to her name. In what is perhaps her best-known novel, *The Joys of Motherhood* (1979), which has been translated into many languages, the main character is Nnu Ego, the daughter of an Ibo chief in the first half of this century. Her story begins in a village in Iboland, where the life of the people is predetermined by the rules which govern their society. A woman's position depends first on her father and later her husband. Nnu Ego's first marriage fails because she is childless. Her husband's reaction is: "I am a busy man. I have no time to waste my precious male seed on a woman who is infertile" (p. 32). Later she is married off to a second husband, Nnaife; she despises him but has no say in the matter. It is only after she becomes pregnant that Nnu Ego manages to resign herself to her fate. She lives in the slums of Lagos, where she raises a great many children under difficult conditions, in a spirit of loving sacrifice. In the course of the book the title acquires ironic overtones, though the author recounts with considerable humour the experiences of an African woman in her relationships with men, with children and with other women.

Emecheta believes that the image of African women which commonly emerges in novels by male authors is to some extent a distorted image. In their eyes, the only good woman is the woman who slaves for her children, no matter what the cost. She must ask nothing for herself. Nnu Ego in *The Joys of Motherhood* is that kind of mother. But when a woman fails to fit this stereotype, when she takes an independent and critical stand, people conclude she must be a prostitute. Emecheta said in the same interview in 1983: "Take a writer like Cyprian Ekwensi, for example. He has brilliant daughters, so why should he portray the women in his novels the way he does? Without generalizing, I do think there is a tendency to consider a woman who works outside the home, and is thus not a mother in the traditional sense, as a threat to her husband. The image of men in novels is much more varied and often more positive. Of course writers like Sembène Ousmane (Senegal) and Ngugi wa Thiongo (Kenya) are exceptions to the rule."

In 1980 Buchi Emecheta returned to Nigeria after an absence of many years. Her sojourn as guest lecturer at the University of Calabar in 1981 provided the inspiration for her novel *Double Yoke* (1982). The title refers to the impossible double burden which African women must bear in a modern, rapidly changing society. They must meet the demands of tradition as well as those of contemporary society. The author put both lines of thought, male and female, as she discusses such topics as the myth of virginity, the idealization of the traditional mother role, etc. In doing so she obviously flew in the face of tradition, for this was the first time the women's standpoint had been presented with such a degree of frankness. The generally accepted views always favoured men. A woman who was not a virgin when she married was called a whore. Men were free to have illegitimate children, but it was a disgrace for a woman to have a child out of wedlock. Emecheta's novels are extremely popular in Nigeria and elsewhere, but they have sometimes been coolly received or even been ignored by African critics.

The writers mentioned above are all from English-speaking West Africa, but a number of women writers are beginning to make themselves heard in East Africa as well. There, too, innumerable prejudices must be overcome, especially as not all women writers concern themselves with these problems. A writer like Grace Ogot (Kenya), for example, may seem more inclined to conform to certain norms than to condemn them, and she is sometimes harshly criticized by more progressive colleagues, who regret that one of the few women writers does not use her talent in a better cause (Condé 1972).

The same can certainly not be said of someone like Rebecca Njau, who writes in both Swahili and English. Her novel

Ripples in the Pool (1975) was well received inside and outside of Kenya. The book gives a balanced view of a number of contrasting ideas in which good, evil, the occult and other forces run counter to the often artificial lines of demarcation between tradition and Westernization, village and city, male and female. Njau's plays are a plea for more individual freedom. *The Scar* (1960) centres on the subordinate position of women in a rural Kikuyu society. The central character is Mariana, a prominent local figure with "revolutionary" ideas. She tries to persuade the other women to give up such senseless practices as the "circumcision" of girls, and to reject the fear and superstitions which are designed to keep them in their place. Not surprisingly, the older women are suspicious of her, but Mariana does have some success in awakening the women and girls of the village to the new opportunities awaiting them. In the end, however, she has to leave town when it becomes known that she was raped at the age of sixteen and gave birth to a child.

There are still very few women writers in Southern Africa. The two best known, Bessie Head and Miriam Tlali, come from South Africa. Both women have suffered under apartheid, Bessie Head because she was born of an "illicit" union between a white mother and a black father. She went into voluntary exile, and has lived and worked in Botswana for many years. In her novel *When Rain Clouds Gather* (1968) the central character, Makhaya, leaves South Africa where he was in the resistance and goes to Botswana. His is a new notion of the relationship between men and women. Working with the women of the village on an agricultural project, he sees how ill at ease they are, unaccustomed to being addressed and treated as equals. In her own characteristic style Bessie Head develops the relationships between those in and out of power, and tells what it is like to be a woman in a patriarchal African culture. She also draws a parallel between sexual and racial discrimination. There are similarities between the inflated male ego and the ego of a Nazi or a white colonial. She

47

recognizes that the need of basically insecure people to feel superior makes victims of women, Jews and "Bushmen" (as the San in Southern Africa are disparagingly called).

Bessie Head's novels have gradually gained in depth, as shown in particular by her 1974 novel *A Question of Power* (cf. Nancy Topping-Bazin 1984). All her writings contain auto-biographical elements, but she does not allow them to play too prominent a role. This is perhaps the secret of the appeal which her works appear to have for readers from different cultural backgrounds.

The second well-known South African writer is Miriam Tlali. While on a visit to the Netherlands her colleague Mothobi Mutloatse (1978) described the situation in South Africa, which made it impossible for black writers like himself to write anything but short stories. The tension and political unrest do not allow writers the extended periods of repose which are needed to set up and work out a novel. For this reason he was amazed to discover that "an important novel" had been written, and "by an ordinary housewife at that!" Miriam Tlali's work is rooted in "the situation". She is outspoken in her criticism of the authorities and "the system" and her books are banned in South Africa.

In Francophone Africa Senegal leads the way, with several writers who have attained some measure of international acclaim, among them Aminata Sow Fall and Mariama Bâ. In addition, I would also like to mention the as yet unknown Ken Bugul, for her striking first novel *Le baobab fou* (1982). For one of her book, *La grève des Bàttu* (1979), Aminata Sow Fall chose the theme of the beggars previously used by Sembène Ousmane in *Xala*. Unlike Aminata Sow Fall, Mariama Bâ's work focuses primarily on the experiences of women. She attained recognition when she was awarded the Noma prize at the 1980 Frankfurt Book Fair for her novel *Une si longue lettre* (1979).

This novel is written in the form of letters, which gives it a very personal impact. The letter-writer speaks directly to her correspondent and in the course of the book a clear picture emerges of both women. After the death of her husband Modou, Ramatoulaye, mother of a large family, writes a long letter to Aïssatou, an old school friend. She confides to Aïssatou her feelings at the time of her husband's death, his funeral and the subsequent period of mourning. She recalls the time she and Aïssatou spent together at school, when they were young and expected great things of life. For Ramatoulaye the blow came after twenty-five years, when Modou suddenly took a second wife (a young girl named Bineta, one of his daughter's friends) without telling her in advance. Nevertheless she remained faithful to her husband up to his death, as dictated by Islamic tradition. Her friend Aïssatou met the same fate but she reacted quite differently. As soon as her husband took a second wife she divorced him. Then she went to university, got a degree and went into the diplomatic service. Ramatoulaye is one of those working women who spend their whole lives trying to combine a job and a home in such a way that no one suffers (except they themselves). After the death of Modou, Ramatoulaye rejects new suitors. She wants to start a new life and, in spite of disappointment and humiliation, she is "filled with hope":

> My heart rejoices each time a woman emerges from the shadows. I know that the field of our gains is unstable, the retention of conquests difficult: social constraints are ever-present, and male egoism resists.
>
> Instruments for some, baits for others, respected or despised, often muzzled, all women have almost the same fate, which religions or unjust legislation have sealed. (English edition, p. 88)

Mariama Bâ died suddenly, before the publication of her second novel *Le chant écarlate* (1981), which brought her promising career to a premature end. She believed that women must fight for their place in society. She herself was active in African women's movements aimed at awakening women and teaching them to stand up for their rights. In an interview (1981) she once said that writers have a very special task, because of the injustice of the position of women in Africa. In spite of the attention which women have received during the United Nations' Decade of Women little if any progress has been made in the fight against discrimination:

> Social pressure shamelessly suffocates individual attempts at change. The woman is heavily burdened by mores and customs, in combination with mistaken and egoistic interpretations of different religions.(. . .) As women, we must work for our own future, we must overthrow the status quo which harms us and we must no longer submit to it. Like men, we must use literature as a non-violent but effective weapon. We no longer accept the nostalgic praise to the African mother whom, in his anxiety, man confuses with Mother Africa. Women have a place within African literature, the place due to them on the basis of their participation — side by side with men — in all phases of the liberation struggle, and their contribution to economic development. But women will have to fight for that place with all their might.

At the 1982 conference in Mainz on African women and literature, there was criticism of the way in which men point to the symbol of Mother Africa as an ideal for ordinary African wives and mothers to follow. This was in line with the views of Mariama Bâ expressed above. Another woman present at that conference, the South African Miriam Tlali, described the process thus: "Men call you Mother Africa and put you on a pedestal. But they want you to stay there for ever — and unhappy you if you want to step down and live as an equal human being!"

It is always difficult to share power when you are used to being lord and master. For people who have never enjoyed power, the changes can only be for the better. This was true in the past, when colonial rule was forced to make way for independence. But one cannot help wondering who has actually benefited from this new power structure. Very few women, it would seem.

At the Second International Book Fair of Radical Black and

Third World Books in London in April 1983, it was clear that while a number of African male authors have already made a name for themselves in international literary circles, black women writers are still fighting for recognition. They have only begun to write about the feelings and experiences of their sisters who, as Jane Bryce (1983) put it, "are silenced by tradition".

The Critics Criticized

Literary criticism, no less than literature itself, bears the stamp of male domination, according to the African women writers present in Mainz. I was reminded of this when I went in search of literary criticism and comments on the work of women writers. In the more important anthologies, essays on East and West African women writers are still practically non-existent. There is one book entitled *Women Writers in Black Africa* (Brown 1981) and Oladele Taiwo recently published his *Female Novelists of Modern Africa* (1984). This raises the question of whether it is wise to exercise apartheid in the evaluation of literary texts, by dealing separately with women's literature. One runs the risk of creating two mutually exclusive categories, enabling male authors to continue to represent "official" literature, to which women writers would have no access. The critics themselves must be on the alert if it is to be avoided.

With regard to literary criticism I would like to distinguish between what I have termed *exclusive* and *inclusive* criticism. In the exclusive approach certain literary (aspects of) texts are often passed over or ignored on the basis of a dominant set of norms. Exclusion has often been used for the purpose of subjugation. This was common policy in the colonial era, when the rulers excluded Africa from what they called civilization.

Both approaches are to be found in literary criticism. According to the exclusive method the critic — consciously or unconsciously — takes his own culture, history and ideology as a model and proceeds to examine every text on the basis of that model. The second approach is generally used by the more open critic, who is not out to accept or reject a work on the basis of his own current scale of values, but considers literary texts against the background of the contexts where they originated. The inclusive method clearly puts greater demands on the critic because nothing is predetermined. This is especially so when the texts are by authors from other cultures or ideologies, or of the other sex. The critic must know his material; he must be erudite in a new, universal sense of the word (and modest!) for he must be familiar not only with his own cultural history, social context and aesthetic norms, but also with those of the authors and the texts he is studying. The advantage of the inclusive approach is that a critic·is less likely to allow himself to be swayed by standard Western or male values (or both).

This is of course no easy task, in particular for those who are unable or unwilling to acknowledge the existence of values other than their own. African writers and critics know from experience to what extent judgements used to be dictated by a Eurocentric, exclusive method of criticism. They are only too aware of the drawbacks of such a system. But what has this experience taught them?

I shall give examples of both kinds of criticism, as applied to the work of women authors. Femi Ojo-Ade of Nigeria (1983) is an example of the exclusive critic. In his article ''Female Writers, Male Critics'', he dictates to African women writers what they ought to do, or rather what they ought not to do:

> The (women) writers that we have studied dwell too much upon the malady of male chauvinism, a phenomenon that, in its most famous aspect, is no less a Western way than the notions of feminism espoused by some female writers. Blackness, African-ness (. . .) is almost foreign to others who have let the questions of male domination blind them to the necessary solidarity between man and woman. (p. 176)

Women writers consider this an unfair argument, as was

made abundantly clear at the Mainz conference.

In an interview Buchi Emecheta (1983) put it this way:

> It is much too simplistic to argue that women who stand up for their rights are contaminated by Western feminism — as if that's all there is to it. Naturally it is true that Western women sometimes have problems that aren't so important here. The mother/daughter conflict, for instance, is not really a problem here, because families are so much bigger. You don't live at such close quarters, as in the nuclear family, so a mother doesn't continually concern herself with one daughter. Loneliness and isolation aren't as common here as in the West. Nevertheless I believe the demand for equality is becoming stronger and stronger, here in Africa as well, where women now dare to break with tradition, sometimes at great cost to themselves.

Another common contention is that women are in danger of losing their femininity as soon as they demand equal rights. Ojo-Ade used this argument in another article, "Still a Victim?" (1982), which is devoted to Mariama Bâ. According to this critic, "Ramatoulaye's feminism as an expression of freedom constitutes only a partial aspect of the totality of African life. Femininity is the virtue of the traditionalist; feminism, the veneer of the progressive striving to become a man" (p. 84). Here again femininity and submissiveness are equated (cf. Simone de Beauvoir).

Eustace Palmer (Sierra Leone) approached the question quite differently and his work can serve to illustrate the inclusive method. In an article entitled "The Feminine Point of View: Buchi Emecheta's *The Joys of Motherhood*", he takes an impartial look at this novel, without contrasting feminism with being black. He respects Emecheta's approach to the reality of Africa, which he sees as a genuine contribution to African literature and not (like Ojo-Ade) as a "deviant" view:

> The picture of the cheerful contented female complacently accepting her lot is replaced by that of a woman who is powerfully aware of the unfairness of the system and who longs to be fulfilled

in her self, to be a full human being, not merely somebody else's appendage (p. 39).

Palmer shows that he is aware of the problems which beset the critic when he is faced with a new or different approach to "reality":

What gives this novel its particular quality is the unashamed presentation of the woman's point of view. This comes out not merely in the powerful evocation of Nnu Ego's misery but even in the narrator's own omniscient comments. (. . .) There will be many who will find Emecheta's analysis of the female controversial.(. . .) But *The Joys of Motherhood* is an imaginative and not a scientific work, and the artist is surely within her rights to exaggerate or even to depart from sociological authenticity. The novel must be judged as a work of art and it is difficult to deny the accomplishment of the artistry. (op. cit. pp. 44, 55)

In the closing passages of his article the critic tempers these broadminded views by casting doubts upon Emecheta's "sociological authenticity". He seems almost to revert to the safe old contention that there is only one scientifically sound "reality".

And yet Palmer's relatively open attitude is encouraging, the more for being uncommon. The main problem is that men are not used to taking the female perspective into account when it does not coincide with their own. And women have often kept their own opinions to themselves, out of fear or for personal motives, just as in the past African views and opinions were often disguised or concealed from the white colonials.

There are women today who have had the courage to speak up, to tell of their encounters with hierarchic role patterns. Moreover, through their heroines they have shown us that it is possible to attack the status quo. We may applaud or deplore this development, but if we reject these views we are again supporting one perspective to the exclusion of all others, and denying the "other" the right to his or her own view of "reality".

Therefore I would like to remind the reader of an old statement by one of the nestors of African literature, Chinua Achebe of Nigeria. I have altered it slightly, with his permission, but the words have lost neither their original wisdom nor their relevance:

> The *male* critic of African literature must cultivate the habit of humility appropriate to his limited experience of the *female* world and purged of the superiority and arrogance which history so insidiously makes him heir to. (Achebe 1975:6)

Achebe used the word *European* instead of *male* and the word *African* instead of *female*, for he addressed the Eurocentric Western critic. He later disclosed that this statement, which dates from 1962, made him "quite a few bitter enemies", one of whom took the matter so seriously that he launched a number of bitter attacks on Achebe. One wonders how much critics — and writers — have learned since.

REFERENCES

Achebe, Chinua, 1958, *Things Fall Apart*, London, Heinemann.
Achebe, Chinua, 1975, *Morning Yet On Creation Day*, London, Heinemann.
Aidoo, Ama Ata, 1970, *Anowa*, A Play, London, Longman.
Aidoo, Ama Ata, 1977, *Our Sister Killjoy*, London, Longman.
Bâ, Mariama, 1979, *Une si longue lettre*, Dakar, Nouvelles Editions Africaines; trans. 1981 by Modupé Bodé-Thomas, *So Long a Letter*, London, Heinemann.
Bâ, Mariama, 1981, *Le chant écarlate*, Dakar, Nouvelles Editions Africaines.
Beauvoir, Simone de, 1949, *Le deuxième sexe I, Les Faits et les mythes*, Paris, Gallimard; trans. 1953, *The Second Sex*, London, Cape.
Beier, Ulli (ed.), 1966, *The Origin of Life and Death*, London, Heinemann.
Brown, Lloyd W., 1981, *Women Writers in Black Africa*, Westport/London, Greenwood Press.
Bryce, Jane, 1983, "Book Fair Blazes Trail", in: *The New African*, May.

Bugul, Ken, 1982, *Le baobab fou*, Dakar, Nouvelles Editions Africaines.

Chemain-Degrange, Arlette, 1980, *Emancipation féminine et roman africain*, Dakar, Nouvelles Editions Africaines.

Cleaver, Eldridge, (1968) 1969, *Soul on Ice*, London, Jonathan Cape.

Cock, Jacklyn, 1980, *Maids and Madams. A Study in the Politics of Exploitation*, Johannesburg, Ravan Press.

Condé, Maryse, 1972, "Three female writers in modern Africa: Flora Nwape, Ama Ata Aidoo and Grace Ogot", in *Présence Africaine*, 2nd trimestre, pp. 132-43.

Diop, Birago, (1947) 1961, *Les contes d'Amadou Koumba*, Paris, Présence Africaine; trans. 1966, *Tales of Amadou Koumba*, London, OUP.

Ekwensi, Cyprian, (1961), 1975, *Jagua Nana*, London, Heinemann.

Emechetan Buchi, 1974, *Second-Class Citizen*, London, Allison & Busby; New York, Braziller.

Emecheta, Buchi, 1979, *The Joys of Motherhood*, London, Heinemann; New York, Braziller

Emecheta, Buchi, 1982, *Double Yoke*, London/Ibuza, Ogwugwu Afor.

Emecheta, Buchi, 1983, Interview with —, by Mineke Schipper in: *NRC-Handelsblad*, 21 May.

Fanon, Frantz, 1952, *Peau noire, masques blancs (Black Skin, White Masks)*, Paris, Seuil.

Head, Bessie, 1968, *When Rain Clouds Gather*, New York, Simon & Schuster; 1972, London Heinemann.

Head, Bessie, 1974, *A Question of Power*, London, Heinemann; New York, Pantheon.

Imbuga, Francis P., 1973, *The Married Bachelor*, Nairobi, East African Publishing House.

Kourouma, Ahmadou, (1968) 1970, *Les soleils des indépendances*, Paris, Seuil; trans. 1981 by Adrian Adams, *The Suns of Independence*, London, Heinemann.

Leacock, Eleanor, 1979, "Women, Development and Anthropological Facts and Fictions", in G. Huizer & B. Mannheim (eds.), *The Politics of Anthropology*, The Hague/Paris, Mouton.

Liking, Werewere, 1979, *La puissance de Um*, Abidjan, Céda.

Liking, Werewere, 1980, *Une nouvelle terre*, théâtre-rituel, Dakar, Nouvelles Editions Africaines.

Liking, Werewere, 1983, *Elle sera de jaspe et de corail (Journal d'une misovire*. . .), Paris, Harmattan, Collection Encres Noires.

Liking, Werewere, 1983, Interview with —, by Sennen Adriamiredo, in: *Jeune Afrique*, no. 1172, 22 June.

Lopès, Henri, 1976, *La nouvelle romance*, Yaoundé, Editions CLE.

Molefe, Sono (ed.), *Malibongwe, ANC Women: Poetry Is Also Their Weapon*, African National Congress (n.d.n.p.).

Mugo, Micere Githae, 1976, *Daughter of My People, Sing*, Nairobi, East African Literature Bureau.

Mugo, Micere Githae, 1978, *Visions of Africa*, Nairobi, East African Literature Bureau.

Mugo, Micere Githae, and Ngugi wa Thiong'o, 1976, *The Trial of Dedan Kimathi*, Nairobi/London, Heinemann.

Mutloatse, Mothobi, 1978, Interview with —, by Mineke Schipper, in *NRC-Handelsblad*, 16 June.

Ngandu Nkashama, P., 1982, "Le théâtre: vers une dramaturgie fonctionnelle", in: *La littérature zaîroise*, numéro spécial de *Notre Librairie*, January-March.

Ngugi wa Thiong'o, 1967, *A Grain of Wheat*, London, Heinemann.

Ngugi wa Thiong'o, see Micere Githae Mugo, 1976.

Njau, Rebecca, 1960, *The Scar*, A play, Nairobi, Kibo Art Gallery.

Njau, Rebecca, (1975) 1978, *Ripples in the Pool*, London, Heinemann.

Nwapa, Flora, 1966, *Efuru*, London, Heinemann.

Nwapa, Flora, 1969, *Idu*, London, Heinemann.

Nwapa, Flora, 1971, *This is Lagos and Other Stories*, Enugu, Nwamife.

Obbo, Christine, 1981, *African Women. Their Struggle for Economic Independence*, London, Zed Press.

Ojo-Ade, Femi, 1982, "Still a Victim? Mariama Bâ's *Une si longue lettre*," in: *African Literature Today*, 12, pp. 71-87.

Ojo-Ade, Femi, 1983, "Female Writers, Male Critics", in: *African Literature Today*, 13, pp. 158-79.

Ousmane, Sembène, 1960, *Les bouts de bois de Dieu*, Paris, Le livre contemporain (1962 trans. *God's Bits of Wood*, New York, Doubleday; 1969, London, Heinemann).

Ousmane, Sembène, 1964, *L'harmattan*, Paris, Présence Africaine.

Oyono, Ferdinand, 1956, *Une vie de boy*, Paris, Julliard (1966 trans. *Houseboy*, London, Heinemann; 1970, *Boy*, New York, Macmillan).

Oyônô-Mbia, Guillaume, 1964, *Trois prétendants . . . un mari*, Yaoundé, Editions CLE (1968 trans. *Three Suitors: One Husband*, London, Methuen).

Palmer, Eustace, 1983, "The Feminine Point of View: Buchi Emecheta's *The Joys of Motherhood*", in: *African Literature Today*, 13, pp. 38-55.

Paulme, Denise, 1975, *La mère dévorante*, Paris, Gallimard.

p'Bitek, Okot, 1966, *Song of Lawino*, Nairobi, East African Publishing House; 1969, Cleveland, World (Meridian Books).

Schipper, Mineke, 1973, *Le blanc vu d'Afrique*, Yaoundé, Editions CLE.

Schipper, Mineke, 1980, *Black Paradise, African Creation and Origin Myths* (in Dutch), Maasbree, Corrie Zelen.

Schipper, Mineke, 1983, *African Literature. Traditions, Genres, Authors and Developments in the Literatures of Subsaharan Africa* (in Dutch) Utrecht/Antwerp, Het Spectrum, Aula-reeks.

Senghor, Léopold Sédar, 1974, Interview with —, by Mineke Schipper, in: *NRC-Handelsblad*, 25 October.

Socé, Ousmane, 1937, *Mirages de Paris*, Paris, Nouvelles Editions Latines.

Sow Fall, Aminata, 1979, *La grève des Bàttu*, Dakar, Nouvelles Editions Africaines; trans. 1981, *The Beggar's Strike*, London, Longman.

Thadani, Veena, 1976, "Women in Nairobi: The Paradox of Urban Progress", in: *African Urban Studies*, 3 (Winter 1978-9), p. 67-83.

Topping-Bazin, Nancy, 1984, "Feminist Perspectives in African Fiction: Bessie Head and Buchi Emecheta", paper read at the *African Literature Association Conference*, University of Baltimore, Maryland, April.

Wachtel, Eleanor, 1977, "The Mother and the Whore: Image and Stereotype of African Women", in: *Umoja*, 1 (2), p. 31-48.

INTERVIEW WITH MIRIAM TLALI
(SOUTH AFRICA)

MINEKE SCHIPPER

Miriam Tlali (b. 1933) spent several years at Witwatersrand University on a student grant awarded for scholastic merit. She wanted to become a physician, but the only study open to her was African Administration. For two years she tried to find a way to study medicine, and finally enrolled at the medical school of the University of Roma in Lesotho. But a year later her money was gone and she had to give up her studies. She returned to Johannesburg, where she went to secretarial school and later found an administrative job in a shop. She was by that time married and had two children.

Miriam Tlali has published her stories and articles in a number of newspapers (*The Rand Daily Mail, The Star, Staffrider* and *Fair Lady*) and in anthologies such as Mothobi Mutloatse's *Forced Landing* (1981) and Charlotte Bruner's *Unwinding Threads: Writing by Women in Africa* (1983). Her novels *Muriel at Metropolitan* (1975) and *Amandla* (1980) are banned in South Africa, as are a number of her short stories. A collection of short stories *Mihloti* (Tears) appeared in 1984 and she has nearly completed another collection *Mehlala Khatamping* (Imprints in the Quag). She is also working on a new novel. During a six-month stay in the Netherlands in 1984 she gave the interview which follows. The grant which made that stay possible gave Miriam Tlali a welcome break from the hectic life she leads at home in Soweto, where she makes a living selling kitchenware door-to-door, and has to do her writing in the few spare hours she can find in the evening.

I see culture as a way of life. To us it also means trying to survive. That takes up most of our time. Fighting for a living every day, and if you want to write there are a lot more problems. You need material and many libraries are inaccessible because they are so far away or in a white area. In many ways you can't compare our situation with that of white women. We're hemmed in on all sides by the political system, and they are not. Of course that goes for black men as well as black women, but women have so much less time, because they have to run the house in addition to holding down a job. It is very rare for a black man to help with domestic chores. All of which means that women don't write as much as men.

Do women generally have a lower level of education than men, and is illiteracy widespread?

Women aren't necessarily less educated, but the emphasis is on other things. Most women have jobs in the service sector or education, and very few get the chance to study medicine or law or technical subjects. Of course in our country these are professions that not many black men have access to either. There is a fairly high level of illiteracy, but I'm not sure about the difference in numbers between men and women in South Africa. In Lesotho there are more educated women than men, because the men go off very young to work on the land or in the mines, as migrant labourers. The women stay at home, so they have more opportunity for schooling.

Is oral literature still alive in the black neighbourhoods?

In our country women have always been the storytellers. The children sat in a circle and listened for hours to the old stories. There was time for things like that then. But as a result of industrialization, women became breadwinners too. There was the rent in the city and so many other expenses. And since then there's been less and less time left for things that aren't really necessary. I think a lot of women still remember the traditional stories. Some of them are good storytellers and very imaginative, but you need time for that and peace and quiet — which we don't have. And children today aren't that interested in stories. They'd rather watch TV.

It would be a good idea if younger women were to record the stories, as told by the older ones. Otherwise our oral literature will die out with the older generation. Some of us realize how important this is, and we've gotten together a group of women writers, to work out plans along those lines. The hardest thing is trying to find the time. Besides the day-to-day things there are social obligations too. With so many accidents and fights, there are always funerals and a funeral is a social event which you are expected to attend. The same thing is true of church festivals and weddings. There's less and less time these days for oral literature.

Which genres do women writers prefer?

We have a number of women journalists. There is one playwright who is really good, Fatima Dike. She is the only one who has had a play published. Most women authors write mainly poetry. Short stories and poetry are naturally the most popular genres, because of the situation. Short pieces of text can be mulled over while you're busy with other things, and it doesn't take long to write them down once you've got it all clear in your head. Most women writers have never published a book. They write mostly in newspapers and magazines. There are still only very limited opportunities for black South Africans to publish anything in book form.

In 1975 it was considered exceptional when you published a book that was written in Soweto. How did it all come about and what happened after that?

I actually owe it to my position as a woman that I'm a writer today: I was forced to leave my job because my mother-in-law was incurably ill. Hopeless cases are sent home because there's no room and no time for them in the hospital. I nursed her right up until her death, four years later. Whenever she groaned or called out I went to her right away. And the rest of the time I sat at a forty-year-old Remington and worked on my first novel. It wasn't published until five years later. The publisher wanted to make a lot of changes because he was afraid it would be banned. For a long time I refused to give my permission, until one day my own mother said she probably wouldn't live long enough to see my book. That was when I agreed to the "censored" version. Later Longman's in London took over the international edition from Ravan Press and published the integral text. That edition attracted the attention of the Censorship Board and the book was banned in South Africa, both editions at once. From then on I was determined to continue writing, and to make no more concessions to any kind of self-censorship. I've become a lot more outspoken since then. When I wrote *Amandla* there was a lot going on politically. The book is about the events in Soweto in 1976, which resulted in a great many casualties. Before *Muriel* was banned I received a lot of letters from so-called white liberals in Pretoria, Bloemfontein and other such places. They wrote in Afrikaans: "Oh, Miriam, we've read your book, but things are not really as bad as that." Maybe that was their opinion, but they have a different way of looking at things. I thought I had taken a fairly moderate stand in that book. *Amandla* is actually a much more political book than *Muriel*. Again the publisher tried to get me to give it a different title and make other changes. I refused. It didn't take long for the book to be banned, but the first edition of five thousand copies was already sold out. *Amandla* means *power* and in South Africa *Amandla Ngawetu* is often used as a slogan, it has become a symbol of resistance. I think the title alone was enough to alarm the Censorship Board. I have also written a great many stories. Thanks to my work I was invited abroad, and I've learned a lot from these trips. You have no idea how isolated we are in South Africa. In Iowa I took part in an International Writers' Workshop, with writers from all over the world. A marvellous experience. Contact like that is so important, so stimulating. Back home I try to share my experiences with others, my own people. I am one of them. There is no distinction made between élite and working-class literature. In the eyes of the authorities we are all rejected blacks, even though they are now doing their best to create a black middle class. The greatest thing I could ever achieve would be to become an example to a new generation of younger women, to show them that it is actually possible to achieve something, if you show some initiative of your own. I've always admired women who stand up to a superior power, like Lilian Ngoyi.

Have you ever considered leaving South Africa?

I would never choose exile, not as long as I could keep on writing in my own country. Leaving South Africa means leaving your land, pulling up your roots. When terrible things happen I suffer along with the others. In exile you lose your ties with the people, and you're liable to forget. I belong with my people.

Is there such a thing as escapist literature in South Africa? Are the women's magazines important in your country? And what about films?

You mean the kind of thing that ends with: "and they lived happily ever after"? They exist in South Africa; they're all written by whites. Stories like that are rather childish and once people grow up they have no time for them. In South Africa blacks are forced to grow up. There's no time for dreams. You have to think about the real world; there's no escaping it.

Films are very popular. You see people racing home to catch the latest instalment of "Dallas". I think most people are motivated by curiosity. At the same time a lot of blacks criticize the characters in this sort of series. The way they act, the kind of world they live in. They devour each other, out of jealousy and greed.

As far as the women's magazines are concerned, they're usually cast-offs the white ladies give to their black servants.

63

The last few years the white ideal of beauty you see in those magazines is not as popular as it once was, when black women tried to lighten their skin and straighten their hair, in order to look as much as possible like white women. There has been a change in attitude, due largely to the influence of Afro-Americans and black South Africans who preach "Black is beautiful" and "Black Power". Of course women still try to look attractive, but their standards are no longer those of white women. That is a thing of the past.

How are women presented in literature? Is there a difference between the writings of men and women in this respect?

That's impossible to say since there is so little written by women in my country. African-language literature, too, is written almost exclusively by men. Women are referred to as tender-hearted and of course motherly and, once in a while, pretty. In urban theatre you find characters who emphasize the contrast between the maternal figure and the woman who wants to be independent, goes her own way and is therefore suspect. Like in the plays of Gibson Kente. Women like that are uncommon, they've turned their backs on the ordinary pattern of life, which means they are usually portrayed in a negative way.

In my own work I try to present as varied a picture as possible of womanhood in all its facets. Using my own experiences and the contacts I've had with other women. I don't idealize women, there are no superwomen in my books. Heroines are still above all the symbol of the *mothers* at home. The same goes for women in the resistance. They represent both images, that of mother and of liberated woman. Lilyan Ngoyi once turned down an invitation to study in China because she didn't want to give up her life as a wife and a mother. She refused this opportunity to add a new dimension to her life, preferring the obligations of her traditional role as mother.

My female characters are portrayed realistically. In *Amandla* the women are no weak, docile creatures. They don't just sit at home; they comment on what men have to say. They are combative. They are mothers and militants at the same time. The way they speak up doesn't always meet with the approval of the male characters. The problems presented by the combination of militancy and motherhood are an entirely new experience for women in our society. We know what it means to combine political militancy with ironing shirts and washing socks — that's what we've always done, along with all the rest. Our way of looking at things, rooted in our own experience, supplements and complements reality as it is seen and described by men.

Have you defied taboos in your work, and what were the reactions?

The real taboo is for a black woman to be found in a compromising situation with a white man. That's something you don't even talk about, let alone write about. And yet it happens every day, ever since the first coloured baby was born nine months after the first Boer, Jan van Riebeeck, landed at the Cape. There are many women in our family who carry around light or even near-white babies on their backs, and we refuse to talk about it. That's the theme of my story "Just the Two", which is banned in South Africa. I read it out in Iowa and the three male Africans who were present, from Cameroon, Ghana and Botswana, protested vehemently. The story is about a train conductor who chases a black girl the length of the train until they end up alone in a compartment, where the scene they objected to takes place. Those writers thought the girl ought to have murdered the man if he couldn't keep his hands to himself. People react like that. They're hurt and afraid because a stranger has violated "one of ours".

I think Western men know that feeling too, the fear that a black man might run off with one of "our white women" . . . .

65

Yes, it's the same sort of thing. Women have always been considered as property. And in our case there's the added political dimension. The writer from Botswana said "Every day I see them crossing the border, Boers who get our girls. Each month more coloured children are born, but Miriam, that's no subject for a story by one of us!" I still wonder why not. In the train I often meet girls who tell me about their affairs with white men. Lots of strangers tell me about their life, the things they've experienced. And sometimes I use this material in my books. But I can't help thinking it's ironic that in a previous session one of those three writers read a poem about a Russian girl who had stood him up! Apparently there's nothing wrong with talking about a relationship between a black man and a white woman!

The same thing goes for the question of virginity, another taboo. If she's had other men before her marriage a woman is never allowed to talk about it. The reverse is true for men. They're proud of their experiences with women and talk freely about them. They say things like "I've been out with so-and-so, but she's nothing special." A man brags about it, something he would never permit his wife to do.

How do people feel about feminism in South Africa?

As you know, up to this moment I'm still the only black woman who has ventured to write about feminism. There is no equality. If you do something out of the ordinary men are more inclined to see you as a kind of "fellow man" than to acknowledge that you have accomplished something important as a woman. That would present too much of a threat. In South Africa white women have more rights now than they used to. Their legal status has been improved to the extent that their husbands no longer have to sign for the purchase of a refrigerator, furniture or a car, or for a contract. But that's still the case for us. I wasn't allowed to sign my own contract with the publisher. My husband had to sign, even though it was *my* book! Even though we're both fighting against white male domination, there is no real solidarity between black women and white women, because we are fighting on different levels. Apartheid stands in the way of true sisterhood in South Africa. This was the conclusion reached by an English journalist who came here to study the question. She asked white women why they didn't fight alongside their black sisters to help improve the position of black women, who lag so far behind. The answer was: "Our men wouldn't be very pleased if we were to stand up to the authorities for that sort of reason." Which means that in the end white men decide which activities "their" women are permitted to take part in. We try to set up our own women's organizations but, as I said in the beginning, it's an uphill struggle. Just trying to keep your head above water seems to take up all your time.

Black men don't give their wives much encouragement either. A lot of men don't want their wives to read things they don't know anything about.

We have seen that a woman must be very strong indeed if she is to overcome all these obstacles, and keep on reading and writing, in spite of everything. What is your secret?

My mother always encouraged me. My father, who was a teacher, died young and left us his books. I enjoyed writing compositions at school, and they were considered very good. And yet at that time I never thought about the possibility of becoming a writer. The two years at university in Witwatersrand did make a difference though. We had teachers who encouraged us to think for ourselves, to be critical, and to question what we read. I didn't start writing until I was much older, as I've told you. Up to now the reviews of my work have almost all been favourable. Maybe I've been lucky, but I do know I'm strong-willed. I believe that writing is important, and that it can really help to bring about changes. That has

67

been proved many times in the past. Otherwise why would there be so much censorship in the world? Why are authorities so afraid of books? They consider knowledge dangerous; they want to have people around them who know nothing of what is happening in their country and elsewhere. We must combat and prevent ignorance. There are inadequate educational opportunities for blacks in South Africa. Countless books are denied us. In spite of all that, we must keep on reading. And I see it as my task to go on writing, as long as I can.

If you could speak to women all over the world, what would you say to them?

I would say: strive for unity, set up a platform you can use to bring down all the barriers that have been raised around you. Educate yourselves and others, so that women will at last have a voice of their own and make that voice heard. Life is only worth living when *everyone* has a chance to work and develop his or her talents.

II.   THE ARAB WORLD

(*Foto* : Jan Stegeman)

PROVERBS

1. Brides will start loving their mothers-in-law when charcoal turns white. (Morocco)
2. My mother-in-law (with her leathery face like a water-skin) is as sour as her son is sweet. (Morocco)
3. Cares and suffering I left at my father's house, but in my husband's house I found them again. (Morocco)
4. If a man has no daughters, no one will know why he has died. (Morocco)
5. If your daughter leaves home, plant onions in her place. (Morocco)
6. A woman who puts kohl on her eyes while her husband is away is suspect. (Morocco)
7. A dissolute man guards his wife the way a thief guards his home. (Morocco)
8. Whatever a bleary-eyed woman cooks, her husband eats. (Morocco)
9. Tie up a woman's tongue and a mule's legs. (Morocco)
10. With a vegetable garden and a second wife, the good life is over. (Morocco)
11. If you dress a one-eyed woman well, she'll look beautiful. (Berber, Algeria)
12. A house without a woman is like a sea without fish. (Berber, Algeria)
13. Look for an ideal woman and marry her daughter. (Algeria)
14. I can't see anything since I started taking care of my eyes. (Algeria)
15. A man to whom God has not given a surfeit of sons to carry on his name is cursed by the Almighty. (Algeria)
16. A proud woman has no secrets. (Algeria)
17. To say "be quiet" means "shout". (Algeria)
18. Evil, thy name is woman; Good, thy name is woman. (Algeria)
19. You don't marry your brother or his father, you only marry an enemy. (Algeria)
20. Don't get upset if a man rebukes you, but if your wife insults you you'll be tormented by sleeplessness. (Algeria)

21. Paradise is under a mother's heel. (Algeria)
22. Don't marry a thin wife; someone's trying to make trouble for you. (Tunisia)
23. All through life it's the mother who counts. (Lebanon)
24. The husband earns the living and the wife builds the home. (Lebanon)
25. A woman just snaps her fingers and she's already thought of a plan. (Lebanon)
26. If you're lucky you'll have a wife and a workhorse, if not you'll have grumbling and quarrels. (Yemen)
27. A woman is like the scent of a sweet-smelling herb. (Yemen)
28. When a man gets old, bring him a young girl. When a woman gets old, throw her away. (Yemen)
29. God gave us ten sorts of gossip, and women have taken nine of them. (Israel)
30. The strong men have gone to sleep, the weak women have got up. (Israel)

ACKNOWLEDGEMENTS

Myriem Fasla, Algeria (18 through 21). *Lourina de Voogd*, selection of 1–10 from Moh. Kabbaj and Moh. Cherradi, 1981, *Bāqa^h min al-amṯāl al-maġribiyya^h* (Un bouquet de proverbes marocains ou l'authenticité du Maroc à travers ses proverbes), Casablanca, Idéale. *Flora van Houwelingen* (11–17, 22, 29, 30), selected or heard from: M. T. Amrouche, 1966, *Le grain magique*, Paris, Maspéro, p. 38 (11); C. Lacoste Dujardin, 1965, *Traductions des légendes et contes merveilleux de la Grande Kabylie*, collected by A. Mouliéras, Paris, Imprimerie Nationale p. 211 (12); *Louisa Berkaïne*, Algeria (13, 14); Aïcha Lemsine, 1976, *La Chrysalide*, Paris, Eds. des Femmes p. 77 (15); *Bahaouda Abd-el-kader*, Algeria (16); *Sabrina Belkheir*, Algeria (17); *Dardar Khaled*, Tunisia (22); *Jehuda Sofer*, Israel (29, 30). *Hilary Kilpatrick*, selection of 23-5 from: F.-J. Abela, 1981, *Proverbes populaires du Liban Sud. Saïda et ses environs*, G.P. Maisonneuve et Larose, 1345, 1678, 810; and 26-8 from S. F. D. Goitein, 1934, *Jemenica. Sprichwörter und Redensarten aus Zentral-Jemen*, Leipzig, Otto Harrassowitz, 160, 1140, 66.

WOMEN AND LITERATURE IN THE ARAB WORLD

THE ARAB EAST — HILARY KILPATRICK
Translated from the Dutch by Hilary Kilpatrick

Language Situation and Literature

A number of languages and dialects are spoken in the Arab world. Arabic, the language of the great majority of the inhabitants of the area, exists everywhere in two forms. On the one hand there is "literary", standard Arabic, which has no regional variations; it is learnt at school and used in the press and all kinds of printed works, in news programmes on radio and television and in conversation between educated people who do not know each other's dialect. On the other hand there are the spoken dialects which differ from standard Arabic and each other and are almost exclusively used in speech. In practice there are innumerable gradations between standard Arabic and the dialects, but it is still true that standard Arabic, even when it is influenced by a dialect, is always recognizable as such.

In some parts of the Arab world other languages have been spoken from ancient times, such as Kurdish in northern Iraq and Berber in North Africa. As a result of European cultural influences French and to a much lesser extent English have been adopted by some writers. Here a distinction must be made between North Africa, where French almost became a national language and a regional school of writing in French has developed, and the eastern Arab world (including Egypt), where writers who use French or English can be considered exceptions; most of them come from Lebanon.

In the Arabic dialects a rich but almost unknown literature of poetry, songs for all occasions, epic and other stories and innumerable proverbs and idioms exists. In the written language, which in contrast to the dialects enjoys high prestige, the first literary texts to have been preserved are poems dating from the sixth century AD. Classical Arabic

72

literature, of which these poems are the earliest monument, flourished between the eighth and the twelfth centuries. In modern times a new Arabic literature has arisen, initially profoundly influenced by Western models but now pursuing its own independent course.

The Historical Context of Modern Arabic Literature

Modern Arabic literature is a child of the encounter between Arabs and Western Europeans in the last two centuries. This encounter has changed Arab society radically; new political, economic and social structures have arisen and modern ideologies have been introduced. Education has been expanded and largely secularised, and new aspirations have appeared in all sections of society. Determining factors in this process of change have been admiration for the technical and scientific progress of the West, resistance to Western colonialism and ambitions to dominate, and the endeavour to preserve the Arab identity, partly by revitalizing the Arab cultural heritage (Allen 1982: 19-26).

Women and Literature in the Arab East

The fact that women writers have made a significant contribution to modern Arabic literature is in itself a sign of the changes which have taken place in the Arab world. Women have always taken part in the composing and transmitting of oral literature as poets and narrators of all kinds of stories. In pre-Islamic Arabia it was women who by custom composed elegies for the dead, and their role as mourners has continued up to today. In the early Islamic period, when women of all classes still appeared freely in public, some of them played an important part in literary and musical life as poets and singers, and also as connoisseurs of poetry and patronesses. Even when women of the higher classes were banished from public life, there is evidence that in families with a tradition of learning and literary interests women continued to take part in these activities (Nègre 1978:

122-6; Minai 1981: 37-42). The first woman in the Arab world to have a book appear in print, Warda al-Yāziḡī,* belonged to one of these families; her thoroughly conventional collection of poems *The Rose-garden* was published in Beirut in 1867 (Al-Ḡundī n.d.: 19).

Pioneers

In the nineteenth and early twentieth centuries poetry and journalism were the main areas in which literary innovations took place, innovations to which women made a modest contribution.

Poetry has always occupied a special place in Arabic literature; composing poetry is the literary activity *par excellence*. But by the beginning of the nineteenth century Arabic poetry had degenerated into hackneyed repetition of traditional themes and images, while originality was sought only in the use of ever more artificial language. The first reaction against this decadent tradition came when poets turned back to the lofty style and clear diction of the masters of the golden age of classical Arabic poetry, and towards the end of the nineteenth century this "neo-classical" tendency had become firmly established. Beside numerous poets there was already a poetess composing in this style, the aristocratic ᶜĀiša at-Taymūriyya (1840-1902). It is perhaps no accident that her poems which betray the deepest emotion and were most appreciated were elegies for her daughter; in this she is continuing the pre-Islamic tradition of poetry by women.

The purified poetry of the "neo-classical" school maintained the rigid traditional form of a fixed metre, lines of uniform length and the same rhyme throughout the poem. Under the influence of Western literature and models from the Bible and Quran young poets began to experiment, searching for forms which were better suited to the themes of the

---

* Arabic names which have no recognized form in the Roman alphabet are transcribed according to the ISO/UNESCO system.

modern age. One experiment concerned a "poetry-in-prose" form, which owed much to the style of Walt Whitman. This form was used by the Lebanese Mayy (Ziyāda; 1895-1941) among others. Mayy grew up in Palestine and as a young woman moved to Egypt with her parents. There she earned the title "Princess of Poetry" and her salon was for a number of years a fixed meeting-point for poets and writers in the Egyptian capital.

Mayy was interested in other literary forms besides poetry, and she published short stories, literary studies and translations of French, English and German works. As a literary journalist she was following in the footsteps of a few women who had earlier been active in journalism. The second half of the nineteenth century was a time when the press in Egypt flourished, largely thanks to the initiative of emigrants from Lebanon and Syria. The press was the ideal medium in which to discuss problems of reform, the introduction of Western ideas and the relationship to the Arab cultural heritage, and the position of women was certainly not neglected. Hind Nawfal, who was born in Beirut, sensed the need for a journal specifically directed towards women, and in 1892 she published the first women's magazine in Arabic in Alexandria, *Young Woman*. Although it disappeared two years later (after the founder's marriage!), other women carried on the torch, first in Egypt and later in the Arab provinces of the Ottoman empire.

Women writers also had the opportunity to publish in newspapers and general cultural magazines. Around the turn of the century the well-known journal *al-Muqtataf* included articles by Zaynab Fawwāz, who is best known for her book of biographies of prominent women in the Arab world and abroad. Zaynab Fawwāz (1845-1914) was herself exceptional; she was born in a village in southern Lebanon and started work young as a servant. After her first marriage failed she married a Syrian and later a high-ranking Egyptian army officer. Despite her lack of schooling and her secluded life behind the veil she was able to occupy a prominent place among the women writers of her time.

It was above all the newspapers which advocated the modernization of Arab society which accepted articles by women. *Al-Ġarīda* (Cairo 1907-15), the mouthpiece of the liberal reformers, published articles by Malak Ḥifnī Nāṣif, one of the first Egyptian women to call for emancipation. After the First World War *al-Ahrām* (still today one of the most authoritative Egyptian newspapers) opened its columns to women, and in the 1930s newspapers and periodicals which published articles by women were no longer an exception.

From the Sidelines to the Centre of Literary Developments

None of the women writers who have been mentioned so far made a significant contribution to the Arabic literature of her time. Others too, such as the Egyptian poetess Ǧamīla al-ᶜAlā'ilī, who was a member of the Apollo Group in the 1930s, were only marginal figures. Their importance lies above all in the fact that they expressed the desire of women to improve their situation. (And in this period there were men too who protested against the oppression of women in novels and short stories, such as Ǧibrān Ḫalīl Ǧibrān in Lebanon and Maḥmūd Ṭāhir Lāšīn in Egypt.)

After the Second World War, however, women begin to contribute to literature in a way which, qualitatively speaking, is in no sense inferior to that of their male colleagues. The first woman who plays a central part in modern Arabic literature is the Iraqi poetess, Nāzik al-Malā'ika (b. 1923), one of the two founders of so-called "free verse", a poetic form based on one of the verse-feet of classical Arabic metre which is repeated, but with the length of the lines and the rhyme-scheme being left free. Since its first appearance in 1947 this poetic form has become the most productive one in modern Arabic poetry, above all thanks to Nāzik al-Malā'ika's efforts in her critical writings as well as her poems to refine and develop her theories.

The thorough knowledge of Arabic poetry on which the theories of the "free verse" movement were based was something Nāzik owed to her family background. Both her father and her mother had a certain reputation as poets, and her mother was the first Iraqi poetess to call for an improvement in the position of women (Boullata 1978:15). But Nāzik's poetry was also influenced by the conservative attitude of the wealthy circles in Baghdad in which she grew up; the melancholy tone and pessimistic view of life which are especially noticeable in her first collections of poems are partly a product of this. Although she devotes most of her attention to the world of the mind and the spirit, she can, when looking at the outside world, react forcefully and profoundly to political and social injustice. She herself ascribes the melancholic tone of her poems to her fear of death, her lack of inner freedom, the defeats and reverses in the political sphere which her people have suffered and the humiliations which she as a woman has experienced (Boullata 1978:15).

Two other women poets of the same generation have achieved an international reputation. Both are from Palestine. The older, Faḍwà Ṭūqān, born in 1919 in Nablus, comes, like Nāzik al-Malā'ika, from a family with a tradition of poets. Her early poems concentrate on her emotions, but even when they speak of lost love and the end of youth they radiate a warmth derived from a fundamental vitality and an optimistic attitude to life. In her later poems she has mastered the techniques of the "free verse" movement, but she is known chiefly because in these poems she has introduced what for her are new themes. The situation on the West Bank since the Israeli occupation in 1967 has extended her experience and her poetic range; her poems dealing with the tragedies of separated families, the suffering and humiliation which are part of life under the occupation and the unbreakable will of the Palestinians to liberate themselves often attain an epic tone. Her language is rich in allusions to themes and images of classical Arabic poetry and full of references to the well-loved land, its olive and orange trees and its rich fertility so typical of Palestinian poetry.

The second of these women poets is Salmà al-Ḥaḍrā' al-Ǧayyūsī, a Palestinian of the diaspora. She was born in 1928, grew up in Akka and Jerusalem and married a Jordanian diplomat whom she accompanied in various postings abroad. In 1969 she defended her thesis on modern Arabic poetry at the University of London and since then she has taught at universities in the Arab world and the United States. She is currently directing an extensive programme of translations of Arabic literature into English. It is thanks partly to her thorough knowledge of both European literature and her own Arabic poetic heritage that she is considered one of the authoritative critics in the Arab world. Her poems reflect her own revolt against the limitations which Arab society imposes on women, and she does not conceal the pain which the conquest of freedom brings with it. Moreover, her life of wandering and struggle has made her deeply conscious of the tragedy of her people and contributed to the metaphysical despair and the loss of faith in religious and other values which, together with the celebration of love and the unspoilt beauty of nature, characterize her work.

Two other writers of this generation should be mentioned here, the Lebanese-Egyptian Andrée Chedid (b.1921), and the Lebanese Etel Adnan (b.1925). Andrée Chedid has lived in Paris since she was 21 and is a highly respected author of poems, novels and plays in French. Although her poetry must be considered as belonging to French literature, she derives from her background a feel for nature and a sensitivity which distinguish her from other French writers. The works of Etel Adnan (see also p. 114ff.) reveal a deep involvement with the fate of her country and of the Palestinians, and she is able unerringly to put her finger on the mechanisms of repression which are employed against women, the poor and other weak members of society. The apocalyptic tone of her political poems is in strong contrast to the gentleness with which she sings of love.

Since poetesses like Nāzik al-Malā'ika and Salmà al-Ğayyūsī made their breakthrough, younger women have been contributing to the continuing developments in poetry. Themes such as the search for one's own identity and for love, fear of death, resistance to paralysing traditions and commitment to one's people in weal and woe are combined in their poetry with new diction and experiments in form. It depends on the individual's background and attitude whether she decides to emphasize the specific women's aspect in her approach to her themes. The Saudi-Arabian Fawzīyya Abū Ḥālid (b. 1955), for instance, attacks the oppression of women in many of her poems, while the Palestinian Ḥanān Miḥā'īl (b. 1946), who writes in English, often chooses situations of life under occupation for the subjects of her poetry. Men and women have the same themes and possibilities of expression open to them, and women, like men, are exploring them to the full.

It took longer for women to make a name for themselves in the field of prose. The novel and the short story are both forms which Arabic literature adopted from the European tradition in a process which began with translation and continued with adaptation and imitation before original work appeared. The novel and short story were accepted relatively late — in Egypt in the thirties and in the Asian Arab countries after the Second World War — as serious literary forms.

Of the two, it was the short story which was first successfully cultivated by women, and in this they distinguish themselves from their male colleagues, who at an early stage also showed interest in the novel. In 1935 the Egyptian Suhayr al-Qalamāwī (b. 1911) published *Stories my Grandmother Told me*, in which an old woman's reminiscences about life in Cairo towards the end of the nineteenth century are recorded simply and attractively by her granddaughter. The theme of the contrasts and tensions between old and new is to be found here, as frequently elsewhere in prose literature. It is

79

also worth noting that in this book a woman plays her traditional role of storyteller and historical memory. Suhayr al-Qalamāwī chose an academic career and as a result had hardly any leisure to devote herself further to creative writing. Her contemporary, ᶜĀ'iša ᶜAbd ar-Raḥmān (b. 1912), whose early stories are noteworthy for their concern with life in the countryside and the position of women, made the same decision; her considerable scholarly and journalistic oeuvre is published under the pen-name *Bint aš-Šāṭr*.

The first women to devote themselves almost exclusively to the short story are the Syrian Ulfa al-Idlibī (b.1912) and the Palestinian Samīra ᶜAzzām (1927-67). Ulfa al-Idlibī belongs to the first generation of Syrian writers who understood how to make use of the possibilities of the genre. In her four collections of stories, the first of which appeared in 1945, she analyses the every-day life of women of the traditional Damascene middle-class with sensitivity and sympathy, paying particular attention to the fragility and suffering inherent in human relationships (Sālim 1974:12; Fernea 1985: 49-55, 353). She published a novel, *Damascus, Smile of Sorrow*, in 1980, and here she combines the themes of the attempt of Syrian women shortly after the First World War to emancipate themselves and the struggle for independence which reached its climax in the same period. One reviewer has considered this book the crown of her literary career (al-Baġdādī 1981:105). Although it is set in the past, the novel can be seen as an indirect comment on the present situation of Syrian women.

Samīra ᶜAzzām could profit from the experience of some older short-story writers in Palestine when she began to publish in the forties. Although the establishment of the state of Israel in 1948 was a disaster for all Palestinians, among whom Samīra shared the uncertain lot of the refugees, she found time beside her work as a teacher and later journalist and broadcaster to continue writing. Her stories were published in the leading literary periodical in Beirut and when she died prematurely she left five collections of stories. She occupies an important place in Palestinian literature as one of the few people who bridged the gap between the first writers of fiction in Palestine and the younger generation who grew up in the diaspora. She is also distinguished by her technical mastery, her concision and her rejection of the sentimentality and romanticism which were then common in much narrative prose. Her stories examine a variety of forms of economic and social oppression to which not only women but also children, the poor, and the elderly fall victim; the stream of consciousness technique allows her mercilessly to expose the inhuman aspects of society which her characters experience. The reprinting of her books in 1982 indicates how important her work is still considered.

More and more women have followed in the footsteps of these "pioneers", continually expanding the range of themes they deal with. One of the best known of these short story writers outside the Arab world is Dr Nawāl as-Saᶜdāwī (b.1930), who is famous above all for her sincere and courageous struggle against the oppression, both mental and physical, of women. She has written three novels as well as four collections of short stories, and all her writing can be said to further her struggle against the oppression of women in the Arab world. When the literary qualities of Nawāl as-Saᶜdāwī's stories and novels are examined, however, some weaknesses may be discovered: a commonplace style and rather limited vocabulary, sometimes a slovenly construction and an occasional tendency to fall back on sugary romantic endings. In a few of her works she even shows all the male characters without exception in a bad light. But her commitment and the gripping quality of many of her themes are points in her favour. Her most convincing works are those in which she shows an awareness of other forms of oppression as well as those to which women alone are subjected; an example is the short story "She was the weakest". A more discrete, but from a literary point of view much more mature treatment of subjects connected with

81

women's lives, including women's sexuality, can be found in the works of her fellow countrywoman Alīfa Rifᶜat, a contemporary of hers, who has published a collection of stories in book form and a number of others in newspapers.

From the foregoing it will be clear that two approaches can be distinguished in the work of women writers. One is inspired by concern for the individual and society as a whole and treats the position of women as one of a number of important themes, while the other is a product of a particular concentration on the oppression of women in Arab society which pretty well excludes any other themes. This second approach was forcefully exemplified in one of the first Arabic novels to be written by a woman, *I'm Alive!* by the Lebanese Laylà Baᶜlabakkī (b.1936). This book caused a sensation when it appeared in 1958 and it is still cited as the most remarkable expression of feminist literature in Arabic. The title suggests the writer's individualism and her violent protest against the values of the Lebanese bourgeois milieu in which women can merely be decorative. The main character looks for a job, breaks away from her parental home and begins a stormy, passionate friendship with a student who is a Communist. In the end she has to face the impossibility of living independently of her family. The book is written in a staccato, nervous style well suited to the atmosphere of challenge and self-affirmation which the author seeks to express. No wonder that it excited a storm of protest in the Arab world when it was published; no woman had ever dared to accuse society in this way in black and white (Fernea and Bezirgan 1977:273-90) Laylà Baᶜlabakkī has published a few other works since, but she withdrew from literary life some years ago.

A number of other women have followed in Laylà Baᶜlabakkī's footsteps, choosing the theme of the revolt and search for identity of a female main character for their books. One of the best known in Lebanon is Amīlī Naṣrallā, who has published several novels and collections of short stories. In her first novel, which was awarded a prize, she attacks the traditional value-system of the Lebanese village as far as it concerns women, her special targets being arranged marriages and the age-old custom of killing any girl who has violated the code of honour and thus brought shame on her family. The savagery of this system of values is brought out all the more clearly because it is portrayed in the beautiful surroundings of the Lebanese mountains which Amīlī Naṣrallāh knows so well how to evoke. In her most recent works, however, she has turned her attention away from the theme of the position of women to concentrate on the war in Lebanon and what it means both to the ordinary citizens and to the Lebanese emigrants abroad, who must stand by impotently and watch (Fernea 1985:183-90, 355).

Round 1960 a handful of novels written by women came out in Damascus, the best known being *Days with Him* (1959) and *One Night* (1961) by Kūlīt Ḥūrī (b.1935). The main character in these novels is a woman who is searching for a relationship based on mutual love and respect. The focus is on her emotional development and her outbursts against the limitations imposed on her as a woman. An interesting feature of these Syrian novels — and to some extent of *I'm Alive!* — is that they share characteristics such as narcissism, romantic outbursts and an inability to analyse social reality with some Egyptian novels written by men thirty years before; in the meantime the predicament of the (male) intellectual has been superseded by the position of women as the central theme, at least as far as these women writers are concerned.

The emancipation of women, especially in the intellectual and emotional sphere, has formed the starting-point of the work of the most prominent Syrian woman writer of fiction, Ġāda as-Sammān (b.1942). She has published four collections of short stories as well as two novels and innumerable articles. One of her novels treats the civil war in Beirut, where Ġāda as-Sammān has lived for a long time. Her stories and novels owe their effect above all to her remarkable style, characteristics of which are original, striking images, a rich, carefully chosen vocabulary and an ironic undertone. Gāda as-Sammān has gradually widened her scope to include all aspects of oppression and lack of freedom in Arab society and her more recent books are a courageous call for the liberation of the individual in the Arab world from all that corrupts his humanity and hampers free development of his potential (as-Sammān 1974: 114; Fernea and Bezirgan 1977:392-9).

In Egypt, where the tradition of writing novels goes back further than in other Arab countries, two women have treated the theme of women's emancipation in novels which are artistically more mature than those of their Syrian sisters. Laṭīfa az-Zayyāt (b. 1925) published *The Open Door* in 1960. In it she situates the struggle which her heroine must wage to control her own destiny and lead a decent life as an independent person in the framework of Egypt's struggle for complete independence and national dignity in the period 1946-56. By letting her two themes follow a parallel course the author makes clear that she sees women's emancipation as inextricably bound up with national liberation — though the latter appears easier to achieve. In *The Confessions of a Mannish Woman* (1961) by Suʿād Zuhayr (b. 1925), the heroine's opposition to social conventions is the central theme of the book and it takes a more unambiguous form. Not only does the heroine overcome her family's resistance to her continuing her studies, but she marries a man she has chosen, and when her marriage fails she gets divorced and moves to a flat where she lives alone. Later she remarries and this time the future seems to promise her more happiness.

The Palestinian Saḥar Ḥalīfa (b.1941), who occupies a special position as the most important novelist in the Occupied Territories, combines the theme of women's emancipation with other, more political ones. Her *The Cactus* (1976) and *The Sunflower* (1980) chronicle the social and economic changes which have taken place in society on the West Bank of the Jordan since 1967. They treat such themes as the role of the guerrilla fighters, the economic dependence of the Palestinians on the Israeli occupiers, the relationship with the other Arabs and the suffering which springs directly from the occupation. Whereas in the earlier book the focus is on the changes which have taken place in society as a whole, the later book is more explicitly concerned with the position of women. A very unusual feature of *The Sunflower* is that a woman of the working classes (who is most convincingly portrayed) is one of the main characters.

This brief survey shows that most women writers of fiction are tending more and more to consider the theme of women's emancipation within the wider context of injustice and oppression in society. The result is that their work gains in variety, as is shown in a recent article on novels and poetry written by women about the civil war in Beirut (Cooke 1982). This article rightly avoids lumping the works together because they are written by women, and instead shows that each author's socio-religious and literary background, her personal experience of the war and her individual character determine her work; these all vary widely. Only the fact that in all the novels discussed the main character is a woman may have some connection with the fact that the author is a woman!

Women writers of novels and short stories have extended the scope of the themes they treat to more and more aspects of life. Their treatment of women characters and the position of women is also becoming increasingly varied, as is shown by a recent novel, *Aisha* (1983), written in English by a young Egyptian woman, Ahdaf Soueif. It portrays a sharp contrast between on the one hand a Western-orientated intellectual milieu, in which the main character grows up, where emotions are suppressed and culture and rationality are the highest virtues, and on the other the grandparents' world, still dominated by a traditional, religiously orientated way of life, and the lower-class milieu of the children's nanny where feelings of love, hatred and revenge and women's solidarity with one another can be experienced to the full. The main character, torn between these worlds, is destroyed; the writer leaves no doubt where her own sympathies lie. Another example of the questioning of Western models of emancipation is the short story "Lulu" by the young Lebanese novelist and short story writer, Ḥanān aš-Šayḫ. Here a Westernized main character compares her life with that of her friend who lives in a traditional milieu. When they meet each other again after a number of years, the main character realizes that her friend, whom she used to pity, is now happier than she is and has achieved a maturity which the "modern" women cannot pretend to. These two works can be considered as a literary expression of the increasing rejection, in the Arab and Muslim world, of a vision of women's emancipation which adopts certain Western ideas uncritically. At the same time aspects of traditional social structures which offered women many and varied opportunities to develop solidarity with each other are being appreciated anew (cf. Minai 1981:239-45). It is to be expected that those sections of society which were relatively less receptive to Western ideas will in the future attract the attention of women writers increasingly and traditional patterns of life will be examined to ascertain their good and weak points rather than being automatically condemned.

This survey of women writers of poetry and prose does not pretend to be complete. It shows, however, that Arabic literature today is the concern of all Arab writers, both men and women. Although the number of women writers is smaller than that of men, the unavoidable conclusion is that in the literary sphere Arab women can make a real contribution to mapping out the future of themselves and their people. The guiding principle of their work is liberation, in the first place women's liberation and also liberation of the human being in the Arab world, and in the second place concern for all endeavours to achieve liberation in all parts of the world (as-Sammān 1974:122-3).

The Woman Writer in Society

The fact just mentioned that there are fewer women than men writing in the Arab world fits into the pattern of women's literary activities the world over. A woman in the Arab world who wants to be a writer encounters obstacles above all in her family circle, and these obstacles are economic and above all social in nature.

In the first place, families of the poorer sections of society are more inclined to make their daughters leave school early than their sons if they are in financial difficulties. Moreover, in some circles it is still the custom to keep girls at home when they have reached the age of eleven or so, regardless of the family's financial position. That a lack of education in exceptional circumstances may not be an obstacle to a literary career is shown by the life of the already mentioned Zaynab Fawwāz. It is also worth noting that not all the Egyptian women who contributed to the short story anthology published by aš-Šārūnī (1975) had completed secondary school. But in normal circumstances a woman who has not pursued higher education will be completely occupied by the traditional tasks which society imposes on her and which leave no free time for intellectual pursuits. Hence it is even more difficult for her than for a man who is self-taught to win fame as a writer.

The social background of women writers is thus more limited than that of their male colleagues; this has led to the striking fact that certain female characters, for instance peasant women or women from the old quarters of the cities, are rarely portrayed in works by women writers although they regularly attract the attention of male writers who sometimes present them with great insight. This phenomenon can also be observed in North African literature, as Lourina de Voogd has pointed out in her contribution (p. 98). Even a wealthy background is, however, no guarantee that a woman can begin a literary career. A great deal depends on the attitude of the members of her immediate family, in the first place her parents and later her husband. Some women, such as Fadwà Ṭūqān and Ġāda as-Sammān, received much encouragement from their close relatives, but others have had to overcome much opposition. Biographical information shows that the greatest resistance comes from husbands who are jealous of their wife's success and consider it unfitting that they should be active in public life. Women with a strong personality and an equally strong urge to write choose to separate from their husbands, either through divorce or merely by living apart, but how many others bind themselves to silence in order to save their marriage?

Outside the family circle the obstacles confronting women who want to write do not differ in essence from those facing men. When Nawāl as-Saᶜdāwī complains of problems of censorship and self-censorship, and of the publishers' habit of pocketing the profits from her books (Latumahina and Van Hoek 1982:256), she is expressing the grievances of many Arab writers, irrespective of sex. The only thing one can say is that readers are more inclined to consider a book as autobiographical when its author is a woman. The resulting gossip can damage her social standing, especially if her family doesn't approve of her writing.

Women's Magazines

Two categories of women's magazines can be found in the eastern Arab world. The first consists of periodicals which are published by official organizations, such as the General Federation of Iraqi women. The aim of these magazines is to further the official policy towards women and to involve women actively in the process of social change. To the extent that they widen women's intellectual horizons and make them aware of their rights they have a positive effect, but they do not allow any fundamental discussion about the role of women in society or the direction in which society as a whole is developing.

The other type of women's magazines corresponds in the

main with women's magazines in the West and is published commercially. The public for these magazines is limited mainly to urban middle-class women. They cover the usual topics of cooking, fashion, child care, health and marital problems, and some of them include gossip about film stars and other celebrities. But the hasty conclusion that these magazines merely imitate Western models is not necessarily justified, at least not in the case of one of the most important, the Egyptian women's magazine *Ḥawwā' (Eve)*. An analysis of the contents of the short stories in this magazine showed that the mentality they reflected was closer to a Western one than to that of the mass of the Egyptian population, but that there were some significant differences between the Egyptian middle-class attitudes and Western patterns of behaviour. In the sphere of personal and especially intimate relationships many limitations were accepted as normal and the themes of family and sexual relationships were treated with caution. As far as work was concerned the Egyptian women had greater freedom to continue working after marriage than in corresponding sections of Western society. And finally in these stories it was not so much greater freedom for women which was advocated as more limitations on the freedom of men (Suleyman 1978:369).

REFERENCES

Allen, Roger, 1982, *The Arabic Novel. An Historical and Critical Introduction*, University of Manchester Press.

Baġdādī, Badīᶜ, 1981,* "Book of the month: *Damascus, smile of sorrow*, interview with the author and critical study", in *Al-Maᶜrifa*, Damascus, no. 228, February, pp. 98–129.

Boullata, Kamal, 1978 (ed. with trans.), *Women of the Fertile Crescent*, Washington D.C., Three Continents Press.

Cooke, Miriam, 1982, "Beirut . . . theatre of the absurd . . . theatre of dreams. The Lebanese civil war in the writings of contemporary Arab women", in *Journal of Arabic Literature*, 13, pp. 124–41.

Fernea, Elizabeth Warnock (ed.), 1985, *Women and the Family in the Middle East. New Voices of Change*, Austin, University of Texas Press.

Fernea, Elizabeth Warnock, and Basima Qattan Berzirgan (eds.), 1977, *Middle Eastern Muslim Women Speak*, Austin, University of Texas Press.

Al-Ġundī, Anwar, n.d.,* *Literature by Arab women. Development and prominent contributors*, Cairo/Beirut, Maktabat al-anǧlū al-miṣrīyya/Dār al-maᶜrifa/Maktabat al-maᶜārif.

Latumahina, Roos, and Albert-Jan van Hoek, 1982, "Nawal El-Saadawi, doctor and writer" (in Dutch), in Ed de Moor *et al.* (eds.), *Vrouwen in het Midden Oosten*, Bussum/Nijmegen/Antwerpen, Het Wereldvenster/MOIdPublications/Standaard Wetenschappelijke Uitgeverij, pp. 254-62.

Minai, Naila, 1981, *Women in Islam. Tradition and Transition in the Middle East*, London, John Murray.

Nègre, Arlette, 1978, "Les femmes savantes chez Dhahabi", *Bulletin d'Etudes Orientales*, XXX, pp. 119-26.

Sālim, Ġurǧ, 1974,* "Introduction to the novel and short story in Syria", in *Al-Ma ᶜrifa*, Damascus, no. 146, April, pp. 7-22.

as-Sammān, Ġāda, 1974,* interviewed by Muḥyı ad-dīn Ṣubḥī, in *Al-Ma ᶜrifa*, Damascus, no. 145, March, pp. 113-24.

aš-Šārūnī, Yūsuf (ed.), 1975,* *The 1002nd Night, A selection of stories written by Egyptian women*, Cairo, Al-hay'a al-miṣrīyya al-ᶜāmma li-l-kitāb.

Suleyman, Michael, 1978, "Changing attitudes towards women in Egypt: The role of fiction in women's magazines", in *Middle Eastern Studies*, 14, 1981, pp. 352-71.

Titles marked * are in Arabic.

ARABIC LITERATURE IN NORTH AFRICA

LOURINA DE VOOGD

One day a scholar at the Karaouine University in Fes said to a group of students seated in a circle around him, "Anyone who is afraid of his wife, please stand up." The whole group stood up, with the exception of one man who was leaning against a pillar. The scholar said to him, "Why aren't you standing? Does that mean you are not afraid of your wife?" The student answered, "Of course I am, Professor, but I can't stand up without the help of my friends. Yesterday my wife beat the soles of my feet until they bled!" (Lamalif 1980: no. 115).

The Moroccan sociologist Fatima Mernissi uses this characteristic anecdote circulating among progressive Moroccan intellectuals to show that even the most creative thinkers in Moroccan society are reduced to the level of a well-worn gramophone record the moment they are forced to contemplate their relationship with the female sex. The question is not whether the anecdote itself is significant. Generally speaking research into the social position of Arab women does not concern itself with the amount of psychological influence they exercise within the home. To Fatima Mernissi the important thing is to demonstrate the extent to which economic, social and political innovation depends on a revolution in relations between men and women. It is understandable, says Mernissi, that a man who has been taught from childhood who is master and who is slave will always remain susceptible to a strict hierarchy. The road to democracy begins more or less in the marriage bed.

In recent years numerous studies have been published on the position of Arab women, most of them by men or by women researchers from the West. This does not raise hopes regarding the contribution of North African women to literature. But what more effective way is there to express your world, your feelings, your joys and frustrations than by writing about them? It is for this reason that the work of Arab women from North Africa is worthy of our attention, even though these writers are unknown beyond the boundaries of their own country.

Writers from the Middle East, in particular Lebanon and Egypt, have always been in the forefront of modern Arab literature. North African authors who write in Arabic are still confronted with the almost unassailable image of those neighbours to the East, as they struggle with cultural and historical complexities at home, in an effort to create better conditions for a literary climate in their own country.

Algerian literature, for example, has become fairly well known simply because, being written in French, it could be published in France, and thus had no trouble reaching an international public. Algerians who write in Arabic, however, must be ever on the lookout for new ways to promote their work.

In Morocco only the French-language authors like Tahar Ben Jelloun, Driss Chraïbi and Abdellatif Laabi have managed to reach a foreign public. Even in their own country the Arabic authors are almost unknown outside literary circles. The same is true in Tunisia, where Albert Memmi and Jean Amrouche were read and admired in French while of the Arabic writers, only Mahmud Mas῾adī and the poet ăs-Šabbī have made a name for themselves in the entire Arab world. Most Tunisian writers are part of a national literature which has gradually come to be known as the Tunisian tradition. In all these developments women play their role, albeit a peripheral one. Their opportunities and obstacles, in the field of literature at any rate, are no different from those of their male colleagues.

Little has been recorded of the early contributions of women to the literature of these countries. But we do know that through the oral tradition women have been instrumental in preserving a rich heritage of folk art and literature.

The population of the North African countries includes Arab, Arabized and Berber women. A Moroccan literary scholar has published a collection entitled *Rubaᶜiyȳat nisā Fās* (Quatrains of the women of Fes). It contains love songs which are sung by the Arab women of Fes and regularly broadcast on Moroccan radio.

> Beloved, I will be your slave, if you will, my sultan
> and my mother and sister your servants in the house
> your mouth smells sweetly of musk, blossoms and carnation
> dust still on your feet, thank you (for coming)
> you, with your lovely (crystal) face. (al-Fāsī 1971:150)

Romantic, urbane poetry which harks back to classic Arab literature: "We pay reverence to the love of Fes/and the Bani Udra" (ibidem 149). This refers to a type of love poetry dating from the eighth century AD and characterized by a form of platonic love.

The songs of the Berber women are known for their realism. Their pride, their vitality and their love of freedom all find expression in their music.

> Poor naïve young man, stop hassling me!
> I came to the village to visit my parents,
> Not to look for a husband — God preserve me from that!
> And soon I'll go back to Azilal, if God so wishes it.
> You say you want me to be your wife
> After just one night of my lovemaking.
> Well, I know how long your desire would last!
> And what can you offer that's sweeter than freedom?
>
> (Fernea 1977:133)

In the folk tales which are part of the Berber oral tradition the heroine is not the unapproachable beloved, but a lady of character. A number of the stories from Kabylia which Mouloud Mammeri (1980) has collected illustrate this point. This oral tradition has always been very important to Arab women, but with the advent of television, the transistor radio and the cassette recorder, which make it possible to import music from all over the world, these songs and stories are bound to lose some of their appeal.

Morocco is a country where books do not flourish. The majority of books published are textbooks and yet Morocco, of all the Arab countries, imports the most schoolbooks. Moroccan children's books are practically nonexistent, and university students read mainly French literature or Arab writers from the Middle East. Fortunately there is a writers' association which is active among the literary élite.

At the moment there are two women writers in Morocco who are fairly well known. Rafīqa aṭ-Ṭabiᶜa has published three collections of short stories and Ḥanāta Binnūna also has three books of stories to her name, as well as a novel which appeared in 1981. Both women teach and are presently employed as headmistresses of girls' schools. The stories of Rafīqa aṭ-Tabiᶜa are set in the reality of everyday life, fleeting images captured in her subtle and very personal style. Ḥanāta Binnūna's work has philosophical undertones and everything she writes echoes a deep involvement with the political situation in the entire Arab world. She has an exceptional style, which Mona Mikhail (1982:55) refers to as "agonized prose".

Mikhail characterizes Binnūna as follows:

> She is a writer whose impulse is turned inwards rather than outwards. The reality she depicts is not observed and then recreated in a sociological manner, but rather is set as a mirror which reflects the drives, the flaws and the deep anxieties of a society at large. . . . (Mikhail 1982:55)

Although Binnūna's "mirror" also reflects the fate of the less fortunate members of society, women among them, this image is supplanted by a flow of ideas emanating from the main characters, who are labouring to express their individual dissonance with the surroundings and the political situation.

The most prominent woman in the field of Moroccan emancipation is Fatima Mernissi. In her well-known study *Beyond the Veil; Male-Female Dynamics in a Modern Muslim Society* (1975) and in *Sexe, idéologie, Islam* (1983), she analyses sexual relationships in an Islamic society.

It was Fatima Mernissi who replied to the critic whose extensive review of Binnūna's novel appeared in the Moroccan newspaper *al-ᶜAlam*. She exposes his review as a sample of typical male thinking. "You are still the master and you conduct yourself as master, as one who understands nothing of women, who does not listen to her words and cannot accept her writings." (cf. *al-ᶜAlam* 1981,12) In her article she stresses her own responsibility, and that of every women who is capable of expressing herself on paper, to communicate to the opposite sex some understanding of feminine nature.

In 1982 a French-language novel was published in Morocco which caused something of a sensation. The novel, entitled *Aïcha la rébelle* is somewhere between a love story and a historical novel and it was written by Halima Ben Haddou, who has been an invalid since she was nine. She is an Algerian (from Oran) but now lives near Nador in Northern Morocco. The newspaper *al-ᶜAlam* published a short interview with her at the time her novel was published (see *al-ᶜAlam* 1982,8).

The story is set on a farm in Northern Morocco during the Spanish occupation. The heroine Aïcha, who rides, runs a farm, practises free love and hates her father from the bottom of her heart, is not only a symbol of opposition to the foreign rulers. She is also a woman in search of *Lebensraum*, a woman of passion and character, demanding the freedom that she considers her due. The price she must pay is loneliness and the contempt of society. The character of Aïcha would be at home in any Western adventure story, but in a Moroccan novel she is a remarkable figure. It is not without reason that Aïcha's nickname is *L'Espagnole* while she alone knows that she is Moroccan and Moslem to the core.

The relatively liberal climate in Tunisia is favourable to literary work. Development in other art forms, such as music, painting, films, the media and in particular theatre, are also promising. The excellent educational facilities which are enjoyed by a great number of girls, ensure that women are represented in all sectors of community life. Most of the writers are professional women, with jobs in education, journalism, radio or television. Layla Bin Mami (b. 1944) went to university and is now a journalist. She published her poems in various journals and in 1968 her collection of short stories *The Burning Minaret* appeared. The title is a symbol of the collapse of traditional values. Thanks to the *Code du Statut Personnel* the rights of Tunisian women are safeguarded under the law, and their position is better than that of their sisters in the surrounding countries. What Bin Mami is seeking above all is equality of feeling, esteem and sexuality.

The poet Zubayda Basir (b. 1938) works in broadcasting and in 1968 published a volume of poetry *Hanīn* (Desire). Nagiya Tamir, a Tunisian who was born in Damascus, has lived in Tunis since 1946. She has written short stories and a large number of plays, many of which have been adapted for radio. Hind ᶜAzūz, who received a traditional upbringing, was for many years associated with the Tunisian women's movement and also worked in broadcasting. Her stories in the collection *Fī ad-darb aṭ-ṭawīl* (In the long alley, 1983) are true to life and written in easy, uncomplicated prose. Often, however, the "message" underlying the story destroys the original spontaneity of her style.

The work of ᶜArūsiyya an-Nālūtī (b. 1950) is much more revolutionary in character. In addition to her involvement in the emancipation movement, she is very much alive to the realities of social injustice. In her collection *al-Buᶜd al-ḥāmis* she describes in gruesome detail how a man, hallucinating as a result of hunger and cold, is driven to cannibalism.

One of the most recent works published by Tunisian women is a volume of short stories by Hayā ibn aš-Šayḥ (1983), some of which are politically oriented. She has also written poems and a number of novels. The novel *Āmina* by Zakkiyya ᶜAbd al-Qādir appeared in 1983. She is well known as a singer and gives readings of poetry from all over the Arab world.

The heroine of her novel has had a musical and literary

upbringing and her whole personality bears the stamp of a classical education. The novel is particularly interesting because it proves that the values of classic Arabic culture need not be sacrificed for a modern education. It is Amina who teaches her unlettered sisters-in-law (great fans of Elvis Presley) to appreciate classical Arab music. The novel also illustrates the conflict of views and opinions between the various milieux which exist in the different Arab countries.

Amina marries a man from a neighbouring country, probably Algeria or Morocco, and finds herself in a highly traditional environment. The father-in-law is given a sympathetic portrayal but as a result of the dominating influence which the mother has on her son, Amina finally refuses to live with her husband's family any longer. Amina becomes the breadwinner and pays her husband's college fees. When the young couple, now with two children, moves to the country, the man gradually disclaims all responsibility for his family and a serious breach develops between them.

The novel is sensitive but not dramatic. Amina's personality is so all-of-a-piece that she is able to cope with the most desperate situations. Her psychological victory is offset by the realization that the emancipation of Arab women must be accompanied by a transition within society. Otherwise the price of their success may be their own happiness.

As we have already seen, Arab literature in Algeria is still in its infancy. The country was under French rule longer than the others and the stamp of French culture has been indelibly imprinted on Algerian society. The work of Algerian women writers is also part of French-language Algerian literature. They too express themselves better in French than in Arabic, due to their educational background. Arabization is proceeding steadily, but French is still the language spoken among the literary élite. For many Berbers, who learned French from an early age and speak only Berber at home, Arabic is a completely new language. In the light of government measures aimed at arabization, it is not surprising that many

Berber intellectuals are working to revive Berber culture and language.

The novel *Une femme pour mon fils* is by a male writer, the Algerian Ali Ghalem (b. 1943). His portrait of a woman in conflict with her traditional role and with her mother-in-law is not without merit. Abdelhamid Benhedouga, a male author who is working to promote the use of Arabic in Algeria, has published a number of novels, among them *Rih al Djanub* (Wind from the South) and *Nihijat al-Ams* (Yesterday is Past). It is to be hoped that Benhedouga will also succeed in persuading women to write in Arabic about their experiences. Of the novels by Algerian, Moroccan and Tunisian writers which have been published in French, many are highly autobiographical, so that women are portrayed in many different roles, as mothers, sisters and lovers. The great merit of these novels lies in the fact that the heroines come from a wide range of social milieux. In the earlier novels by women from the various Arab countries the heroines are usually from middle- or upper-class backgrounds. The work of these men is also extremely helpful in forming an impression of what life is like in a typical Arab society. But in order to know how women really think and feel, it is above all important to read what they themselves write. In short, women must publish.

Within the limited oeuvre of recent North African Arabic literature by women, many works will inevitably display technical imperfections, and authors will not always make the best use of their literary potential. A new literature needs feedback. Feedback to learn from and to enrich one's work, as a literary channel for individual expression. A wailing woman easily becomes tiresome, but a woman with a haunted face awakens interest in the causes of her grief. One of the main themes in the French-language works by women is the conflict created by biculturism. *Aïcha la rebelle* is a prime example. The Algerian Kabyle and Christian writer Fadhma Aïth Mansour Amrouche (1882-1967), mother of Marguerite Taos Amrouche and Jean Amrouche, also touches upon this theme in her moving autobiographical novel *Histoire de ma vie* (1979). She lived much of her life in Tunisia and France and in her foreword she says: "In spite of the forty years I have spent in Tunisia, in spite of my French education, I have never felt that I was one with the French or with the Arabs. I have always remained the eternal exile" (Amrouche 1979:9).

Nina Moati describes the same conflict in her trilogy *Les belles de Tunis* which is set against a Jewish background, while it also plays a role in several of Assia Djebar's novels. This theme is absent, however, from North African Arabic literature. Here women are one with their background, and their upbringing as Arabs and as Moslems enables them to view the problems of the Arab women on the road to equality in the right perspective. This fact can be a great stimulus to Arab women writers.

What other media can women employ besides the printed book to make their voice heard? We have seen that a number of Tunisian women are involved in radio work or employed as journalists. But how free are women to express themselves? Most of the better magazines on the Tunisian market come from Saudi Arabia or the Emirates, and are published or distributed via central offices in Europe. This type of magazine is modern, full of expensive (European) advertisements for clothes, perfumes, cosmetics and jewelry. One example is *Sayyidatī* (Mrs), which is comparable to, say, *Vogue* and comes from Saudi Arabia via London. *Hiyā* (She) from Abu Dhabi runs the same type of advertisement but it is a much less expensive magazine. These magazines are largely concerned with typical women's affairs such as children, cooking, etc. *Sayyidatī* also devotes a great deal of space to art and literature, and to the position of women, usually in the form of an interview with a well-known philosopher, or a piece about the influential role of women in certain African tribes. A prominent feature is the letters-to-the-editor column, devoted mainly to marital problems. *Sayyidatī* invariably advises readers to seek help and consolation in religion. The problems are usually handled with a personal touch and the classic clichés are absent. The price of these magazines is such that only a limited group can afford them.

The top Arab newspapers in North Africa are in the hands of men, and outside of incidental contributions by women journalists, there are very few sections that cater to women's interests. But around 8 March (International Women's Day) entire pages are devoted to women's news.

Progressive and radical women's groups are not encouraged in Morocco and the media are no exception. There is the middle-of-the-road magazine *Aïcha*, headed by Princess Lalla Fatima Zohra (also president of the National Union of Moroccan Women). And there is also a *Health Magazine*, especially for housewives and mothers, which reports on new gains in medicine, such as echography and test-tube babies, all illustrated with photographs of European women. A newcomer appeared in 1983, *Democratic Youth*, which highlights the position of women within the political structure. *March 8*, which first appeared in 1984, offers well documented articles. In Morocco magazines and newspapers disappear as quickly as they appear, and it takes quite some time for a publication to really establish itself. Generally speaking, the media do not present any real women's perspective at all.

REFERENCES

ᶜAbd al-Qādir, Zakkiyya, 1983, *Amina*, Tunis, Dār al-qalam.

Aicha, măgallaᵗ al-mar'a al-maḡribiyya (Aicha, magazine for women in Morocco), 1983, Rabat.

al-ᶜAlam, 19 July 1982, *Sudūr awwal kitāb lī-Halīma bin Haddū*, Rabat.

al-ᶜAlam, 1982, 633, *Fatima Mernissi, Hawla kitāba Ḥanāṭa Binnūna*, Rabat.

Amrouche, Fadhma A.M., (1968) 1979, *Histoire de ma vie*, Paris, Maspéro.

ᶜAzūz, Hind, 1983, *Fī ad-darb aṭ-ṭawīl*, (In the long alley), Tunis, ad-Dār at-tunisiyya lil-našr.

Ben Haddou, Halima, 1982, *Aïcha la rebelle*, Paris, Jeune Afrique.

Binnūna, Ḥanāṭa, 1981, *al-Ġad wa-al-ġaḍab* (Tomorrow and the anger), Casablanca, Editions Maghrébines.

al-Fāsī, Muḥammad, 1981, *Rubāᶜiyyāt nisā' Fās* (Quatrains by the Women of Fes), Fes.

Fernea, Elizabeth Warnock, and Basima Qattan Bezirgan, 1977, *Middle Eastern Muslim Women Speak*, Austin/London, University of Texas Press.

Hiyā; al-usra al-ᶜarabiyya (She; the Arab family), 1983, Abū Dhabī, de Verenigde Arabische Emiraten.

Ibn aš-Šayḫ, Hayā, 1983, *Wa-ġadan tušriq šamš al-ḥurriya* (Tomorrow the sun of freedom will rise), Tunis, Dār al-qalam.

Lamalif, April 1980, Fatima Mernissi, *Un futur sans femmes*, pp. 27-30, Casablanca.

al-Maǧalla as-sihhiyya (Health Magazine), 1983, Rabat.

Mammeri, Mouloud, 1980, *Tellem chaho! Contes berbères de Kabylie*, Paris, Bordas.

Mernissi, Fatima, 1980, see Lamalif.

Mikhail, Mona, 1982, "Ambiguity and relevance in the works of Khannāthah Bannūnah", pp. 53-64, in: *Arabic literature in North Africa: critical essays and annotated bibliography*, Cambridge, Mass., Dar Mahhar.

Moati, Nine, 1983, *Les belles de Tunis*, Paris, Le Seuil.

an-Nālūtī, ᶜArūsiyya, 1975, *al-Buᶜd al-ḫāmis* (The Fifth Dimension), Tunis, ad-Dār al-ᶜarabiyya lil-kitāb.

aš-Šabāb ad-dimuqrātī (The democratic youngsters), 1983, Rabat.

Sayyidatī; maǧallaᶜal-usra al-ᶜarabiyya (Mrs; magazine for the Arab Family), 1983, London.

FRANCOPHONE LITERATURE IN NORTH AFRICA

FLORA VAN HOUWELINGEN

When Westerners speak of the daily life of women in the Maghreb (Morocco, Algeria, Tunisia), the land of the "setting sun", they generally point to their rejection and oppression within these societies. This state of affairs is not due solely to French colonialism, as many Algerian men claim, but is clearly bound up with the culture of the area itself. This is made abundantly clear in a study by Fadéla M'Rabet, one of the few feminist sociologists from the Maghreb. In *La femme algérienne, les Algériennes* (1969), M'Rabet maintains that emancipation will not make much progress until there is a change in the attitude of men as well. As long as patriarchal standards and traditions, combined with an Islamic-political ideology, continue to dominate and the National Association of Algerian Women remains an appendage of the Party, the outlook for women is a sombre one. M'Rabet's book ends with the following words:

> If a feminine vanguard does not continue the daily fight against stupid prejudices and shameless privileges, then this hope will remain — and for how many generations yet to come? — an illusion.

Although the political situation in Morocco and Tunisia has altered, the position of women in general is not much different from that in Algeria. It is only in Tunisia that future prospects for women are somewhat more promising. The situation sketched above cannot help but affect literary criticism, (state) publishing and the public itself. Nevertheless in the last few decades more and more North African women writers have gained a place for themselves in the field of literature. In order to understand why they very often write in French, we must consider this literature against an historical and sociological, as well as a literary, background. It is also important to

102

determine whether North African male writers have contributed to any changes that have been brought about in the image of women.

The seeds of the present cultural alienation of the Maghreb were sown in the nineteenth century, when French colonizers made the French language compulsory at the executive and administrative level, and established French schools open to only a small portion of the original population. There remained only a few Arabic (Koran) schools. When the revolution broke out in Algeria in 1954, over 75 per cent of the population was illiterate (Bonn 1974:156). Although illiteracy has decreased in recent years, there is a noticeable trend towards arabization, so that today the market for French-language literature in the Maghreb is limited to readers educated at French schools. The Maghreb has a very large rural population, where illiteracy is very high, especially among older women. These people are cut off from formal literary activities, and until recently they have succeeded in preserving the traditional culture solely by means of oral transmission in an Arabic or Berber dialect. By reciting folk tales and legends, singing songs and poetry, using proverbs and dancing to their own music, they have significantly influenced the development of French-language North African literature.

Since the end of the last century the oral tradition has been recorded mainly by men. As early as 1890 Mouliéras wrote down eighty-five Kabyle legends and fantastic tales in a Berber dialect, and these were later translated into French (Lacoste-Dujardin 1965 and 1970). This collection includes not only traditional folk tales, in which women appear in the role of wife and mother, but also a number of "Oriental" tales, in which white princesses spend all day doing nothing, while black slave girls minister to them and perform all the necessary domestic activities.

The traditional folk stories often make mention of the *teryel* (the anti-woman), a myth which was later recorded in German by Frobenius (1922). The *teryel* lives in the undergrowth or in a cave where she is in contact with the powers of the underworld. She is free to go wherever she wishes, while the civilized woman attends to her housekeeping. She hunts like a man, but devours her prey raw. Her favourite victims are young women and children. Sometimes she pretends to be a civilized woman and mingles with the womenfolk. Then the hero arrives and unmasks her. In many stories the *teryel*, symbol of anti-fertility, is associated with old women who, because of their infertility, are thought to be evil. Myths like these were often used to frighten young girls.

In the oriental narratives, on the other hand, the daughter or the wife of the sultan often occupies a position of influence. The daughter dresses up like a man and sometimes takes the sultan's place, until the time comes to yield her place to the husband of her choice. Her position of influence was often attained at the expense of others, usually black women. Children do not play any significant part in these stories, and even infertility is not considered a serious problem. Lacoste-Dujardin (1970:331) believes that these stories may indicate the rise of a new consciousness among these women storytellers with regard to their position in traditional society.

The first Francophone literary activities on Algerian soil were initiated by the Algérienistes (ca. 1900-35) and the *École d'Alger* (ca. 1935-50). It was not until the 1940s that indigenous Algerian authors entered onto the scene, and they remained faithful to French literary norms and traditions.

The essays and novels of Djamila Debèche also date from this period. Debèche, who was born in Rhiras and received an excellent French education, had her first book, *Leila, jeune fille d'Algérie* (1947), published in France. It was followed several years later by *Aziza* (1955), in which the author describes the difficulties facing Algerian women whose schooling has given them a modern Western orientation, but who are seen in their own culture as objects, at the disposal of father, brother or husband. While Westerners are inclined to see in Debèche the first Algerian woman writer to champion the rights of the women of her culture, many Algerians consider her a prime example of cultural alienation.

Biculturism also appears in the work of other women writers. About the same time as Debèche was writing, Marguerite Taos Amrouche published her first novel *Jacinthe noire* (1947). Taos was born in Tunisia and lived there for many years, until her family emigrated to France. Her early autobiographical novels *Jacinthe noire* and *Rue des Tambourins* (1960) make no secret of the frustration she feels at having no true home. As a Berber who converted to Catholicism she feels suspended between two cultures, a feeling shared by her mother Fadhma Aïth Mansour. It was not until years later when, at the urging of her brother the well-known poet Jean Amrouche, she decided to write *Le grain magique* (1966), that she appears to have accepted her fate. In the foreword to this collection of Berber stories, poems and proverbs from Kabylia which she translated into French, Taos says that French has become almost as familiar to her as her native language (Berber), so that it can no longer be considered an obstacle in the struggle to save the Berber oral tradition from extinction. Taos died in 1976, leaving behind not only her mother's autobiographical story *Histoire de ma vie*, but also three gramophone records with her talented interpretation of the Berber songs of her people. Despite considerable political opposition, she also succeeded in creating a chair of Berber literature and sociology at the University of Algiers.

In the fifties a new generation of Algerian authors went in search of their own culture, under the influence of a growing nationalism. The "generation of '52" spoke to its own people, even though most of them did not read French. During the war of independence, many people with no literary gifts took up their pens to describe, in simple school French, the horrors of what they had endured. Poetry by women writers such as Nadia Guendouz (1968), Anna Gréki (1963, 1965), Danièle Amrane and Leila Djabali (Barrat 1965) dates from this period.

Very little has been heard from them since the war; some are dead and others have given up writing. In 1963 the Association for Algerian Writers (UEA) was founded; fifty-six members signed the manifesto, only five of whom were women (Déjeux 1973:29). Especially after the coup in 1965 many authors relinquished their freedom of expression, in the belief that self-censorship was the price they had to pay for the privilege of being spokespersons of their people. Social realism became the official literary line. Publication and distribution came under the control of the Government Printing Office (SNED). Authors who did not intend to waste their literary gifts on a political dictatorship emigrated to France and published their work there. They referred to the revolution as "abortive" because the country had again become the victim of cultural alienation (Nisbet 1980:31). Today the majority of French-speaking Algerian women writers live in France.

Since 1969 the Ministry of Information and Culture has encouraged young people to write by awarding an annual prize to the author of the best French or Arabic-language short story based on the war of independence. These stories, which the ministry publishes in its magazine *Promesses*, are written and read almost exclusively by men. The literary quality is not very high and women invariably play a subordinate role in the struggle, though in reality they contributed much to the liberation of their country. A poll conducted by Charles Bonn (1974:164) showed that younger women are not greatly interested in the war of independence. They concern themselves more with emancipation, free love and other topics found in Western women's magazines, literature and films. French-language Algerian literature published in France, in which these themes also appear, is almost unavailable and is even smuggled into the country. Many younger women deliberately speak, read and write French because it gives them access to modern Western society and some hope of changing their situation. They associate Arabic with tradition and religion, a view diametrically opposed to that of established literary opinion. To speak and write in French about Algerian women, especially mothers, is a violation of the traditional closed environment and is akin to sacrilege. Traditionalists contend that this worldly approach is only possible if one adopts the Western attitudes of the former oppressor. Authors who adopt this approach and moreover publish their work in France are seen as "prostitutes" in the service of the consumer society (Bonn 1974:225). In 1971 the newspaper *El Moudjahid* even published a poem by Moustapha Toumi in which he vehemently denounced the emancipation of Algerian women, invoking all the standard clichés about eternal femininity". In "Femme, femme, femme", his target is that standard troublemaker, the woman who complains because her husband comes home late:

> Let me believe, let me dream;
> Just stay what you have always been
> That is: Woman, Woman, Woman
> To the tips of your fingers
> To the curve of your lips.

This poem was met with a storm of protest from young women like Tania, whose reply was published the following week:

> In answer to your article in today's paper, I say no!
> I shout no!
> No, we do not want to remain what we have always been.
> We no longer want to be what women mean to you.
> We do not want men to talk about us without consulting us. No!
> You ought to know, Mr. Toumi, that there is no longer such a thing
> as the traditional feminine personality.

And yet public opinion considers women like Tania aliens. Even a young man of her own age felt called upon to lecture her:

> There are girls, girls like you perhaps, who want to live the American way, whose parents work day and night and sacrifice

their whole lives so that their daughters will never know what poverty is. They didn't have the chances that you had — they fought in the war and worked their whole lives. If they can't read and write, blame it on colonialism (Bonn 1974:131).

This boy, and with him most Algerian men, believes that literacy is enough to emancipate Algerian women, and that they will be free as soon as the social revolution is a fact.

Male authors now living in France, like Rachid Boudjedra (1969, 1972), Mohammed Dib (1962, 1968) and Yacine Kateb (1956) from Algeria, and Driss Chraïbi (1954, 1972) and Mohammed Khaïr-Eddine (1964, 1968, 1970) from Morocco, do endow their autobiographically inspired heroes with psychological insight into the suppression of North African women. But it is unfortunate that these heroes choose to take out their frustration on European women, who are highly sexualized, while their own mothers, sisters and wives are symbolized by "land", "cave" and "sea". These writers are primarily interested in their own bodies, which it seems they have only just discovered. The role reserved for women is one of accomplice. Though they denounce the (sexual) oppression of their women, they offer very few new perspectives. Or do they consider women liberated when they are available for the pleasure of any man, which is the image which these authors present of European women?

Assia Djebar (the pseudonym of Fatima Zohra Imalayen) is the first Algerian writer to study the plight of her sisters. Her novels describe the mental and physical frustration of Algerian women from a fictional female perspective. After the publication of *Soif* (1957) and *Les impatients* (1958), Djebar was rebuked by literary critics because her work was not rooted in the war of independence and because she wrote about the kind of women's problems that only affected upper middle-class society. She retired to Tunisia, later Morocco (Merad 1976:72, 73), where she came into contact with Algerian refugees, and for the first time understood what her people were thinking and feeling. In her next novels *Les enfants du nouveau monde* (1962) and *Les alouettes naïves* (1967), her heroines are conscious of their political role in the reconstruction of their country. But at the same time she shows that Algerian women are still the victims of patriarchal standards and traditions:

> Yes, it is almost easy to forget, he thinks as he comes home in the evening and looks at this wife whom the all-powerful oppressor out there will never know. People say she is "imprisoned", but her husband thinks "liberated"

and later on in the same passage "a body that submits without response, because the dialogue of mutual contact is missing" (Djebar 1962:18).

In 1970 the Algerian radio put on an adaptation of her play *Rouge l'aube* (1969), but cut out all passages which referred to the part women played in the struggle for liberation. And for a long time after that Djebar wrote nothing. It was not until 1979 that her next novel *Femmes d'Alger dans leur appartement* was published in Paris by the feminist press Editions des Femmes. At present she is involved in film-making, because this enables her to reach women who are illiterate. Djebar's work is regularly imported into Algeria. Younger women see her as the symbol of their emancipation (Bonn 1974:130).

Zoubeïda Bittari is an extremely realistic Algerian author, who shortly after independence published her first and only novel-essay. The drama of her own life, as described in *O, mes soeurs musulmanes, pleurez!* (1964), reveals the primitive methods of subjugation which Algerian women still face every day. The price which Bittari had to pay for her freedom was her health and her son. She is now employed as maid with a family in France. Aïcha Lemsine, in contrast, is an Algerian writer who was originally fairly optimistic about the eventual emancipation of Algerian women. In *La Chrysalide* (1976) she relates how for generations women have resisted the status imposed upon them by men. However in *Ciel de Porphyre* (1978), which appeared two years later, Lemsine has become more circumspect. The principle character is man and women play only a subordinate role in the story.

In Algeria there is little or no criticism on the basis of literary criteria. Literature is judged by its socio-political content, and there is no place for the evaluation of literary forms. Female literary critics carry little or no weight. Once in a while they also publish a short story or poem of their own in a newspaper like *Moudjahid* or the weekly *Algérie-Actualité*. In the West, on the other hand, literary studies on North Africa are not uncommon. Thus Evelyne Accad, who was born in Beirut and continued her studies in the United States, goes into the role of women in contemporary fiction from North Africa and the Arab world in *Veil of Shame* (1978).

During the colonial era the French did not succeed in getting as firm a foothold in Tunisia and Morocco as they did in Algeria, and French-language literature in those countries is much less extensive. In the previous article Lourina de Voogd has already referred to *Aïcha, la rebelle* (1982) by Halima Ben Haddou as an example of the very limited oeuvre of Moroccan women writing in French. The climate for Francophone literature is much more liberal in Tunisia, as shown for example in *Cendre à l'aube* (1975) by the Tunisian woman journalist Jelila Hafsia. In this novel, which was published in Tunisia, the author champions the cause of emancipation. Her heroine Nabila is an intelligent young woman who married three times. All three marriages end in divorce and she finally chooses to live alone. In Algeria and Morocco a book like *Cendre à l'aube* would probably have been censored out of existence. Katia Rubinstein, a Tunisian author of Jewish origin, is at present a teacher of philosophy in Paris. In her autobiographical novel *Mémoire illettrée* (1979) she describes, in a mixture of French, Arabic, Italian, Sicilian and Spanish, the life of a little girl in Tunis at the time of French colonial rule. When the girl grows up and goes to Paris, all her dreams are shattered. Paris is not at all the heavenly city which she remembers from the novels of her youth. Rubinstein's book is striking above all because of the unusual form: it is interspersed with news bulletins and songs, which evoke the social, political and cultural climate in Tunisia during the colonial period.

It is time that the authorities and the literary institutions in the entire Maghreb recognize that the work of French-language Maghreb authors who choose to or are forced to live and work in France is part of the literary history of their country. The gradual arabization of the Maghreb bodes ill for this French-language literature. It is possible that in thirty or forty years' time it will exist only in France. There a new literary trend is making its entrance: expatriate literature. One of the forerunners of this trend is Leïla Sebbar (1978) who was born in Algeria but moved to France at a very young age. As her mother was French, she was given a French education. All her literary work deals with the Algerian expatriates in France. In *Fatima, ou les Algériennes au square* (1981) and *Shérazade, 17 ans, brune, frisée, les yeux verts* (1982) she paints an extremely realistic picture of the problems facing Algerian women in France. Shérazade even leaves home and becomes a squatter. Although women still form a minority within French-language literature, they are gaining a firmer foothold. Their prose is vivid and realistic and they experiment very little with literary forms. They prefer the novel, short story and essay, although women like Anissa Boumedienne (1980) and Hakima Tamani Redjimi (1979) have also written magnificent poetry. In spite of opposition on all fronts, more and more women are starting to write, in order to express their indignation at the status which men have imposed upon them. Aïcha Lemsine's characters in *La Chrysalide* (1976:126) are all too aware of this:

> Khadidja, who was illiterate, had the feeling that she was born too soon. She knew that, by contrast, Faïza's salvation lay in books. A woman who can read and write, she always said, was better able to cope with the problems of life. She herself had suffered in silence under the superiority of men.

REFERENCES

Accad, Evelyne, 1978, *Veil of Shame*, Sherbrooke, Naaman.

Amrouche, Fadhma A.M., 1968, *Histoire de ma vie*, Paris, Maspéro.

Amrouche, Marguerite Taos, 1947, *Jacinthe noire*, Paris, Charlot.

Amrouche, Marguerite Taos, 1960, *Rue des Tambourins*, Paris, La Table Ronde.

Amrouche, Marguerite Taos, 1966, *Le grain magique*, Paris, Maspéro.

Barrat, Denise, 1965, *Espoirs et Paroles, poèmes algériens recueillis*, Paris, Seghers.

Ben Haddou, Halima, 1982, *Aïcha, la Rebelle*, Paris, Jeune Afrique.

Bittari, Zoubeïda, 1964, *O, mes soeurs musulmanes, pleurez!*, Paris Gallimard.

Bonn, Charles, 1974, *La littérature algérienne de langue française et ses lectures*, Ottawa, Naaman.

Boudjedra, Rachid, 1969, *La répudiation*, Paris, Denoël.

Boudjedra, Rachid, 1972, *L'insolation*, Paris, Denoël.

Boumedienne, Anissa, 1980, *Le jour et la nuit*, Paris, Saint-Germain-des-Prés.

Chraïbi, Driss, 1954, *Le passé simple*, Paris, Denoël.

Chraïbi, Driss, 1972, *La civilisation, ma mère! . . . .*, Paris, Denoël.

Debèche, Djamila, 1947, *Leila, jeune fille d'Algérie*, Algiers, Charras.

Debèche, Djamila, 1955, *Aziza*, Algiers, Imbert.

Déjeux, Jean, 1973, *Littérature maghrébine de langue française*, Ottawa, Naaman.

Dib, Mohammed, 1962, *Qui se souvient de la mer*, Paris, Seuil.

Dib, Mohammed, 1968, *La danse du roi*, Paris, Seuil.

Djebar, Assia, 1957, *La Soif*, Paris, Julliard.

Djebar, Assia, 1958, *Les impatients*, Paris, Julliard.

Djebar, Assia, 1962, *Les enfants du nouveau monde*, Paris, Julliard.

Djebar, Assia, 1967, *Les alouettes naïves*, Paris, Julliard.

Djebar, Assia, and Wallid Carn, 1969, *Rouge l'aube*, Algiers, SNED.

Djebar, Assia, 1979, *Femmes d'Alger dans leur appartement*, Paris, Eds. des Femmes.

Frobenius, Leo, 1922, *Volksmärchen der Kabylen*, Iena, E. Diederichs.

Gréki, Anna, 1963, *Algérie, capital Alger*, Tunis, SNED.

Gréki, Anna, 1966, *Temps forts*, Paris, Présence Africaine.

Guendouz, Nadia, 1968, *Armal*, Alger, SNED.

Hafsia, Jelila, 1975, *Cendre à l'aube*, Tunis, Maison Tunisienne de l'Édition.

Kateb, Yacine, 1956, *Nedjma*, Paris, Seuil.

Khaïr-Eddine, Mohammed, 1964, *Soleil arachnide*, Paris, Seuil.

Khaïr-Eddine, Mohammed, 1968, *Corps négatif*, Paris, Seuil.

Khaïr-Eddine, Mohammed, 1970, *Moi l'aigre*, Paris, Seuil.

Lacoste-Dujardin, Camille, 1965, *Traduction des Légendes et Contes merveilleux de la Grande Kabylie*, collected by Auguste Mouliéras, Paris, Imprimerie Nationale.

Lacoste-Dujardin, Camille, 1970, *Le Conte Kabyle*, Paris, Maspéro.

Lemsine, Aïcha, 1976, *La Chrysalide*, Paris, Editions des Femmes.

Lemsine, Aïcha, 1978, *Ciel de Porphyre*, Paris, Jean Claude Simon.

Merad, Ghani, 1976, *La littérature algérienne d'expression française*, Paris.

M'Rabet, Fadéla, 1969, *La femme algérienne, les Algériennes*, Paris, Maspéro.

Nisbet, Anne-Marie, 1980, *Maghrebian Studies Conference*, Kensington, New South Wales University Press Limited.

Rubinstein, Katia, 1979, *Mémoire illettrée*, Paris, Stock.

Sebbar, Leïla, février 1978, "Si je parle la langue de ma mère", in: *Les Temps Modernes*, Paris.

Sebbar, Leïla, 1981, *Fatima ou les Algériennes au square*, Paris, Stock.

Sebbar, Leïla, 1982, *Shérazade, 17 ans, brune, frisée, les yeux verts*, Paris, Stock.

Tamani Redjimi, Hakima, 1979, *Des mots de la vie*, Paris, Saint-Germain-des-Prés.

Tania I, 28 mai, 11 juin 1971, "Polémiques sur l'émancipation de la femme algérienne", in: *El Moudjahid*, Algiers, SNED.

Toumi, Moustapha, Printemps-été 1970, "Femme ... Femme ... Femme ...", in: *El Moudjahid*, Algiers, SNED.

INTERVIEW WITH ETEL ADNAN
(LEBANON)

HILARY KILPATRICK

Etel Adnan, who was born in 1925, writes in both French and English. She lived for many years in France and the United States, before returning to Lebanon in 1972, as art editor of Beirut's principal French-language newspaper. She now lives in France but regularly visits the United States. Her writings include the following volumes of poetry: *Moonshots* (Beirut, 1966); *Five Senses for One Death* (New York, 1971); *"Jebu" suivi de "L'Express Beyrouth-Enfer"* (Paris, 1973); *L'Apocalypse arabe* (Paris, 1980); *From A to Z* (Sausalito, California, 1982). She has also published a novel, *Sitt Marie Rose* (Paris, 1978), which has been translated into a number of languages.

Etel Adnan also has to her credit the text of two documentaries on Lebanon at war. In addition to writing, she also paints and designs ornamental rugs. Her work has been exhibited in the United States, France, Morocco, Tunisia and Lebanon.

When did you start writing?

I began when I was about eight years old. I remember at school we were sometimes asked to make up sentences based on certain words. I always looked forward to assignments like that and I used to write long paragraphs on each word. That was in Beirut, in Lebanon. I went to a neighbourhood school, a private school run by French nuns. I liked it there since I was an only child and at school I could play with other children. I disliked the nuns, but once in a while there was one who was especially nice to me, one I considered "beautiful". That was what I always looked for in people, "beauty". In the other children, the teachers, my mother's friends. I always used to be in awe of beautiful people. I came to love words and sentences and people in that same way.

Later on we had to write long compositions. Some of my

compositions were actually short stories. Once, when I was about 14, I wrote a story that was so good that I was punished for it, because everyone thought I had copied it out of a book. The French nun refused to believe I had written it myself. Another time we were asked to write a composition in class, under the supervision of the teacher. They told me my composition was so beautiful that I couldn't possibly have written it myself. According to the nun, I had read it somewhere, learned it by heart, and then written it down in class. When they questioned me I was so flabbergasted that I couldn't manage more than a feeble "no". So I was punished again.

How did your family and friends feel about your going to university and about your writing?

When the Second World War broke out inflation was high, my father was old and my mother, though younger, had no "respectable" profession. So at the age of 16 I went out to work. I got a job in a French office, filing and stapling documents together. It was fun because I was out in the wide world. There I was, at 16, a working girl. The war was then in its third year and I had left school without getting the French *baccalauréat*. When October came I started to cry because I wanted to go back to school. In October of the following year my boss came up to me, a Frenchman who had been a university lecturer. He encouraged me to register at a secondary school, and through a combination of courses and private lessons before the office opened at 10 a.m., I finished the last two years of high school and passed the examinations required for university entrance. I wanted to become an engineer — which then included architecture — but my mother said that was men's work and that I ought to be ashamed of myself for even considering the idea. Then she registered me at the Arts Faculty, partly because most of the classes were in the late afternoon and that way I could keep my job.

115

There I met an extraordinary French essayist, Gabriel Bounoure, who was head of the faculty. Gabriel Bounoure was one of the most gifted critics of French literature and he loved poetry as if it were a mystical experience, in fact the only mystical experience of value. I found myself overwhelmed by poetry. I suddenly realized that we were put on earth to read poetry. I loved Baudelaire and Rimbaud and Gérard de Nerval. Everything else sort of receded into the background. My office job began to seem like some kind of bad dream, and I spent less and less time at work. I changed jobs several times and each time I was given work that was less demanding, less interesting and less well-paid. My head was buzzing with poetry.

I had also found a friend, the ideal friend for an 18- or 19-year-old girl like me. She was Russian, but her parents had emigrated to Beirut after the revolution. She knew a lot about music and read nothing but poetry and philosophy. Her name was — and is — Lydia. She read so much of Rainer Maria Rilke's poetry that it seemed to me that Rilke must have once lived in her room in that little flat in Beirut with the lone palm tree in front.

I was living in a world of ideas dominated by poetry. For years I was convinced that the whole human race was created in order to sit on sidewalks and read poetry. I often read poetry while I was walking, and sometimes I sat down on a stone or on the sidewalk to continue my reading. Some people thought I was crazy, worst of all my mother. The situation was getting out of hand, and she saw every young man I talked to as a potential husband. She wanted to get me married off before books "drove me crazy".

I wrote my first poem "The Book of the Sea" when I was about 22. I loved the sea and until I was 18 or 19 it was my one great love. The affairs I had had were hasty and surreptitious, out of fear of my mother and the neighbours. All my sensuality was absorbed by the beauty of the sea all around Beirut. Swimming became an almost complete sexual

116

experience. I saw the sun as masculine (*le soleil* in French) and the sea both as myself and as a woman distinct from myself. The poem, which is some fifteen pages long, is about a long love affair between the sun and the sea. About a kind of cosmic marriage, and the essence of the meeting of sky and water and the strange relationship between these two elements. Later on I went to Paris on a scholarship from the French government. My father had since died and my mother was heartbroken at the separation. In Paris I wrote "The Book of Night" and years later, after the death of someone I had loved carelessly, I wrote "The Book of Death". That was during the first or second year I was in California.

As a woman in the Arab world, have you had major difficulties to overcome in order to become a writer?

In Arab countries society does not like women in politics, but does respect women writers. There is such reverence for literature in the Arab world and such love for poetry, that even women share in that respect. Women writers have no great problems in the Arab world. At times they are subjected to censorship, but in this they are no different from their male colleagues. They are not censored because they are women.

As far as my own experience is concerned, while in the States I started sending pieces to a Beirut magazine *Šiᶜr* (Poetry), which translated my poems faithfully and encouraged me to send more. One day a French-language Moroccan review, founded shortly before by Abdellatif Laabi, wrote to me in California, saying that they were putting together a special issue on Palestine. That was how I came to write my first "political" poem, a long piece entitled *Jebu*, which refers to the Jebusites, the Canaanite tribe that founded the city of Jerusalem, which King David later captured from them.

When did you first begin to write in English?

About the same time. It was not something I planned, but as I was active in the anti-Vietnam movement in America, I had to write in English. But I continued to write in French whenever a text was destined for Beirut or North Africa. I am happy to be able to say that my "political writings" encouraged many — mainly younger — women writers in the Arab world. My work was immediately translated and appeared in Arab magazines and literary reviews. I have no complaints on that score.

Because of the civil war in Lebanon I spent some time in Paris, and it was there that I wrote my first novel, in French, *Sitt Marie Rose*. The fact that it was banned in some parts of Beirut was due to the ideas expressed in the book, and not to the fact that the author was a woman.

How does the Arab world view authors who, like you, write in French or English?

A poet of my age is happy to receive recognition, since you know that the time that remains to you is limited. When the Syrian poet Naḏîr al-ʿAẓma wrote that I was the greatest Arab woman poet since al-Ḥansâ' of pre-Islamic times, I was delighted and profoundly moved. Not only was this a great compliment, but it also allayed one of my greatest fears, that because I wrote in a foreign language, my work would not be considered part of Arab literature. I have always regretted not writing in Arabic, and therefore running the risk of not actually being accepted as an Arab writer. You may be wondering why I don't write in Arabic? Well, it is such a beautiful language, it almost breaks my heart not to write in Arabic. But the main reason is the colonial school system that was imposed on Lebanon during my childhood. We didn't speak Arabic at home either, because my mother was Greek. After that I was always travelling, working first in one country and then another, so that I never learned Arabic well enough to be a poet in that language. But perhaps it is also true to say that I don't want to give up my "long-distance" love affair with the Arabic language. Who can say?

In 1960 I began to paint, and I heard myself say out loud, "I paint in Arabic!" At that moment my soul was at peace, as if I'd been given the answer to an important problem.

Are there certain standard images of women in modern Arab literature, certain taboos which women writers defy?

There is something I would like to mention here, something which although it is extremely personal, has an objective value. About 1970 I wrote a long poem in English which I called "Five Senses for One Death". It was published in New York by The Smith. This poem is a kind of funeral oration, something I wrote from deep down in my soul, after the suicide of a friend. A few years later Yûsuf al-Ḥâl and I were translating the poem into Arabic, in order to publish it in book form. Yûsuf, who is the editor of the magazine *Ši‘r* and an excellent poet himself, saw it as a love poem, and wanted to use the masculine form for my friend. I said, no, it wasn't a man but a woman, a young woman, and I wanted it to stay that way. Yûsuf said that it was a literary convention. I said, no, women have a right to their own feelings. And this is perhaps the first poem in Arab literature written by one woman for another. It did not cause a sensation. On several occasions it was broadcast in Arabic, and I am particularly pleased that many poets, most of them men, have admired it and taken it seriously. For me it represents a sort of feminist declaration. Of course it is also — and mainly — something else.

Women are the theme of my novel *Sitt Marie Rose*, women within the Arab context and more particularly against the background of the Lebanese civil war. In my view it is not in the literary world but in the political world that men resent women who express themselves freely. When *Sitt Marie Rose* came out I was on leave from a French-language newspaper in Beirut, *L'Orient-Le Jour*. The paper had been threatened, or at least strongly advised never again to publish my work. So when in 1978, during one of the cease-fires, I returned to Beirut to take up my work again, the editor-in-chief said literally, "Who asked you to write what you think?" I replied, "But your paper was paying me to write what I thought." There was a long pause. I was paid to write on painting, not on politics!

III. ASIA

PROVERBS

1. It is a waste to name your daughter, since you will always lose her — to death or to a husband. (Bengal, India)

2. An educated woman is sure to become a widow and then she behaves like an unmanageable ox. (Bengal, India)

3. The shade of a fig tree is the coolest, the love of a mother the best. (Bengal, India)

4. Sad is the life of a man who has no mother at home. (Bengal, India)

5. Virtuous is the girl who suffers and dies without a sound. (Bengal, India)

6. God save the family where two wives are in charge. (Bengal, India)

7. Better to be mud than a barren woman. (Andhra, India)

8. Woman's character and man's fate, inscrutable even for the gods, let alone for mankind. (Sanskrit, India)

9. Four heads will agree, four nipples — never. (Kerala, India)

10. Beware! A beautiful girl is useless for work. (Kerala, India)

11. Woman and money tempt even the Creator. (Andhra, India).

13. Women are like shoes (they can always be replaced). (Andhra, India)

14. A daughter and a cow will go whichever way you choose [neither has a will of her own]. (Andhra, India)

15. A woman, a Miri [a tribe of northeast India], a parakeet and a crow: these four you cannot trust. (Assam, India)

16. One should not trust rivers, women or horned beasts. (Bangladesh)

17. Persistent low fever and a nagging husband are not dangerous, but they can make one's life miserable. (Bangladesh)

18. An indulgent husband would rather live on uncooked rice than insist on having meals cooked by an unwilling wife. (Bangladesh)

19. When one's purse is empty, even the wife at home is not one's own. (Bangladesh)

20. A bad king ruins his kingdom and fortune flees his land. A bad wife ruins a man and he goes starving. (Bangladesh)

PROVERBS

21. Poverty ruins a man's character, pimples ruin a complexion, too much rain ruins a field and beating ruins a wife. (Bangladesh)

22. If you love your wife, you must leave her regularly; if you love your child, you must beat it regularly. (Indonesia)

23. If the wife is smart and the husband stupid, she can hide a thief in her hair. (Indonesia)

24. If you lose your wife, you can find another, if you lose your senses, disaster has struck. (Indonesia)

25. However smart a woman may be, she'll end up in the kitchen. (Indonesia)

26. Always marry an older woman; you won't starve and you'll benefit from her experience. (Indonesia)

27. A wife follows her husband to heaven, she follows him to hell. (Indonesia)

28. She may not be the submissive type, but she'll wash the napkins. (Indonesia)

29. A woman is like a chipped plate [you can do with her what you like]. (Indonesia)

30. No matter how beautiful and talented a girl is, a boy — even deformed — is always more valuable. (China)

ACKNOWLEDGEMENTS

Sanjukta Gupta, India (1-6), and selection of 7-15 from Sen Gupta (ed.), *Women in Indian Folklore*, Calcutta, Indian Publications, 1969, as well as help in obtaining 16-21 from *Nihar Karim*, Bangladesh; *Tineke Hellwig* (22-9), selected or heard from Abdullah Hussein, *Kamus istimewa peribahasa Melayu*, Kuala Lumpur, 1975 (26); M. K. Hasyim *et al.*, *Peribahasa Aceh*, Banda Aceh, 1977 (23); S. Keyzer, "A collection of Javanese proverbs and proverbial expressions" in *Language, Geography and Ethnography of the Dutch East Indies* (in Dutch), 1863 (28); W. Hoezoo, "Some Javanese Proverbs" in *Monthly Bulletins of the Dutch Missionary Society* (in Dutch), 1865; *T. Iskandar*, Indonesia (22 and 24); *Sylvi W. Puntowati*, Indonesia (25 and 27); recalled having heard 30.

WOMEN AND LITERATURE IN ASIA

SOUTH ASIA — SANJUKTA GUPTA

Introduction

The history of written literature in South Asia goes back almost three thousand years. At the very beginning of this period there were women like Vāk and Gārgie, who composed hymns together with the male poets. These were the poets of the Vedas, the most ancient of Hindu sacred writings. In the Middle Ages, too, there were many women who ranked among the most sophisticated and cultured writers of their time. A relatively large number of women in the upper classes could read and write, and the daughters of aristocratic families were encouraged to practise writing poetry, as part of their education. Moreover, during ancient and medieval times Indian literature had a strong oral tradition, so that it was even possible for women who could not read and write to achieve lasting fame. There were also women who excelled in the composition of hymns.

The vast South Asian subcontinent is comprised of no fewer than five countries. The people of these countries belong to different ethnic groups and often differ widely in culture, language, customs and religion.

In India, Pakistan, Bangladesh, Sri Lanka and Nepal there are about twenty-three major spoken languages, almost all of which are also written. Most of these languages have a significant literature of their own. Linguistically they belong to two major families, the Indo-Aryan and the Dravidian. Urdu, the official language of Pakistan and the majority of Moslems living in India, comes from both the Indo-Aryan and the Indo-Iranian, which are in turn part of the Indo-German family. Urdu originated in the military camps of the Moslem soldiers who invaded India from the northwest. It is predominantly a mixture of Persian and North Indian languages, but it also shows traces of Arabic influence. By the

124

seventeenth century AD Urdu had developed into a beautifully polished and elegant language, in use at the Mughol and Luknow courts, the medieval centres of Moslem culture. But even before that it had acquired a literary dimension at the courts of the Moslem kings of South India. Its literary motifs and idiom were drawn largely from Persian, the official court language of the Mughol princes of Delhi.

The beginning of the modern period in Indian literature dates from the encounter with Western philosophy and literature in the early decades of the nineteenth century, through contact with the British officers of the East India Company, and the introduction of the English educational system in several metropolitan cities. It was the middle-class intelligentsia who benefited most from this new form of education. Many of them had liberal views and were aware of the terrible social injustice and exploitation inherent in the position of women. By the end of the nineteenth century male champions of the women's cause had brought about a number of social reforms and done much to foster education among Indian women. The latter was perhaps the most important reform of all, for at the end of the Middle Ages women of all classes had sunk back into illiteracy. Even among high-caste Indians, educated women were thought to bring bad luck.

Contemporary literature reflected this new awareness of discrimination against women. In the early decades of the twentieth century many male authors were writing on social themes, such as the pitiful condition of child-widows, and the torments to which child brides were subjected by mothers-in-law and other members of the family. They also wrote about the horrific consequences of the dowry system and the evils of polygamy.

Although these authors showed great humanity and compassion for the victims of these abuses, they took quite a conservative view of the ideal woman, whom they saw as a protective, indulgent, self-sacrificing mother, a docile, self-effacing, long-suffering martyr of a wife. Women's strength lay in their capacity to patiently and cheerfully accept life's trials, more often than not at the hands of men. The epitome of womanhood was Sītā, Queen of Rāma, the tragic heroine of the Indian epic *Ramayana*. The emancipation of women was to be brought about by men, and women were to accept all that befell them as their fate or *karma*.

The Early Modern Period and the Image of Women in Literature
From the early period of modern literature there have been female poets of considerable stature. Women rapidly distinguished themselves as novelists and short story writers as well, the two genres which were characteristic of the new literary development during the modern period. Most of these authors upheld the conservative values of the androcentric society. They idealized the child-widows and the neglected wives, whom they saw as meek and passive creatures who succeeded in transforming their misery and frustration into religious fulfilment, in the service of God or family. This was seen as their ultimate duty. Like their male counterparts, these women writers reserved their highest praise for the female character who showed herself to be an ideal mother. Women writers were usually housewives or young widows and any attempt to challenge the male norms and values of their society would have put an end to their literary activities. The respectability of a woman, especially one who had neither husband nor son to protect her, was easily compromised. The women's welfare organizations had their work cut out for them rescuing young women victimized by their families. Women had no right, let alone the freedom, to settle important issues for themselves. The birth of a girl was a regrettable occurrence in the eyes of parents and other members of the family. The marriage bond was subject to such rigid rules and the general opinion of female morals was so low that the only way that a woman could safeguard her life and character was to marry as quickly as possible, and thus secure the protection of a husband.

To ensure a prepuberal marriage it was imperative that a girl be married off before she was ten, as a guarantee of her virginity. Female infanticide, neglect of girl babies and cruel marriage alliances were not uncommon. Her utter helplessness and the lack of any economic rights often meant that a married woman living with a large extended family was little better than a slave, unless she could count on the protection of a sympathetic husband and later sons. Her redemption lay solely in motherhood and the bearing of a son. It was common for young or childless wives to commit suicide when their husbands died, often under pressure from the husband's family. As a result of child marriages and polygamy there were many widows, whose only salvation lay in becoming the willing handmaidens of families who were willing to take them in. Although it was not forbidden by law, the remarriage of a widow was a social taboo. Needless to say, the situation sketched above applied to the upper and middle classes. Lower down the social scale, among the working classes, conditions were different, though male oppression was present there too.

Up to the 1930s, movements concerned with the emancipation of women concentrated mainly on the more practical problems arising from the oppression of women, and there was very little regard for their spiritual emancipation. There were, however, a number of female poets, such as Radharani Devi (who wrote under the pseudonym Aparajita Devi), who had the courage to challenge the traditional ideal of womankind, and tried to show that women, too, are individuals. They were seen as nonconformists and often came in for harsh criticism.

A New Social, Political and Economic Status

The 1940s, and the granting of independence to the countries of South Asia, marked the beginning of a new era for women authors in India. Together with their male contemporaries they began working towards a new kind of self-determination in which sex played no part. The new Indian constitution granted Hindu women political equality, as well as equal rights of inheritance, and introduced monogamy and divorce. Moreover, rapid urban expansion and the economic deterioration of the middle classes have produced two new phenomena: more and more women are receiving an education, and many women are leaving the confines of the home to take an outside job. As a result a number of good women writers have emerged, whose work is a valuable contribution to Indian literature. Many of them are highly educated women, aware of the changing patterns of Western social philosophy and literature. They are well read, travelled, progressive and emancipated. Some of them, such as Kamala Markandeya and Usha Priyamvada, live in the West. Some, like Chitra Fernando of Sri Lanka and Anita Desai of Delhi, write exclusively in English.

Although traditionally the literary activities of women have centred mainly on poetry, most of the well-known women authors today choose prose as their literary medium, usually in the form of essays and novels. Talented writers like Amrita Pritam and Nabaneeta Deb-Sen began their literary career as poets, but later took up prose because it is a more popular and effective medium. A number of the above-mentioned writers also teach at universities. They are keenly aware of the problems which women face today and they closely follow developments in women's movements all over the world. Many of them are involved in emancipation in their own country, and contribute to modern feminist magazines such as *Manushi*, published in Delhi.

Women and their Problems in Modern Women's Literature
Women in South Asia have many problems to contend with. Some of these are caused by the chronic poverty which is characteristic of most Third World countries, others are bound up with tradition and religion, while still others are common to all viricentric societies. Writers have always been interested

in the difficulties of middle- and upper-class society, but the progressive ideas of both Gandhi and Marx have also made modern writers aware of the hardship and suffering of the lower class, the working class, the poorest of the poor. Most women authors write mainly about women, and all these problems are reflected in their work.

The main character in Chitra Fernando's *Missilin* (1981) is a poor village woman who works as a cook for a middle-class family in Colombo, Sri Lanka. In her village she had an identity of her own, a sense of belonging. In Colombo everything is different, and her individuality is swallowed up by her work. To her employers she is a "convenience", but she has no real place in their family. Her employers are neither cruel nor insensitive, but they do not see her as a person. There are many Missilins in modern cities like Calcutta, Bombay and Delhi.

Ismet Chugtai, too, depicts the unwanted and uncared-for who exist on the fringe of society. In *Tiny's Granny* (1976) she portrays a Moslem woman who is never seen as an individual by the people around her.

Shanta Rama Rau lived for many years in England, and her autobiographical stories "Home to India" and "Gifts of Passage" and the novel *Remember the House* all display a proud awareness of her Indian identity. Like all contemporary writers, she is aware of her own modernity and defends the freedom she has won from orthodoxy and narrowminded bigotry. In *Nectar in a Sieve* (1954) and *A Silence of Desire* (1960), Kamala Markandeya relates with sympathy and understanding the frustrations of poor country families.

Ashapurna Devi is at her best when dealing with socio-historical themes. Her recently published trilogy is the chronicle of three generations of women, mother, daughter and granddaughter. These novels, which span some one hundred years, are concerned with the struggle of well-educated middle-class Bengali women to free themselves from the social chains of a male-dominated society.

The heroine of the first novel *Pratham Pratisruti* (1964) is Satyavati, the only child of a progressive father. She grows into an intelligent and spirited young woman, and with determination and self-confidence she resists the narrow-minded orthodoxy of her mother-in-law. She persuades her weak and docile husband to move to Calcutta, where their sons will be able to get a better education. There a third child is born, a girl called Suvarnalata. She is intelligent and Satyavati is determined to see that she gets a good education. She hopes to be able to delay the girl's marriage until she is of age. But her husband is fearful of incurring the disapproval of society and, with his mother's help, he marries Suvarnalata off from his mother's house in the village. The second novel, *Suvarnalata*, tells of the miserable life to which the girl is doomed in the house of her authoritarian husband. Her education, her writing talent and her intelligence are all wasted in the rigid orthodox atmosphere within her husband's family. The only one who understands her is her youngest daughter, Bakul, who inherits her writing talent. The last novel in the series is entitled *The Story of Bakul* (1973). Calcutta is developing rapidly and changing circumstances enable Bakul to defy her despotic father. Not only is she able to avoid an arranged marriage, but she succeeds in fulfilling her literary talent. She is unlucky in love and chooses to remain single, but she finds independence, harmony and commitment in life. She achieves the things which her simple, poetic mother dreamt of and her strong-willed and spirited grandmother fought for. But she is also painfully aware of the crisis of modern womankind. The conflict between old values and new produces an ambivalent situation which is a danger to less strong-minded individuals. This seems to be the message which the author is trying to convey. Ashapurna Devi, now in her seventies, is among the foremost Bengali writers.

The crisis described in her book is indeed the result of a changing culture and changing values. The women of today are faced with problems of adjustment which are often the cause of intense suffering. Divorce is one of these problems. Though it is a fairly recent phenomenon, it is already threatening social stability in certain sectors of Indian society. The conflicting values of husband and wife, combined with the ambivalent attitude of the husband, often lead to the break-up of a marriage. There are men who want their wives to be modern and intelligent, but only on the surface. Underneath they must remain chaste and loyal and submissive. Nowadays, however, women are brought up to believe that they are individuals in their own right. The novel *Storm in Chandigarh* (1969) by Nayantara Sehgal highlights this problem, which has become more acute since men and women mix freely before and after marriage.

As more and more South Asians settle abroad, a new problem of adjustment presents itself. In her novel *This Time of Morning* (1965) Nayantara Sehgal relates the story of Leela and Nita, two young girls who live in the United States. Leela has a strong need to feel at home in America, which leads to her becoming pregnant. She never succeeds in reconciling her new life with the traditional values of her own culture, and in the end she commits suicide. Her sister Nita experiences the same sensation of loneliness and alienation, even though she lives with her parents.

One of the most serious problems affecting the expanding cities and industrial towns is that of working wives. Sociologist Pramila Kapur examined this problem in *Marriage and the Working Woman in India* (Delhi, 1970) and *Love, Marriage and Sex* (Delhi, 1973). Until then only male authors had tackled this subject. Anita Desai is one of the women writers who have since successfully broached this theme in a novel. In *Voices in the City* (1965) she presents in Amla the new type of working wife who considers her job as the only lifeline. Manisha, her sister, committed suicide because she could not bear the drudgery of a purely domestic existence. She had no life of her own, no individuality and was not appreciated by her family. To escape the same fate Amla takes a job, hoping to find her identity in her work. Brinda, the heroine of Usha Priyamvada's short story "Paper Flowers", takes a different attitude. She feels imposed upon because she has to go out to work in order to help support the family. She puts the blame on her brother, who cannot find a job.

Feminism and Women Authors

Feminism has also reached the South Asian subcontinent. This is evident from the gulf of protest literature which is the work of the more modern women writers. In the foreword to her novel *The Friend of the Great City* (1969) Rajani Pannikar says: "love, marriage, divorce — these are the phases of our conjugal life in the Indian families. Wherever traditional control is operative there is suffocation and wherever we have freedom there is divorce. This problem is the burning issue of the day. Everybody experiences it, but no one has a solution for it."

Rajani Pannikar's pronouncement is supported by Shanti Joshi's novel *Fish and the Dead Net* (1971). Mandira meets her future husband at a swimming-pool and immediately falls in love with him. After a brief courtship they are married. But then her husband forbids her to go to the swimming pool or to see her friends and family. He is extremely jealous and thinks she is unfaithful to him. In his eyes she must be fickle, otherwise she would not have allowed him to win her so easily. He is suspicious of her individualism, and to demonstrate his authority as a husband, he demands Mandira's constant attention, even at the cost of their children. In the end Mandira leaves, taking the three children with her, and asks for a divorce. The author stresses the ambivalent attitude which the modern male displays towards women. The old standard image of the ideal woman, the epic Sītā, still holds sway and is supported by popular films. No matter how attracted a man may be to a smart, modern, emancipated woman, he will usually find her too complicated and unreliable for a permanent relationship. Although in India the cosmic, active force of the divine is seen as feminine and is thought to be present in all women, in everyday life they must be mastered. Women must be made passive and submissive if they are not to bring chaos and danger. Authority must remain in the hands of men. Modern Indian men seem unable to make a choice, while in the meantime their wives become more and more confused and frustrated until, finally, they rebel.

Pramala, heroine of *Some Inner Fury* (1955) by Kamala Markandeya, has no wish to be a modern emancipated woman, but to please her husband she wears shorts, plays tennis and gives parties. Her husband Kit, however, treats her more as an inferior than as an equal. Pramala, who is childless, is overwhelmed by loneliness. She becomes involved in social work and very much against her husband's will, she also adopts a poor low-caste girl. At the end of the book Pramala impetuously — almost deliberately — rushes into a burning school to rescue the children trapped there and dies in the flames. Women rebel against the double standard and the hypocrisy of their husbands. They refuse to be suffocated, as contemporary literature demonstrates. In the modern novel women regularly defy sexual taboos by having extra-marital relationships, as in *Storm in Chandigarh* by Nayantara Sehgal. Ratti, the principal character in Krishna Sobati's *The Sunflower of the Darkness* (1972), is depicted as a woman suffering from severe psychological problems related to sex. As a child she was sexually molested by an older man; her schoolfriends who found out about the incident taunted her instead of trying to help her. The affair wounded her so deeply that she has become a confirmed man-hater and cynic. She likes to flirt with young men, toying with their feelings, but never lets any of them get close to her. She ridicules marriage, which she calls an empty relationship, but then she falls in love with a married man. She truly loves Divakar and wants to sleep with him, but when he offers to divorce his wife, she begs him not to because she cannot bear the thought of the suffering this would cause his child. Besides, she believes that her temperament makes her unsuited for marriage. She refuses Divakar's proposal of marriage, but accepts a sexual relationship. Divakar is free to come to her whenever he wants to; she will always be waiting for him.

The female characters in Rajani Pannikar's *Duriya* (1974) are no advocates of sexual abstinence either. Namita lives with her lover Hari who has a wife and a child and is awaiting a divorce. At one point, after a quarrel with Hari, she leaves the house and goes to a women's centre run by a militant feminist named Sushila. There she meets a young man and falls in love with him. In the meantime, however, Hari has obtained his divorce, as well as custody of the child. Namita goes back to Hari, to be a mother to his child. Another character in the same novel is Charu, an adventurous young woman who has had a great many affairs. She finally marries and her young husband is willing to forget her past adventures. This novel can be seen as a young woman's somewhat exaggerated protest against the traditional authority of a father or husband.

In her novel *Her House* (1972) Meharunissa Parvez portrays two young women. Elma is a well-educated, cultured and charming young lady, whom her husband divorces because she suffers from chronic asthma. Elma is left to suffer alone and is even exploited by her own brother. The other young woman is Rashma, whose mother is a fanatical Christian who when Rashma becomes pregnant refuses to accept the girl's Hindu lover. She would rather have her daughter remain with her as an unmarried mother, and she sees to it that she cannot marry her lover.

Mamata Kaliya, another young writer, delights in ridiculing the kind of young men who believe in sexual liberation for themselves but demand chastity of their wives. Paramjit, a character in Kaliya's novel *Beghar* (1971), is a member of the intellectual middle class of Bombay. He has a sweet and tender romance with Sanjivani, who comes from the same milieu. She is modern, but also gentle and cultured, and they are very much in love. On their first sexual encounter, however, Paramjit discovers that Sanjivani is not a virgin. He is indignant and rejects her. Later he marries a girl chosen for him by his parents, who is not only uneducated but also narrow-minded. Paramjit cannot put Sanjivani out of his mind and after five years of marriage, he dies of a broken heart.

In her short novel *Inni* (1973) Malati Perulkar shows the other side of the coin. Inni is modern and emancipated, but at the same time she clings fiercely to traditional moral values. She is in love with Raj, a playback singer in Hindi films. Long ago Raj left home, deserting the wife he had married against his will. He is popular as a singer and has had many affairs, but when he meets Inni again, he realizes he still loves her. When he asks her to marry him she refuses, because she could not marry a man who was no longer a virgin. Inni finally marries a childhood friend, a Moslem named Sahil, whom she admires for his shy innocence. But she can no more forget Raj than she can love Sahil. Raj dies a horrible death and at that moment Sahil realizes that Inni has always loved Raj. Knowing this, he is no longer able to love her and they become estranged. By clinging to the empty ideal of chastity, Inni has ruined both their lives. The author wants to show how senseless and dangerous it is to stick to the old myths and values in the rapidly changing Westernized urban society of the modern middle class.

An even more daring iconoclast is Mridula Garg. In her *Sunshine of her Share* (1975) she declares that sexual enjoyment is life's highest good, and the physical ecstasy of orgasm is totally unrelated to romantic love. When two people are attracted to each other's bodies, no hollow ideals or romantic myths should be allowed to interfere. Manisha, the principal character, is a university woman, who writes short stories and teaches Hindi literature at a college. She consistently stresses the physical side of the male-female relationship and rejects the idea that love or loyalty are in any way involved. She even seems convinced that marriage is a hindrance rather than a help in achieving a satisfying sexual relationship. While married to her first husband Jiten, she has an affair with Madhukar. And once she is married to Madhukar, she carries on an illicit relationship with her ex-husband.

But not all women authors are proponents of sexual promiscuity. Some of them are deeply concerned about the effects which the breakdown of a marriage, and later divorce, can have on children. The knowledge that his mother has committed adultery can have grave psychological consequences for a child. Moreover, children always suffer when they are forced to choose between their parents, to decide where their first loyalty lies. This is the theme of Mannu Bhandari's novel *Apki Banti* (1971). Banti's parents are separated and he lives with his mother while she waits for her divorce. During this time he enjoys her undivided attention. But then his mother marries a widower with children from his first marriage, and Banti finds it impossible to adjust to the new situation. His conduct begins to cause problems and he is sent to his father. But the father has also remarried and has a child by his second wife. Banti feels rejected by his mother and cannot accept his little half-brother. He is both miserable and unmanageable, and finally he is sent away to a boys' school. Mannu Bhandari makes no value judgements; she simply depicts the child's emotional anguish at his parents' divorce and remarriage.

Nirode, the principal male character in Anita Desai's *Voices in the City* (1965), discovers very young that his mother actually hates his father. He also sees his mother flirting with another man, and suddenly his affection and love for her vanish. The loving mother he adored, that symbol of perfection, is gone. He is filled with hatred and this brings him to create a new image of his mother, that of the demoness Kali, the dark goddess of destruction.

Anita Desai and Amrita Pritam are the two most talented

Indian woman writers. Their writings have a lyric quality which sets them apart. Desai writes mainly psychological novels. In *Cry the Peacock* (1963) she presents a detailed analysis of the complex personality of her heroine Maya. Superstitition, libido, a father fixation, mental maladjustment and a thirst for life all combine to make her an emotional cripple. As a child her nanny once took her to the temple of Siva to have her horoscope read. The red phallic symbol of the god, the priest standing next to it, his hoarse monotonous voice telling of love and sex and death, as symbolized by the courting and mating peacocks — all this aroused her but frightened her as well. The priest predicted that in the fifth year of her marriage either she or her husband would die an unnatural death. She remembers the priest as a lascivious-looking albino, who described the eerie cry of the peacocks as the haunting call of sex and death — two concepts inextricably entwined. The awful symbolism and the fear of death hanging over her drives Maya to the brink of insanity in the fourth year of her marriage. Her husband, an intellectual, knows nothing of the prophecy and when Maya is again tormented by nightmares in which she hears the peacock cry, he attributes it to a form of suppressed sex perversion, a kind of Electra complex. In a moment of acute mental stress, tortured by the thought that one of them is to die, Maya murders her husband and commits suicide. The book is a remarkable piece of literature, in which the greater part of the story is related in an interior monologue. There are frequent flashbacks interspersed with ordinary conversations between Maya and her husband. It bears the stamp of Anita Desai's personal style, evocative and suggestive, with a charming lyricism and a striking power of expression.

Amrita Pritam began her literary career as a poet and her novels and short stories also have a poetic quality. Her early work focuses on the inner life of her characters, many of whom seem to be projections of the author herself. Pritam's mature work is characterized by a search for harmony and truth. She is strongly influenced by Freud and intrigued by the way in which sentimental young girls always seem to be in search of unselfish mother love. Her story "The Ghost" is narrated by a young girl. She has always been closer to her mother than her father, and feels the need to be loved by other mother figures too. She is crushed by her grandmother's rejection. Then suddenly she is told that her mother is actually her foster-mother, and that the lonely, sad but loving aunt who lives behind their house is her real mother. She cannot accept the truth; shaken and confused, she finally falls ill. Eventually she recovers, only to discover that she has lost both mothers.

The sorrow and loss felt by the little girl and the manner in which she deals with these emotions have autobiographical overtones. Amrita Pritam lost her mother when she was eleven, and with the encouragement of her father, she managed to cope with her loss by writing poetry. In a sense Pritam represents the modern progressive female. Her view of life was radically altered by the political partition of Punjab and the accompanying chaos and cruelty. Much later when she settled in Delhi, she felt strongly attracted to a more radical modernism. In her autobiography she focuses on these events as they have influenced her work.

Conclusion

We have taken a brief look at the image of women as presented in the writings of contemporary women authors. There is an old saying that there is an author behind every story and a society behind every author. Does that mean that the works we have discussed represent the female psyche of South Asia? Not quite, for we have talked mainly about some of the more progressive writers. Only Ashapurna Devi can be regarded as a representative woman author. She belongs to the well-educated middle class, the upper-caste society which has produced most of India's contemporary literature. Typical or not, all these women writers are acutely sensitive to the changes their world is undergoing, and well aware of the fact that they are themselves a product of those changes. They know that urban society is in a state of flux and that modernization can be a painful process. Together with prominent male writers, they are trying to provide models for the world of tomorrow, while keeping sight of the crises in which women find themselves today, in the rapidly changing societies of South Asia.

REFERENCES

Bhandari, Mannu, 1971, *Apki Banti*, Delhi.

Chugtai, Ismet, 1976, *Tiny's Granny*, translated from original Urdu by Ralph Russel, in *Contemporary Indian Short Stories*, vol. I, ed. Sahitya Akademi (reprint), New Dehli.

Desai, Anita, 1963, *Cry the Peacock*, London.

Desai, Anita, 1965, *Voices in the City*, London, Peter Owen.

Devi Ashapurna, 1964, *Pratham Pratisruti* (ed. 1), Calcutta.

Devi, Ashapurna, 1966, *Suvarnalata* (ed. 1), Calcutta.

Devi, Ashapurna, 1973, *Bakulkatha* (ed 1), Calcutta.

Fernando, Chitra, 1981, *Missilin*, in *An Anthology of Modern Writing from Sri Lanka*, ed. Ranjini Obeyesekere and Chitra Fernando, University of Arizona Press, Tucson, USA.

Garg, Mridula, 1975, *Us ke Hisse ke Dhup* (Sunshine of Her Share), Delhi.

Joshi, Shanti, 1971, *Machli aur Mara Jal* (Fish and the Dead Net), Lucknow.

Kaliya, Mamata, 1971, *Beghar*, Allahabad.

Markandeya, Kamala, 1954, *Nectar in a Sieve*, London.

Markandeya, Kamala, 1955, *Some Inner Fury*, London.

Markandeya, Kamala, 1960, *A Silence of Desire*, London.

Pannikar, Rajani, 1969, *Mahanagar ki Mita* (The Friend of the Great City), Delhi.

Pannikar, Rajani, 1974, *Duriya*, Delhi.

Parvez, Meharunissa, 1972, *Us ka Ghar* (Her House), Delhi.

Perulkar, Malati, 1973, *Inni*, Delhi.

Pritam, Amrita, 1977, *The Revenue Stamp: an autobiography*, translated from the Punjabi by Krishna Gorowara, New Delhi.

Pritam, Amrita, 1982, in *Manushi*, Number Ten, Delhi.

Priyamvada, Usha, 1974, "Paper Flowers", in *Modern Hindi Short Stories*, ed. Mahendra Kulasrestha *et al.*, Delhi.

Rama Rau, Shanta, 1956, *Remember the House*, London.

Sehgal, Nayantara, 1965, *The Time of Morning*, London.

Sehgal, Nayantara, 1969, *Storm in Chandigarh*, Delhi.

Sobati, Krishna, 1972, *Surajmukhi Adhere ke* (The Sunflower of the Darkness), Delhi.

TINEKE HELLWIG

Introduction

South-east Asia is a vast area comprising many different countries, among them Thailand, Malaysia, Singapore, Indonesia and the Philippines. It is not possible to discuss here the contribution which women have made to the literature of all these countries. Thus instead of giving all of them superficial coverage, I would like to look more closely at one of them, namely Indonesia. After this country attained its independence from the Netherlands in 1949, it had to break away from the remnants of colonial rule in order to create a new political and cultural identity. The geographical make-up of Indonesia, with its great sprawling expanse of islands, makes it difficult to think of it as one nation. Moreover, the importance of the countless ethnic groups, each with its own language, culture and standards, must not be underestimated. Since independence the government has done all in its power to foster the concept of "unity in diversity", which is the official device of the Indonesian republic. However, it cannot be denied that Java has played a major role in determining the identity of Indonesia. And understandably so, in the light of the Javacentrism which existed even in colonial times. Those developments which favoured or were otherwise bound up with the emancipation of women manifested themselves first in Java. That champion of women's rights Raden Adjeng Kartini was Javanese, and women's organizations and congresses usually originated in Java. The birth of such organizations (Wanita Utomo in 1908, Putri Mardika in 1912) was closely associated with the rising tide of nationalism. In the fifties the *Gerwani,* a progressive women's movement, had a strong following, but when Suharto came to power in 1965 these activities came to an end. Today there is only the Islamic women's movement Aisyah and the *isteri*, the "married women's organizations" which, as the name suggests, have little or nothing to do with emancipation. Feminism in its Western form is unknown in Indonesia.

There is only one official language, introduced in 1945, Bahasa Indonesia or Indonesian, which is based on Malayan. Nevertheless, many Indonesians speak another regional language as their native tongue, and do not learn Indonesian until they go to school. Newspapers, magazines and modern literature almost always employ Indonesian. However, the level of illiteracy (29 per cent) indicates that not everyone has access to the contents of these publications.

Malaysia and Indonesia share a common culture and linguistic background, but as a result of their colonial history they developed along quite different lines. Malaysia, which came under English influence at the end of the eighteenth century, became independent in 1957. The language, Malaysian, is also based on Malayan and closely resembles Indonesian. Malaysian society is characterized by a division between, on the one hand, the Malaysians and on the other, the Chinese, Indians and Pakistanis. The fact that a large proportion of the population is non-Malaysian or of mixed origin has contributed to the extensive use of English. Modern Malaysian literature contains both Malaysian and English works. However, the Malaysians have little regard for the English-language literature, which is mainly the work of authors of mixed race (Lloyd Fernando 1968 and 1981). It is precisely the writings of these authors that make it clear how conscious people are of racial discrimination, how much importance they attach to it, and how it is bound up with social status. The following section deals with the modern written literature of Indonesia.

Literature Past and Present

The traditional written literature of the country differs from one region to another. Literary activity usually centred around the princely courts which were situated in various places on the Malayan peninsula and Sumatra (Malacca, Djohor, Atjeh, Palembang, Riau). This literature is largely anonymous, but we do know that Riau is the only place where there were women writers (see Andaya and Matheson 1979:111 and Hamidy 1981: 28, 31). In addition to the written literature there was, and still is, an oral tradition in which texts were accompanied by music or a dramatic form such as the Wajang, or shadow show. It has not been determined whether women were also involved in these activities nor what their role was. There are a number of female Wajang players today in Java, but they are rare. At the beginning of this century a modern literature began to develop, with genres such as novels, short stories and poetry. During this same period nationalist feeling and the emerging Indonesian identity often found expression in literature. The clash between traditional views (*adat*) and modern Western-oriented ideas is often used as a theme. Jakarta quickly became the centre of literary activity in Indonesia.

The relationship between women and literature can be expressed in three different ways: women can be considered as authors, characters or readers. As very little is known about reading habits in Indonesia, we will concentrate on the first two categories.

There were very few women writers in the early stages of modern Indonesian literature, and it was not until the seventies that their numbers began to increase. According to Chambert-Loir (1977:268) this century has produced 400 authors, only 38 of them women. At first women wrote more poetry and short stories than novels and published their work mainly in magazines. Because so little of their work has appeared in book form, it is very scattered and difficult to view as a whole. In 1979 a collection of poems by women appeared, together with the English translations (Toeti Heraty 1979). Although according to the introduction to this collection there are no impediments to a literary career, very few women ever do make a name for themselves. Not only are there few women writers, but the literary production per writer is also very limited. As poetry is generally employed for the expression of extremely personal feelings, it is difficult to form a clear idea of women writers in general on the basis of poems. We will therefore concentrate on novels and short stories.

Early-Modern Women Writers

Before and after the war works were sometimes published in Dutch, and the writings of three prominent women authors appeared first in Dutch and only later in an Indonesian edition. The best known of the three was Raden Adjeng Kartini (1879-1904). Although she did not see herself as a writer and never intended to publish her letters, Kartini is one of the first women whose works appeared in print. As the daughter of a progressive Javanese prince, she attended European schools until the age of 12. However, from puberty on girls from aristocratic families were expected to remain at home. This only intensified her love of freedom and she spent a great deal of time writing letters to her girlfriends and other acquaintances. She died at the age of 25, but not before she had planted the seeds of an emancipation movement which was to grow and flourish. In 1911 Kartini's Dutch letters were edited by J. H. Abendanon (see Kartini 1911, 1976), and in 1922 the first Indonesian translation appeared, followed by two others in 1938 and 1979. Kartini believed that the best way to make women independent was through education, and her main aim was to promote the founding of girls' schools in her country. Kartini also drew attention to the adverse affects on women of the practice of polygamy, which at the time was common in upper-class Moslem circles.

The subject of education will play an important part in our discussion. Not only was it a prominent theme, but it also helped to stimulate the rise of written literature in Indonesia. Many authors were themselves teachers and the sudden increase in the number of women authors was due in part to the fact that there were more educational opportunities being created, in particular for women (see Soemardjo 1979:115 and 1981:45).

Education is the main theme in the novel *Buiten het Gareel* (Beyond the pale, 1940) by the West Javanese author Soewarsih Djojopoespito. It is the story of idealistic, nationalistic teachers and their struggle to establish an Indonesian education system, separate from the Dutch school system (cf. Termorshuizen 1979). The heroine is a young teacher Soelastri, who chooses to fight for her ideals together with her husband Soedarmo. But Soedarmo is demanding, and he is often disappointed in his young bride. Moreover, he is egoistic and authoritarian, so that Soelastri must fight to retain her independence. But in spite of problems and disappointments, the bond between husband and wife becomes increasingly strong. It was not until thirty-five years after the Dutch version appeared that an Indonesian translation was published, by Soewarsih herself (1975).

Widjawati, het Javaanse meisje (W, the Javanese girl, 1948), by A.P. Djajadiningrat (pseudonym Arti Purbani), appeared in Dutch in 1948, followed a year later by the Indonesian version, which is still being reprinted today. This book actually belongs to the pre-war period which it describes. The story is set in the Javanese princely territories (Jogjakarta, Surakarta), which are characterized by a rigid feudal structure. Aristocratic young girls are allowed very little liberty (cf. Kartini). Widjawati is not herself of aristocratic birth, so that she is allowed to attend a teacher-training school in Batavia; later she goes on to study nursing. But the difference in their rank makes it impossible for her to marry the man she loves. Widjawati's friend, the high-born Roosmiati, is obliged to marry her cousin, who already has two wives and a child by one of them. The difference between girls from higher and lower backgrounds is highlighted by a scene in which Roosmiati sends one of her servants with a message for her lover, to arrange a meeting. For an aristocratic young lady there appears to be no obstacle to an intimate relationship with men, for she does not return home from the meeting with her lover until the early morning (1948:18).

Literature from the Minangkabau

It is somewhat misleading that the women writers mentioned above are all from Java, for it was actually in West Sumatra that modern Indonesian literature first manifested itself during the 1920s. In this region, known as the Minangkabau, a Malaysian dialect is spoken and traditionally the language has always been very close to Malaysian. Thus it was easier for people from this region to write in Indonesian than for those with a completely different dialect. The Minangkabau is one of the few societies within Indonesia where a matrilinear system is in force, one in which property, especially agricultural land, is transmitted through the female line. It is moreover also matrilocal, so that the husband moves into the wife's family home (see Postel and Schrijvers 1977:80-3). The conflict between traditional and modern views is strongly felt and strongly expressed by writers who grew up in the Minangkabau (cf. Teeuw 1979:54-5).

One of the related themes which are still prominent in Indonesian literature is that of the arranged marriage. Young people prefer to marry someone of their own choosing, but the *adat*, as represented by parents and relatives, determines who the marriage partner will be. Several authors have taken up this problem, among them Marah Rusli, Nur Sutan Iskandar, Hamka and Abdul Muis. They protest against the way these young lives are dominated by the *adat*. These writers side with the young people who are the heroes and heroines of their books. The main character is usually a young girl who is faithful to her beloved and, once married, to her husband. She is a docile creature who patiently awaits what fate has in store for her. The young men in these stories rebel against the *adat*, which in Minangkabau society admittedly affects them more than it does the girls. Older women play a prominent role here, arranging their children's lives as they think best.

Polygamy is a fact of life in the traditional Moslem society of the Minangkabau, and the rivalry and jealousy arising from this practice is the cause of great suffering among modern women. In stories which centre on this theme the heroine is usually a tragic figure, while the other woman is portrayed as egoistic and demanding. In the novel *Merantau ke Deli* (Hamka 1939), Leman yields to the pressure of his family and takes a second wife. At first he is enchanted by her youth and the novelty of the marriage, which blinds him to her egoism. Only later, when his first wife has left him, does he begin to realize how much she meant to him. Although young people and their choice of a partner are popular themes, sexuality and sexual relationships are almost never mentioned. All young girls marry — it is unthinkable that they should not — and they are all assumed to be virgins when they enter the married state. There are only two women among the Minangkabau authors, Selasih and Hamidah, and both use the same themes as their male colleagues. There is no sign of rebellion in their writings, in spite of the fact that the young women they portray have very little to say about their own future. The young men are luckier because, aside from the bride whom his parents select for him, a man has quite considerable freedom. The characters seem to have accepted their fate. Selasih and Hamidah both stress how important it is to have children. A childless marriage may lead a woman to give her husband permission to take another wife (Hamidah 1935); even then, one of the relationships is bound to suffer, and divorce is often the only solution.

Female Characters in Novels by Male Authors
Two novels in which one man and two women are the central characters are *Layar terkembang* (With sails unfurled, 1936) by Takdir Alisjahbana and *Belenggu* (Fetters, 1940) by Armijn Pané. In the first book the author draws a sharp contrast between Tuti, an intellectual, emancipated young woman,

who originally rejects the idea of marriage because she does not want to be tied down, and her sister Maria, a happy-go-lucky girl who marries Jusuf. When shortly afterwards Maria dies, her last wish is respected and Jusuf and Tuti marry. It is clear that Tuti is the author's idea of the ideal women.

Belenggu, though quite different, is in its way equally innovative compared to the Minangkabau novels. The main characters are Tono, a doctor, his wife Tini and his mistress Yah. The novel relates the story of a broken marriage which is the result of Tono's liaison with Yah, his childhood sweetheart. The author traces the relationship up until the moment the two women meet, when they both decide to leave Tono. All three characters are carefully developed and worked out; neither Tini nor Yah fits the image of the ideal woman, the virgin bride, which was previously considered so important. Tini is not a virgin when she marries Tono; she has had an unhappy love affair and believes her lover dead. And once she is married she refuses to take up the role of assistant to her doctor husband, and demands the right to lead a life of her own. Yah was married off to a man twenty years her senior, but later ran away from him and was forced into prostitution. As a result of the author's extremely personal style, the reader is made party to the thoughts and experiences of Tono, Tini and to a lesser extent Yah. The author does not take sides and the women are not censured for their behaviour. As the story ends the characters all go their separate ways.

Belenggu created a new role for women in literature, that of sexual partner. After the war this idea was taken up and developed by prominent writers such as Pramoedya Ananta Toer and Mochtar Lubis. Significant social changes were taking place, in particular during the struggle for independence, and in literature, too, attention shifted to the new social situation which was emerging.

Women are often portrayed as victims of this new situation,

and they are sometimes forced by circumstances to prostitute themselves. Pramoedya has described a variety of female characters, many of whom have made this choice, in order to obtain information about a brother from a soldier, to escape an arranged marriage, or simply to keep body and soul together (Pramoedya 1950, 1952, 1954[a], 1957). But sex is also a natural human need. Fatimah is married to Isa, who proves to be impotent, and when she meets the young and high-spirited Hazil she finds his sexual attraction difficult to resist (Mochtar Lubis, 1952). A number of books are set against a corrupt background where sex as a pastime is highlighted, alongside the role played by money, status and male prestige (Pramoedya, 1954[a]; Mochtar Lubis 1964). Here the men run the show and women are kept very much in the background.

In her book *Kedjatuhan dan hati* (The fall and the heart, 1950) S. Rukiah presents another new type of female character: the book follows the heroine Susi from childhood, during which the family is dominated by an ambitious materialistic mother, to adulthood, when she herself becomes a mother. Susi, who is determined not to submit to her mother's wishes and marry a suitable partner — Par — joins a guerrilla group during the revolution. Susi is sullen, unapproachable and unfeminine, until she falls in love with the communist Lukman. But in the end she cannot turn her back on the bourgeois ideas of her childhood, which means that marriage to Lukman is out of the question. When the guerrilla movement comes to grief, Susi returns home and marries Par. She bears a son, whose father is Lukman, and when he comes to see her one last time, she still cannot bring herself to run away with him. No matter how hard she has tried she cannot break loose from her environment. Susi, too, loses her virginity before marriage, although here it is a question of a free choice, a logical consequence of her love for Lukman. But in the end she too bows to the prevailing moral code, marries a man she does not love, and spends the rest of her life guarding a guilty secret. Her older sister Dini, on the other hand, makes no concession to tradition; she remains unmarried, for which she is censured by society. Susi, however, admires her for her stand, because it shows how strong-willed she is.

The Rise of the Popular Novel

As we have seen above, from 1920 to the 1950s there were very few women writing in Indonesia. In their novels the female characters play a more important part than in works by male authors, but the number of writers and the number of works are still insufficient to allow a fair comparison. Moreover, all the authors continue to adhere to certain conventions: the choice of a partner and the female stereotype. The latter is presumably a holdover from earlier literature, the image of a woman who faints or bursts into tears at the drop of a hat.

It would be interesting to know what the reactions of the reading public and the critics were to these first few women writers. An intensive study would be needed to ascertain whether they were judged in the same way as their male colleagues or whether special criteria were used. Initially readers and critics did not see women writers as strange or threatening; they were neither ignored nor particularly encouraged. In an article in which she looked back on her writing career, Selasih (1972) said that she was always accepted as an equal.

During the 1960s short stories became the preferred genre, most of them published in magazines. Women were also active in this genre, among them Nh. Dini, Titis Basino and Enny Soemargono. Dutch women's magazines, which had remained popular long after 1949, made way for Indonesian versions such as *Femina* and *Kartini*. A weekly supply of column space was available for stories, and newspapers began to publish them in instalments. This increased literary activity on the part of female authors continued on into the seventies, when the so-called *poproman* or popular novel began to come into its own. There is a certain resemblance to the Western dime-store novel, but it would not be entirely fair to equate the two. Indonesian popular novels have a character all their own, and are not Western imports. They can be traced back to a Chinese-Malaysian tradition from pre-war days, paperback novels which made their entrance in Sumatra (Medan, Padang, Bukittinggi). They were published as separate issues of various magazines which appeared irregularly (see Sitti Faizah 1963:39). At that time the genre was dominated by men. Since the revival of the last ten years the boundary between popular and serious novels has become less pronounced than before, due in part to the fact that the *popromans* are sometimes carried by well-known publishing houses.

Popular novels are important in the Indonesian context because they stimulate reading. They are printed and reprinted in much larger editions than the serious novels. One publishing house, Pustaka Jaya, prints the latter in editions of about 5,000 (for a population of 145 million!), while popular novels often run to over 15,000. Their popularity increases when they are filmed.

For a number of women authors the writing of popular novels is only a sideline: Aryanti (pseudonym of Haryati Soebadio) is a professor of Sanskrit at the University of Jakarta, Marianne Katoppo is a prominent theologian, Poppy Hutagalung is a journalist aad Marga T. is a doctor. These authors are widely known, their work is discussed and filmed, and they are actually more popular than the serious authors.

This genre is not exclusively the domain of women, for there are at least as many male authors who write *popromans*. The setting of these stories is the big city, usually Jakarta, where the children all go to university, and the parents have a second home in the country, in addition to the comfortable, Western-style house. It is a world where alcohol and drugs are not uncommon. In spite of their dimensions — they often run to 300-400 pages, which is quite large by Indonesian standards — these books often lack psychological depth. The story always centres around young people, their love affairs and the choice of a marriage partner. Sex has become one of the basic ingredients of the plot, but often even the women writers take the male standpoint — sex can provide only physical gratification — confirming the standard pattern of male authority and female subordination. In *Karmila* (1973), the most popular book by the well-known Marga T., the heroine is given too much to drink and then raped. When it becomes clear that she is pregnant, her family arranges for her to marry the man who raped her. No mention is made of the psychological consequences of the affair, nor the reaction of society, nor the fact that Karmila will probably have to give up medical school. Two other books, by Ashadi Siregar (1976[a], 1976[b]) deal with rape in more or less the same way. To women readers in the West this may seem somewhat farfetched, but Indonesian readers devour this type of novel. All three books have been successfully filmed. In a way, the theme of pre-war novels — arranged marriages and unhappy love affairs — has returned to the forefront in the popular novel. Now, however, the marriages are dictated by social circumstances or moral pressures, and sometimes they are even the result of a stupid mistake. Subjects calculated to interest women, such as pregnancy, bringing up children, the relationship between parents and children, the ageing process and financial independence, are only rarely highlighted: they are referred to indirectly if they come up at all. Female homosexuality remains the one great taboo.

Three Authors of Important New Works

In addition to the many writers of popular novels, there is one woman writer in Indonesia who is definitely a serious novelist. She is Nh. Dini. During the 1950s she published short stories in magazines but she owes her fame to the novel *Pada sebuah kapal* (On a ship, 1973). She later wrote three novels and five small volumes of autobiographical material based on childhood memories. Her novels, which are all written in the first person, and often feature a relationship with a Western man, emphasize the inequality between men and women. Her characters are always conscious of that inequality; they strive for a more equitable treatment, but this struggle never seems to rise above the level of their personal needs. In *Pada sebuah kapal* the heroine Sri is married to a Frenchman, but she is not happy. Here again marriage was forced upon the female main character because she had already lost her virginity. Owing to her husband's indifference Sri feels justified in taking a lover. Sexual contact is described from the feminine point of view, as an expression of warmth, tenderness and understanding, and the heroines do not feel they have in any way been "conquered" by the man. Like Dini's other heroines, Sri does not feel guilty about her unfaithfulness, nor does she suffer from the stigma of the "fallen woman".

Dini's writings can be seen as novels of emancipation, in which she appeals to the women of Indonesia to take their rightful place as independent human beings with a will of their own, to renounce excessive sentimentality, and fight the double standard. An interesting sidelight is the fact that although Dini portrays Indonesian (Javanese) characters, they associate mainly with Westerners and her stories are given a Western setting such as France or Japan. Indonesian readers find it more difficult to identify with the various characters, and as a result events are often seen as characteristic of a free-and-easy Westernized society, and not applicable to Indonesia.

Pada sebuah kapal received a great deal of publicity and has virtually made the reputation of its author. Articles and interviews with Dini point up how extraordinary it is for a woman to write freely and frankly about sex outside of marriage without bringing in the matter of guilt. The question which most often recurs and which seems to intrigue readers is, of course, whether Dini's heroines are replicas of herself. She does not comment on this subject.

In recent years female characters have also been given

important roles in the works of male authors. Umar Kayam published two short stories, both of which bear the name of the heroine as title, "Sri Sumareh" and "Bawuk" (1975). Sri Sumareh is a woman brought up according to Javanese tradition. Her ideal is the Wajang character Sembadra: "the true wife, docile and patient, who understands her husband's frailties and admires his strength" (1975:38). Sri accepts the life which fate has ordained for her. Her husband dies young, her daughter has to get married because she is pregnant, the leftist political activities of her daughter and son-in-law lead to his execution and her daughter's imprisonment. Against this background she must bring up her granddaughter, amid serious financial difficulties. She earns her living as a masseuse, and she often has to fight off the groping hands of her clients. There is only one young man, twenty years her junior, whom she allows to embrace her, and whose tenderness awakens her emotions. In spite of her limited understanding of modern society, this ageing woman manages to hold her own.

Bawuk is a completely different type of woman, from a less traditional Javanese background. And yet she too is depicted as someone who is determined to run her own life, and who knows exactly what she wants. Against their family's wishes she marries a communist activist, which does not make life any easier for her. Both stories are refreshing in that they portray the heroines not only against a family background, but within a much broader context.

The third female character is Njai Ontosoroh (Pramoedya 1980[a], 1980[b]). This native woman, second wife of a colonial, develops from an unlettered village girl into the shrewd and capable head of a large livestock farm. These three women, all three Javanese, and all three created by Javanese male writers, are depicted in a situation in which they must rely on themselves, and act as independent human beings. The difference between them and Dini is that she attempts to justify the conduct of her heroines, primarily by having them narrate the story themselves. In Kayam and Pramoedya, on the other hand, it is taken for granted that women have to fend for themselves.

Closing Remarks

In summary we can say that in modern Indonesian literature women writers were rare up until the sixties and seventies, when a group of women authors appeared, most of whom concentrated on the *poproman* or popular novel.

Literature is an élitist occupation. Books are expensive and those who read and write them are all well educated. It is for this reason that education plays such an important role in the development of literature. Initially women were poorly represented in literature because they did not have access to education to the same degree that men did. It was only after the war, when more and more girls started attending school, that a generation of young women writers reached maturity. The limited range of subjects which existed before the war — love, marriage, family — are still in use. The typical wife is described as docile and obedient to her husband, an image which appears to be common among male and female authors alike. Women writers are not militant, but seem rather to have resigned themselves to circumstances which are largely unfavourable to them: dependence, polygamy, the risk of being set aside by their husbands.

Against the background of a new social and economic situation women are often depicted as victims, who have no other choice but to prostitute themselves. During this period, the fifties, women do not seem to react against this image.

The fictional world is generally dominated by male norms and values. This is particularly true of sexual conduct in popular novels. Dini is the only author to portray women who are conscious of male domination and rebel against it.

Literature is a means of disseminating ideas. This can be done by presenting a realistic, recognizable world, in such a way that the reader comes to identify with the characters. To be recognizable the fictional world must not differ too much from the real world.

The relationship between female characters and real women is an important aspect of our subject. In the novels discussed above women are invariably seen within the confines of marriage and family. However, sociological and anthropological studies have shown that in Indonesia a considerable portion of the rice culture and the retail trade is in the hands of women. It is surprising and regrettable that women are never portrayed in these roles, and that the setting is always the city. It is also unfortunate that writers like Aryanti and Marianne Katoppo never write about women who have responsible positions of their own, especially since both of them could speak from experience. While the popular novels present the ideal image, that of women within marriage and the family, it is for the anthropologists and sociologists to ascertain to what extent this ideal of the housewife and mother exists in the reality of modern Indonesian society. It seems almost as if in the very beginning, at the time of the Minangkabau novels, certain literary conventions were laid down which authors have adhered to ever since.

It is possible that these conventions — and with them the image of women in general — will gradually alter, as people become more and more aware of the position of women. If so, this will undoubtedly lead to a more critical and even feminist perspective in the literature of Indonesia.

REFERENCES

Andaya, B., & V. Matheson, 1979, "Islamic thought and Malay tradition: the writings of Raja Ali Haji of Riau (ca. 1809 — ca. 1870)", in *Perceptions of the Past in Southeast Asia*, A. Reid & D. Marr, Singapore, pp. 108-28.

Armijn Pané, 1940, *Belenggu* (Fetters), Jakarta.

Arti Purbani, 1948, *Widjawati het Javaanse meisje* (W. the Javanese girl), Amsterdam.

Arti Purbani, 1949, *Widjawati* (Indonesian translation 1948), Jakarta.

Ashadi Siregar, 1976[a], *Terminal cinta terakhir* (Last Love Terminal), Jakarta.

Ashadi Siregar, 1976[b], *Sirkuit kemelut* (Crisis Circuit), Jakarta.

Aveling, Harry, 1975, *From Surabaya to Armageddon* (translated stories by Pramoedya Ananta Toer, Umar Kayam *et al.*), Singapore.

Biro Pusat Statistik, 1982, *Indikator kesejahteraan rakyat* (Indicator of people's welfare), Jakarta.

Chambert-Loir, H., 1977, "Les femmes et l'écriture: la littérature féminine indonésienne", in: *Archipel*, 13, Paris, pp. 276-82.

Echols, J. (ed.), 1956, *Indonesian Writing in Translation* (translated stories by Pramoedya Ananta Toer, Mochtar Lubis *et al.*), Cornell.

Hamidy, U.U., 1981, *Pengarang Melayu dalam kerajaan Riau dan Abdullah bin Abdul Kadir Munsyi dalam sastra Melayu* (Malay writers in the Riau Kingdom and Abdullah bin Abdul Kadir Munsyi in Malay Literature), Jakarta.

Hamidah, 1935, *Kehilangan mestika* (Bereft of her Magic Jewel), Jakarta.

Hamka, 1939, *Merantau ke Deli* (Going Abroad to Deli), Medan.

Hendon, Rufus S., 1968, *Six Indonesian Short Stories*, Yale University.

Hill, D., 1979, "Alienation and opposition to authoritarianism in the novels of Ashadi Siregar", in *Review of Indonesian and Malaysian Affairs*, 13.1, Sydney, pp. 25-43.

Kartini, Raden Adjeng, 1911, *Door duisternis tot licht* (From Darkness to Light), Semarang/Surabaja/The Hague, 1976[4], London.

Kartini, Raden Adjeng, 1920, *Letters of a Javanese Princess*, translation 1911 by Agnes Louise Symmers, New York; 1976[4], London.

Kartini, Raden Adjeng, 1922, *Habis gelap terbitlah terang, boeah pikiran R.A. Kartini. Dimelajoekan oleh Empat Saudara* (Indonesian translation 1911), Batavia.

Kartini, Raden Adjeng, 1938, *Habis gelap terbitlah terang, boeah pirikan R.A. Kartini. Dimelajoekan oleh Empat Saudara* (Indonesian translation 1911), Batavia.

Kartini, Raden Adjeng, 1938, *Habis gelap terbitlah terang*, translation 1911 by Armijn Pané, Jakarta.

Kartinin Raden Adjeng, 1979, *Surat-surat Kartini, Renungan tentang dan untuk bangsanya*, translation 1911 by Sulastin Sutrisno, Jakarta.

Lloyd Fernando, 1968, *Twenty-two Malaysian Stories*, Singapore.

Lloyd Fernando, 1981, *Malaysian Short Stories*, Kuala Lumpur-Singapore-Kowloon.

Marga T., 1973, *Karmila*, Jakarta.

Mochtar Lubis, 1952, *Jalan tak ada ujung* (A Road with no End), Jakarta.

Mochtar Lubis, 1968, *A Road with no End*, translation 1952 by A.H. Johns, London.

Mochtar Lubis, 1963, *Twilight in Djakarta*, translation 1964 by Claire Holt, London.

Mochtar Lubis, 1964, *Senja di Jakarta*, 1965[2], Kuala Lumpur.

Nh. Dini, 1973, *Pada sebuah kapal* (On a Ship), Jakarta.

Postel, E., & J. Schrijvers, 1977, "Minangkabau women: change in a matrilineal society", in *Archipel*, 13, Paris, pp. 79-103.

Pramoedya Ananta Toer, 1950, *Keluarga Guerilja* (A Guerilla Family), Jakarta.

Pramoedya Ananta Toer, 1952, *Tjerita dari Blora* (Stories from Blora), Jakarta.

Pramoedya Ananta Toer, 1954[a], *Midah, si manis bergigi emas* (Midah, the Sweetheart with the Golden Teeth), Jakarta.

Pramoedya Ananta Toer, 1954[b], *Korupsi* (Corruption), Bukittinggi.

Pramoedya Ananta Toer, 1957, *Tjerita dari Djakarta* (Stories from Jakarta), Jakarta.

Pramoedya Ananta Toer, 1980[a], *Bumi manusia*, Jakarta; English translation 1982 by Max Lane, *This Earth of Mankind*, Penguin Books, Australia.

Pramoedya Ananta Toer, 1980[b], *Anak semua bangsa* (Child of all), Jakarta.

Rukiah, S., 1950, *Kedjatuhan dan hati* (The Fall and the Heart), Jakarta.

Selasih, 1972, "Pengalaman menulis karya sastra pada masa Pudjangga Baru" (My experiences in writing literary works during the P.B. period), in *Budaja Djaja*, V, no. 54 (Nov.), Jakarta, pp. 674-88.

Sitti Faizah, 1963, *Roman pitjisan sebelum perang* (Penny dreadfuls before the war), M.A. thesis, Universitas Indonesia, Jakarta.

Soemardjo, Jakob, 1979, *Novel Indonesia mutakhir: sebuah kritik* (Recent Indonesian novels: a review), Yogyakarta.

Soemardjo, Jakob, 1981, "Rumah yang damai: wanita dalam sastra Indonesia" (A Quiet Home: Women in Indonesian literature), in *Prisma* X no. 7, Jakarta, pp. 44-52.

Soewarsih Djojopoespito, 1940, *Buiten het gareel* (Beyond the pale), Utrecht.

Soewarsih Djojopoespito, 1975, *Manusia bebas*, translation 1940, Jakarta.

Takdir Alisjahbana, 1936, *Layar terkembang* (With Sails Unfurled), Jakarta.

Teeuw, A., 1979, *Modern Indonesian Literature*, Den Haag.

Termorshuizen, G., 1979, "Een leven buiten het gareel" (A Life Beyond the Pale), in *Winterboek Engelbewaarder*, Amsterdam, pp. 109-22.

Toeti Heraty, 1970, *Seserpih pinang sepucuk sirih. Bunga rampai puisi wanita*. (A Taste of Betel and Lime. An anthology of poetry by women), Jakarta.

Umar Junus, 1979, "Betina-perempuan-wanita" (Females-women-ladies), in *Prisma* 4, Jakarta, pp. 23-32.

Umar Kayam, 1975, *Sri Sumarah dan Bawuk* (Sri Sumarah and Bawuk), Jakarta.

Vrouwengroep Antropologie, 1979, *Vrouw in zicht! Naar een feministische antropologie* (Women Ahoy! Towards a feminist anthropology), Amsterdam.

INTERVIEW WITH NABANEETA DEB-SEN
(INDIA)

SANJUKTA GUPTA

Nabaneeta Deb-Sen is professor of comparative literature at Jadavpur University in Calcutta. She attended university in India, as well as in England and the United States. Alongside a full-time job at the university, she also writes poetry, fiction and essays. She has two daughters, who also keep her busy; one is at university and the other is just finishing secondary school.

Nabaneeta Deb-Sen was an only child. Her mother was a poet, and Nabaneeta, too, began to make a name for herself with her Bengali poetry while still at university in the late fifties. She continued to write and publish collections of poetry. In the seventies she turned to fiction, with several novels and a large number of short stories in Bengali. Her best prose works, however, are her remarkable essays. Her style is marked by keen wit, lucidity and quite considerable powers of critical appraisal. Two of her best-known collections are *The Rival of God* and *Nabaneeta, the Actress* (1983). In this last book she has achieved a considerable literary feat by formulating the most profound ideas in a lucid and easy style, with sparkling flashes of humour.

Her parents belonged to the intelligentsia of the Bengali middle class, whose political views correspond to those of liberal humanists in England. Traces of this influence are to be found in her work, although at no time does she display dogmatic ideological views.

This interview took place at Nabaneeta Deb-Sen's home in Calcutta.

How do male critics see women writers?

Not very favourably. I am convinced that women writers have to be exceptionally good and often they must show proof of extensive literary experience before their work is reviewed to the same extent as that of their male colleagues.

Do you think that male authors feel threatened by women writers?

Yes. Men are suspicious of women who write about serious subjects. They consider poetry the proper genre for women — suitable for the emotional outpourings of a sweet young thing! They're even allowed to write fiction, as long as they keep to intimate domestic scenes, which confirm traditional male values, and write in a suitably docile style.

As soon as you start to write seriously — essays on political or economic subjects or on social evils — you feel as if you've just disturbed a hornets' nest. I sense the hostility of men, for instance after publishing critical reviews or an analysis of social problems. Men take criticism as a personal insult and automatically assume that you have a grudge against them.

Men are convinced that women shouldn't try to "mount the wild horse of truth" for — she says it sarcastically — such a distasteful undertaking is best left to unfeeling creatures like men. When a woman writes seriously, her books are received by the public like prisoners drilled each day under the watchful eye of the guard. They are inspected from head to toe by the readers, who are determined to see them solely in relation to the woman writer as a person.

Have you ever tackled subjects that were taboo?

That is really very difficult in Bengal. If you try to live a conventional life and yet write unconventional things, you are going to get into trouble. I feel very strongly the ever-present discrimination on the basis of my sex, discrimination by male colleagues, by critics and by readers. In the case of a woman writer readers aren't satisfied with the literary work itself. They want a glimpse of her private life, they want information about her that has nothing to do with her work. A personal scandal might enhance the reputation of a male author — like the autobiography of a film star — but it would immediately

161

put an end to the aesthetic esteem in which a woman writer was previously held by Indian middle-class readers.

The way in which Indian readers discriminate against women authors is disastrous. I must admit that I am bitter about this situation. The domestic role which the woman writer fulfils dominates her public image as a writer. A male author is free to neglect all his domestic and social obligations. He is an artist, and everyone knows artists are untamed animals, temperamental and chaotic, audacious and irreverent. But women, though they may try something artistic from time to time, will never be real artists.

Suppose that you were a woman writer in Calcutta: you belong to a traditional Indian family and you've just had a rather unconventional piece published in a prominent literary journal. From that point on your family life would become unbearable. Your father would solemnly advise you to put an end to such nonsense. With tears in her eyes, your mother would explain that you were ruining any hope you might have of making a good marriage, your brother would tell you that you've put him in an extremely awkward situation. If you were married, your husband would be deeply unhappy. He would implore you to give up writing and stop debasing his name, and your children would ask why you can't be a normal mother like all the other mothers they know.

In India fathers are allowed to indulge in such escapades, but mothers must be sedate and proper. And of course everything — in particular all those domestic chores — takes precedence over writing. Writing only begins when the last item on the list of duties has been crossed off. For example, Shailabala Ghose wrote her novel *Sheikh Ander* in the thirties. The sheik in the story is a Moslem driver who marries the daughter of his Hindu employer, after first running away with her. The author defied three taboos: class, religion and virginity, and she was bitterly criticized for it too. As a Hindu child-widow of the highest caste, she was ill-advised to tackle so many sacred cows at once!

Is this still the case? Do writers still meet with this kind of censorship, and are they still afraid to defy taboos?

Among the Hindu women writers, there are only a few who dare to broach that kind of problem. In the West women writers are free from every form of obstacle or restraint, thanks to the emancipation of women and the general social trend towards tolerance. But in India and more particularly in Bengal, the literary climate is still such that women must contend with all sorts of taboos. Consciously or unconsciously they heed Mallarmé's advice: "Always use the wrong word." For a woman writer has a solemn and secret duty to express her "un-self". I never write down the first word that occurs to me when I feel inspired to write, not even the second word. I always wait until I have sufficiently camouflaged my original thought. Among the young writers in Bengali there is only one woman — Bani Roy — who has the courage to ignore the unwritten moral codes which are imposed on women authors in Bengal, for the sake of her art. If I were writing in English I would feel more free; I would be able to express my real feelings, my anger and my longings, much more openly and forcefully. I wouldn't have to consider the feelings of readers, because I would be addressing readers I didn't know and who didn't know me. Writing in Bengali for Bengali readers makes me feel "un-free". Moreover, those of us who teach have an extra group of guards, our students. Even as I write I cannot forget that some readers know my face.

What you've just been telling me, does it apply only to your own personal reactions and inhibitions?

Yes, that's true. I'm probably too conventional. I feel the threat; I'm afraid that my children might suffer if I were to write without reserve. The social position of women is precarious and you have to be sure to strike just the right balance. I don't dare take any risks. I believe that I am assured of a respectable future if I identify with my role as a mother — my traditional, Indian role — and not with the role of somebody's wife, or Mrs So-and-so. It is an endless and often unfair struggle which is very wounding to one's self-esteem.

IV.   THE CARIBBEAN

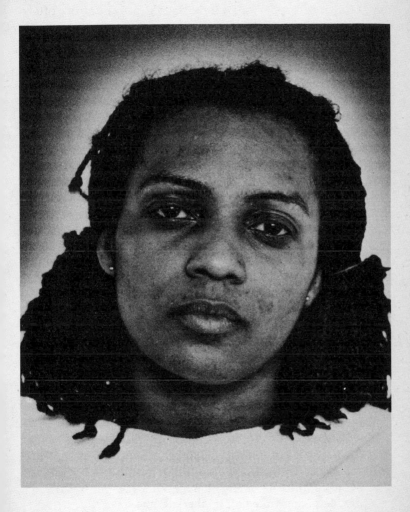

(*Foto:* Robert de Hartogh)

PROVERBS

1. Beautiful woman, beautiful trouble. (Jamaica)
2. If the man had known [what would happen] he would never have planted his yams in a strange woman's ground. (Jamaica)
3. If you need the old woman's pepper pot, you'll have to scratch her back. (Jamaica)
4. Man builds the house, but woman makes the home. (Jamaica)
5. If the old woman is home, the ram goat can't hang himself [i.e. he will not get tangled in the rope] (Jamaica)
6. Perfect women and white John-crow are equally scarce. (Jamaica)
7. When the guinea fowl calls, it says: "Don't play with women." (Jamaica)
8. A woman's mouth is a fowl's mouth [i.e. she is ungrateful]. (Jamaica)
9. If a woman does not want to dance, she says her frock is too short [i.e. she makes up an excuse]. (Jamaica)
10. A woman's pain is never done [i.e. she is always crying over nothing]. (Jamaica)
11. If an old woman wants to cry, she says the smoke got in her eye [i.e. she wants to blame somebody else]. (Jamaica)
12. When man in trouble, woman laughs at him. (Jamaica)
13. If you see an old woman at a crossroad, do not bother her [she might be a witch]. (Jamaica)
14. Ants follow fat, women follow men. (Jamaica)
15. When you see an old lady run, don't ask why, just run too. (Jamaica)
16. Woman's breasts are never too heavy for her [i.e. she can cope with her problems]. (Haïti)
17. You can have several wives but only one mother. (Haïti)
18. Better a good baisait [mistress] than a bad wife. (Curaçao)
19. He is like a child without a mother [i.e. in bad shape]. (Curaçao)
20. He has turned his mother's milk bitter [i.e. got himself into trouble and disgraced his mother]. (Curaçao)
21. The youngest child is his mother's death [i.e. you can't go on for ever]. (Curaçao)

22. A child that doesn't listen to its mother ends up in the snake's mouth (Curaçao)
23. Grandmother's breast is for all children. (Surinam)
24. You can hide your old mother but not her cough [truth will out]. (Surinam)
25. Mother dead, greetings finished [i.e. friendship lasts only as long as there's something to gain]. (Surinam)
26. A woman is like half a cent — you can't make her any smaller. (Surinam)
27. Cook the mother for the children, and they'll eat her; cook the children for the mother and she won't touch it. (Dominica)
28. Every man kisses a woman differently (Guyana).
29. A man who wants two wives must have two tongues. (Guyana)
30. A man must see a woman before he buys a bed. (Guyana)

ACKNOWLEDGEMENTS

Aart G. Broek, Holland/Curaçao (1-14 and 18-22), selected from Martha Warren Beckwith, *Jamaica Proverbs*, New York, Negro Universities Press, 1925, 1970, and from P. Hoefnagels and Shon W. Hoogenbergen, *Antillian Proverbs* (in Dutch), Curaçao, 1981; *Frank Cundall*, Jamaica (15); *H.J. Lamur* and *Arthy Lamur*, Surinam (23-5); *Astrid Roemer*, Surinam (26); *Ovid S. Abram*, Guyana (28-30); *Ineke Phaf* helped to obtain 14, 15, 26, and 28-30; numbers 16 and 17 come from B. David and J.-P. Jardel, *Les proverbes créoles de la Martinique. Langage et société*, s.l.n.d. Cérag.

WOMEN AND LITERATURE IN THE CARIBBEAN

INEKE PHAF

The purpose of this essay* is to determine, first, whether there is a "typical Caribbean" image of women in the literature of the region which points to certain stereotypes, and second, whether women writers respond to this image with a "Caribbean" view of their own.

For our purposes the Caribbean comprises those islands and countries around the Caribbean Sea which in the past had a plantation economy based on slave labour. This means that the Guianas and Surinam are also included (see Sandner 1980). These countries, on the very doorstep of the United States, have a variety of political systems. There is socialism in Cuba and a "capitalist" government in Jamaica. There are departments (Martinique, Guadeloupe) and independent states under French, Dutch (Aruba, Bonaire and Curaçao) or North American (Puerto Rico) flags, as well as governments headed by nationalist leaders, as in Surinam and Guyana.

In the smaller states more and more women are beginning to write and to publish their work. The poetry of Rosario Ferré of Puerto Rico and the folk poet Louise Bennett of Jamaica, the prose works of Jacqueline Manicom of Martinique and Bea Vianen and Sonia Garmers of Surinam and Curaçao — all these are part and parcel of the literary development of these countries. It is not possible to discuss the work of all the women writers now active, nor to study their personal lives. There are too many of them, and in many cases their biographies, or at any rate the problems which affect their writing, are quite similar to those of the women whose interviews appear elsewhere in this book. In the politically turbulent Caribbean it is more important to look for *common*

* The study upon which this article is based was made possible by a grant from the Volkswagen Foundation of Hanover.

social and cultural conflicts which find expression in the literature of the various countries, conflicts which women writers respond to in a specific manner. This approach has been chosen because the study of these questions on a regional level has only just begun, and because up to now the image of women in literature has received very little attention within that study. We shall limit our discussion to those women writers who have given the above considerations a prominent place in their work.

It is only recently that a survey of Caribbean literary history has been undertaken. This is due in part to the fact that the various Caribbean countries did not begin to take an interest in their own literary traditions until about twenty years ago. As the process of decolonization continues, there is an increasing awareness of the importance of cultural developments in the growth of a national identity, while factors which all parts of the region have in common are being "discovered".

In his classic work on decolonization Frantz Fanon of Martinique stresses the importance of maintaining a collective sense of responsibility during this continuing process, and he is addressing not only politicians but also writers and researchers. This is essential in a region which is so divided, not only geographically, but in many other respects as well. Colonization has resulted in extreme social and cultural polarization, the consequences of which are still felt today. The plantation economy which was imported produced the "intercontinental" population we see today. The original Indian inhabitants were unsuited to plantation work, so that the European owners brought in African slaves to work in the fields. When slavery was abolished they were replaced by Asian contract labourers. But emancipation did not automatically put an end to the stark contrast between the European and African sections of the population. In the early decades of this century there was little or no social mobility for the large numbers of free, but unskilled workers. Modernization, chiefly North American-inspired, brought oil refineries and bauxite companies which required technically skilled workers. The others found employment on the sugar and banana plantations, in the ports or on the Panama Canal which was then under construction. The various governments did little to improve the infrastructure of their own countries, and in many cases there was little they could do, due to limited financial resources or the existing political power balance. The measures they did take were aimed mainly at bringing the living conditions of the urban "élite" up to North American or European standards, which only widened the gap between them and the rest of the mainly agrarian population.

While the influence of the historical developments sketched above was not the same in all of the Caribbean countries, the former relationship between slave/black and master/white can be seen even today. Not only is the colour of one's skin a kind of status symbol, but there is a distinct polarization between the international urban community and the poorer classes in the slums and rural areas.

This polarization has considerably affected women's opportunities within society. Sociologists even refer to the *Caribbean phenomenon* with regard to family structures, in which skin colour is of major importance (see Henriques 1976; Nettleford 1978; Cohen Stuart 1979). This phenomenon is rooted in history, notably in the relationships which existed at the time of slavery. Black men and women were the "damned" of colonial society, and for all practical purposes they had no family ties. They could be bought and sold at will, and their living conditions did nothing to stimulate a desire for children of their own. Mothers wanted to spare their children a similar fate, and numerous documents testify to cases of abortion and suicide by black women who were pregnant. Mulattos had more chance of improving their lot in life. As the illegitimate childen of white fathers, many of them were born "free", so that their conditions were better than those of slaves. The planters considered female slaves as their property, and a black girl was in no position to refuse the "wishes" of her master. If she tried to defend herself against such advances the white man was always proved right, and in any case he could see that she paid for her resistance.

And yet black women often preferred a white man to a black, because a slave had nothing to offer them or their children. A white man was not obliged to grant her support but at least there was the possibility of his doing so, especially if she had caught his fancy.

It was also important not to emphasize one's African origins. Language, religion, manners and dress all had to be adapted to the "white" tastes which reigned in the colonies. This process of assimilation started with the outward appearance: the lighter the skin, the straighter the hair, the more chance there was of partial integration into the colonial elite, the only group with money. Of course the aspirations of such women were a threat to the official spouse, who was usually a European woman. She was a prisoner of the Catholic or Victorian conventions of her milieu. She was not permitted to work, but had to supervise the running of the household and keep up appearances. For her no black lovers, let alone children by them. This sort of situation did nothing to promote mutual trust among women; the constant "erotic" rivalry was far more likely to make them enemies.

Not only have researchers begun to study the pattern of conduct of the white husband with his "assimilated concubines", but there is now also more interest in the position of the "authentic" black women. The women who have not adapted to fit a "white world", and are still living in a rural area, or in one of the city slums. Quite often they have no partner and are hard put to find a man who will take on responsibility for them and their children. The severe shortage of jobs which followed upon the abolition of slavery greatly contributed to their present plight. Black men were forced to move away in search of employment. Women and children remained at home without a provider. They had to fend for themselves with at most a tiny plot of land behind the house. This is the origin of the expression "my mother who fathered me", a reference to the hard-working black mother with children by different fathers. Her philosophy of life is quite different from that of "assimilated" black women in the urban context. Her moral standards are based on a different kind of logic, which is often misunderstood.

If we are to measure the influence which such Caribbean factors as these have had on the image of women in literature, then we must first concern ourselves with the material to be studied. As we have already observed, there is as yet no broad view of Caribbean literature as a whole. Many works are difficult to obtain, the editions are limited and there is little communication among writers themselves. Professional writers meet with many obstacles. Widespread illiteracy makes it difficult to acquire a reading public and there are few publishers who specialize in literature. Literary criticism flourishes to a limited degree among insiders — often the writers themselves — which can interfere with an objective evaluation of an author's work. Language presents problems all its own. Those who think in Papiamento, Hindi, Malaysian, Sranantongo, Creole, Yoruba, patois or pidgin English are not much interested in works written in the languages of European colonizers (Spanish, English, French and Dutch). So the authors of these works are dependent on the European book market, where literary critics take exception to their "Caribbean style", which is rather free with the accepted rules of grammar. When these writers attempt to express their experiences in their own way, the wording they choose is often overly emotional. Though they are writing in the European language, their emotional choice of words serves to emphasize precisely those characteristics which are typical of the Caribbean.

In addition to this general problem, women writers are faced with other, quite specific difficulties. When they come to Europe, where there is more interest in their works than at home, the women's movements awaken them to their potential as women. But too often this new awareness is still of little use to them in their own society, due to lack of cooperation from both men and women. The only country in the Caribbean where women's rights are regulated by law and where social conditions exist which guarantee those rights is Cuba. Moreover, the cultural climate there, as regards publishers and reading public, is more advanced than in the other countries in the region, so that women writers in Cuba enjoy a much more favourable position. For this reason we shall turn first to Cuban literary tradition, in order to ascertain to what extent the "Caribbean family pattern" is to be found there and in what ways women authors in Cuba have taken up this theme. Later we shall compare these authors with writers from other parts of the Caribbean. The emphasis will be on the relationship between the *main characters* and *urban society* where, as we have seen, social and cultural differences manifest themselves most clearly. Our study will concentrate largely on *novels*, the genre which provides the most information on the social and cultural situation during a given period. In addition to studying the image of women, we shall also be paying particular attention to the consequences of *decolonization*, as this has been a major factor in determining the attitudes of the central characters to their own country as well as their reactions to encounters with other cultures.

Havana as Caribbean City

The Caribbean polarization described above is reflected in the history of Havana. It is the largest city which dates from the conquest of the New World, and has the most flourishing cultural tradition. As in the other cities of Spanish America, the creoles (i.e. people born in a Spanish- or English-speaking Caribbean area, one of whose parents originally came from Europe) were the first people to produce characteristic art forms of their own: poetry, painting, music and architecture. Due largely to her position as a seaport, Havana gradually

173

became the third largest city on the American continent (see Phaf 1983). By the end of the eighteenth century the citizens of Havana had become sufficiently wealthy and confident to embark on the reconstruction of the colony's economy.

With the help of Spain, the city oligarchy began expanding the system of sugar plantations on the island for the benefit of the export trade, which meant there was a growing demand for African slaves (see Sánchez-Albornoz 1977). These slaves had lived in the city ever since its founding, but they were employed mainly in domestic service or livestock farming in surrounding areas. Life on a sugar plantation run according to a "capitalist system" was a good deal more strenuous and the life expectancy of the slaves was extremely short. Havana grew into the major slave market of the Caribbean area and the fate of the slaves on the sugar plantations became a social taboo. This presented no problem for the Spanish soldiers, the civil servants and the creole landowners. For the "free" citizens of Havana, however, it meant continually having to choose between conforming to urban Catholic society and sympathizing (in secret) with the slaves, whom they provided with assistance during uprisings.

Slavery was officially abolished in Cuba in 1886, but racism actually increased under the influence of the North American ideology of the superiority of the white race (Davis 1982). The economy of the republic, which gained its independence in 1902 (the third former colony in the Caribbean, after Haiti and the Dominican Republic), was still based on sugar. With the introduction of modern technology, the industry was becoming more efficient, and the gap between the slave labourers in the fields and the urban "élite" was widening. Modernization touched off a process of urbanization on the island, which in turn led to the expansion of the civil service and the means of publicity and attracted foreign banks, business and tourists. All this created a demand for personnel, in particular women, and many of them joined the flow of migrants from rural areas to the capital, people eager to flee the oppressive rigidity of the provinces and to try their fortune in the city.

In 1953 Havana became the only city in the Caribbean where there were more women than men, and this was still the case in 1981 (Schroeder 1982). The position of women in this "city of women" changed substantially between 1953 and 1981, and they are today an integral part of the political and economic life of the city. Although women were given the vote in 1940, this initially had no great effect on their participation in political affairs. The majority of women were not interested in politics, and in rural areas in particular they were inclined to follow their husbands' lead. In the cities women were given poorly-paid jobs due to their lack of schooling, and the temptation was great to revert to one of the traditional professions of a seaport, prostitution, in preference to fetching and carrying for an unfriendly employer. In 1959 there were 11,500 registered prostitutes in Havana, not counting those who were supported by their "lovers".

In 1959 the dictator Batista was overthrown and Castro took power. This marked the beginning of a turbulent period of development in Cuba. A number of women who had fought with the guerillas alongside Castro and Che Guevara founded the FDC, Federación de Mujeres Cubanas (Federation of Cuban Women), which since then has served to stimulate political and social consciousness among Cuban women. The activities of this organization included an appeal to the women of Cuba to join the people's militias to help to defend their country, as well as adult literacy programmes, live-in schools for farm women and evening classes for domestic employees living in the city. Prostitutes were offered an opportunity to learn a trade, so that they could be integrated into the "normal labour process".

In 1975 the new constitution created a legal basis for all the new forays women were making into the world of work, and gave working women full equality with working men. The publications of the Central Party Bureau (1975 and 1977) confirm this, and the consequences of these developments are discussed in interviews with representatives of the various female sectors of the population (see Randall 1972; Séjourné 1980).

How have such far-reaching historical changes affected the position of women in a city that in the past two hundred years has evolved from a colonial slave trader into a shining example to the societies of the southern continent? How has the stereotyped Caribbean pattern of family life altered in a society that up to 1886 held slaves, up to 1898 was a Spanish colony, from the beginning of political independence in 1902 has been strongly influenced by North America, since April 1961 has developed a socialist system and by ordering national mobilization has demonstrated that it must always be alert to a possible military invasion? To what degree has this development brought about a heightened consciousness of existing prejudices with respect to women within the literary tradition, in a country where the present cultural policy, on the surface at any rate, offers women the best prospects in the entire Caribbean?

The Female Mulatto as Urban Symbol

It is in the early nineteenth century that the mulatto as female stereotype makes her first appearance in a novel set in Havana. In 1839 she is the main character in *Cecilia Valdés* (Villaverde 1971), a book which is today a "national epic" and which has recently been filmed. The heroine of the title is the illegitimate daughter of a wealthy Spanish slave trader, who is married to a high-born creole woman. He has a daughter by his black mistress and though he supports her, she does not know the name of her father. At a party Cecilia meets her half-brother Leonardo, though neither is aware of this blood tie.

Cecilia, who is "almost white" and very beautiful, has an affair with the law student Leonardo. This leads her to reject the advances of her childhood friend, a musician and a mulatto like herself. The author makes it clear what her motives are, and how they are bound up with the social relationships of the day:

> Cecilia hoped that in the shadow of white people — no matter how illicit their relationship was — she would be able to work her way up, out of the humble surroundings in which she was born. And if she was not able to achieve these goals herself, at least her children would. Marriage to a mulatto would lower her self-esteem. Such mistakes are liable to happen in societies like that of Cuba (p. 129).

The incest motif foreshadows the tragic dénouement. Cecilia becomes Leonardo's mistress but she has a rival in Isabel Ilanchete, who comes from a prominent creole family. Isabel has everything that Cecilia lacks: unimpeachable breeding, a convent education, a healthy outdoor life on her parents' estate, where she goes in for sport and visits with neighbouring families. This tranquil and well-regulated existence contrasts sharply with the turbulent life in the old quarter of Havana where Cecilia lives. Leonardo becomes more and more conscious of this contrast as he climbs the social ladder. He completes his studies and is rewarded with a palace and the title of count. His infatuation with Cecilia comes to an end when she gives birth to their child, a daughter. With the encouragement of his dynamic mother, he proposes to Isabel. In a fit of rage Cecilia, who is now described as a "proud and vengeful mulatto", sends her old friend and protector to the wedding to kill Isabel. But it is Leonardo who dies. Cecilia and her friend end up in jail, and Isabel goes into a convent.

This city novel is clearly based on the Caribbean code of conduct described above, and the "assimilated" figure of Cecilia is seen by Villaverde as a product of her environment. Though he portrays the mulatto girl as a tragic figure, his sympathies obviously lie with a well-regulated married life together with the appropriate partner, in this case Isabel.

The mulatto girl is a standard character in folk drama of the nineteenth and twentieth centuries, alongside the poor

177

Galician immigrant and the comic *negrito* (Fernàndez 1975; Leal 1980; Van Duin/Van Haastrecht 1983). She is attractive and self-assured and her paramount trait of character is an unbridled opportunism in affairs of the heart, in which her prime considerations are money and status. The mulatto previously appeared in Miguel Barnet's *Canción de Rachel* (1969). In this documentary biography in the form of a novel, Barnet has Rachel reminisce about the old glory days at the Alhambra Theatre back in the twenties, when she starred in the role of the mulatto girl. Audiences were made up largely of Spanish immigrants (see Phaf 1982), who received a taste of Cuban customs and "morals". These plays lampooned the political situation and parodied the life of the poor. They were followed by an evening of exuberant dancing, and Rachel's performance of rumba and guaracha provided an exciting finale.

Rachel found her inspiration in working-class neighbour-hoods, where she studied the customs of the black people, how they moved, the way they expressed themselves. Then she went home, blackened her face and practised in front of the mirror. This Cuban girl born of German/Hungarian parents became the most famous *rumbera* of the day. In spite of the fact that her art was based on the rhythmic traditions of Africa, to her dying day Rachel looked down upon blacks. In reality her character, the "white mulatto", was indistinguish-able from the "real" multatto. The erotic appeal which she radiated enabled her to take advantage of all that men could offer her. In his first important works the famous poet Nicolás Guillén showed his contempt for the kind of mulatto who despised black men. His poetry, which was first published during the thirties, was inspired by the daily life of the black people of Havana. He describes the *Mulata* (Guillén 1974:167), as seen through the eyes of a *negro bembón* (i.e. a black man with thick lips), who will have nothing to do with her. She needn't think she's so *adelantada* (i.e. less black than he is), nor that he's sitting around waiting for her. He's quite happy with his own wife, who takes good care of him. But life at home is not always peaceful either, as witness the poem *Búcate plata*, in which his wife demands that he start bringing home some money! In *Rumba* Guillén portrays the *rumbera*, whom he describes as both good and evil. Evil because he associates her with opportunists, prostitutes and the underworld, and good because of her beauty. She enchants the audience — and the poet — with her dancing and after the performance he goes off with her.

This blend of erotic female mulatto and star performer is the great attraction of modern Havana night life in the novels set in the forties and fifties. In *Gestos* (Sarduy 1963) Severo Sarduy's mulatto is a servant girl who performs after hours at the night club Picasso, where she sings "typical tropical" melodies for North American tourists. The period is the Batista dictatorship (1952-8) and although the woman in the book is not interested in politics, her lover ("almost white") who is involved in a resistance movement persuades her to smuggle a bomb into the electricity works. At the risk of her own life she gets past the police checkpoints and places the bomb. It explodes, leaving the city without electricity, but she never hears from her lover again and in the closing pages of the book the author compares the plot with a Greek tragedy.

No less tragic is the fate of Dolores Rondón in *De dônde son los cantantes* (Sarduy 1980). Dolores arrives in the capital together with her friend, the politician Mortal. Drug-dealing, white girls and alcohol prove the undoing of Mortal, and Dolores does not achieve the success she had hoped for. Then, for the best of motives, she organizes a spectacular show for the citizens of Havana in the presidential palace, which turns out to be a failure. After her death her unfulfilled hopes and dreams are etched upon her gravestone in Camagüey.

In the two "Havana novels" by Guillermo Cabrera Infante another poor provincial girl does all she can to find favour with men. *La Habana para un infante difunto* (1979) centres on the erotic development of the narrator from youth to manhood. It seems that he has an irresistible attraction for women. Most of his conquests are unlettered working girls from the provinces who are not overly encumbered with sexual inhibitions. He becomes a journalist and the highpoint of the novel is his love affair with the singer Violeta del Valle, a mulatto girl from the province of Oriente. Their relationship ends prematurely, however, after his Catholic marriage. As Violeta is not prepared to share him with his wife, he finally drops her.

Tres tristes tigres (1971) is the story of a musician and two journalists who in their work are constantly surrounded by women. The story begins in 1958 when the sophisticated singer Cuba Venegas starts to make a name for herself in the entertainment quarter La Sierra. Her great attraction lies not in her singing voice but in the "tropical" eroticism which she exudes. Cuba's real name is Gloria Perez and she comes from a small village with a rigid moral code. To escape from this milieu she goes to Havana, where she makes a point of searching out men who are in a position to further her career. The man who "discovers" her is the musician, a mulatto like herself, but she discards him when a photographer from a well-known magazine shows an interest in her. Cuba dresses and paints her face like her Las Vegas idols, and in addition to her numerous male lovers, she also has relationships with other women who, like herself, are in search of pleasure and "something different". The author also introduces Cuba's alter ego, an actress who used to be involved in "serious" theatre. As a result of her marriage to a man from the urban bourgeois milieu, she has become so confused and unstable that she seeks the help of a psychiatrist. Her altered social status has made her insecure; she feels that she is being manipulated and her jumbled emotions are reflected in the conflicting statements she makes during her therapy sessions. They are a mixture of lies and truth, so that it is difficult to know what she is really thinking.

And finally there is Edmundo Desnoes's *No hay problema!*

(1964), which tells of the love of the hero Sebastian for a mulatto girl. He is a journalist and meets Norma at his parents' home, where she works as a maid. Her family lives in a working-class neighbourhood and her mother takes in washing. Mother and daughter both despise the father, a white man of Spanish origin who has lost his job on account of his political activities.

When Norma starts an affair with Sebastian she quits her job and becomes a prostitute. This makes Sebastian feel guilty and he asks her to marry him. To Norma this proposal is a bad joke — how can he possibly marry someone who used to be his parents' maid? Besides, she actually prefers her black friend Manuel, one of Batista's soldiers. But Manuel has a wife and child, so that he cannot give her much money. When Sebastian realizes that he must share Norma with Manuel, a Negro with frizzy hair and a paunch, he breaks off their relationship, so that in the end she has no one to protect her and is forced to earn her living as a prostitute.

The stereotype of the mulatto girl plays an important part in all these novels, against the fictitious but recognizable background of pre-1959 Havana. She is portrayed both as a radiant object of male passion and as a tragic figure imprisoned in her role.

Does this image alter in those novels which depict the Havana of the post-1959 period, when as a result of social changes her philosophy of life has become useless? Before we attempt to answer this question, I would like to point out that most of the literature referred to above was not written or published until after 1959. Only Villaverde (1903) and Guillén (1930) were previously well known and their work has been reprinted many times. Their nationwide popularity in the Cuba of today is due to the fact that they have given their characters not only an individual, but also a social context. The other writers have "reconstructed" the mulatto girl, following the changes wrought by the revolution. In so doing they have demonstrated that, at least as a masculine projection of the past, she was for them too an important figure. Political and economic considerations are of secondary importance to them, and they even take a conscious stand against this interference in one's personal life. This is particularly marked in the works of Cabrera Infante.

Edmundo Desnoes is the first to describe the mulatto girl in Havana at the time of the revolution. His *El Cataclismo* (1965) is set in 1960 and 1961, and as the title suggests, the city is in a state of turmoil. The rich are losing their money and position and many either leave the country or commit suicide. The "middle group", Catholic and of Spanish origin, has a strong sense of social justice and adapts to the new situation. For the black people the changes offer a new perspective. The servant girl Migdalia can now marry her black boyfriend Evelio and move into an apartment. This Migdalia bears no resemblance to the mulatto girl of the old days. She is just as prudish as her white sisters and she shares their ideas about married life. Evelio is illiterate and works as a coffee vendor and the fact that his whole family is employed in the docks has made him politically conscious. He admires Migdalia for the fine manners she has learned from the family she worked for, but is critical of her tolerance towards her employers. When the whole family prepares to beat a hasty retreat without paying Migdalia her last wages, Evelio keeps the plane on the ground until his girlfriend gets her salary.

For a long time this novel, the title of which is taken from a speech by Fidel Castro, was the only work to refer to the existence of the mulatto girl and her life in Havana at the time of the revolution. Not until 1978, 1980 and 1981 does she reappear. Manuel Pereira describes the part she plays in the life of the schoolboy Leonel in *El Ruso* (1980). Since the missile crisis in 1962 Leonel is overzealous in his admiration of the Soviet Union, which does not make him popular with his classmates. His love life, too, gives cause for concern. The commendable Mariela, the only girl who does her homework with the boys, expects something besides endless tales of "the

182

land of snow" during their outings. But Leonel is shy and inexperienced. Fortunately he has Nieve, a mulatto cabaret entertainer at Tropicana, who instructs him in the ways of love. After that he has more success with Mariela and can boast two girlfriends, one part of his "public" life at school and the other in the background, providing him with tenderness and admiration.

This continuation of the "Caribbean" relationships is not referred to in *El Gallego* (1981) by Miguel Barnet. His "testimonio novel" reconstructs the life of the Galician immigrant Manuel from around 1920 up until the end of the sixties. At first Manuel's ideas about black girls were the same as those of every other European or Cuban creole: fine to go to bed with but not to marry. But many years later he meets a mulatto girl in the house where he works and, after living together for a time, they marry. Manuel, his wife and their two children live in Havana, the Havana of the revolution, and it is a good life. He has a state pension, he is able to send his children to university, and the difference in the colour of their skin is of no importance. But throughout the whole work the emphasis is on what Manuel thinks and feels. There is no mention of his wife's background or her life before they met, and her ideas, to the extent that they differ from his own, are not taken very seriously.

Thus Barnet stresses social integration, without going all too deeply into cultural differences. This is something which Alejo Carpentier does do in his last great novel, *La Consagración de la Primavera* (1978). He even sees these cultural differences as *the* main problem in urban society. His novel describes the discrimination prevalent in the metropolis from the twenties up until the raid on Playa Girón in April 1961.

His heroine Vera was born in Russia and fled to London with her parents before the Russian Revolution. Later she joins a ballet group in Paris, where she meets Enrique, a *habenero* from a rich creole family. When the Second World War breaks out Enrique and Vera go to Havana, where Vera discovers the "invisible ghetto" of the city, the public white section and the hidden black area. The situation is familiar to Enrique from his childhood, but Vera as a European cannot accept it, and this has serious consequences for her future, both personal and professional. Vera sets up two ballet schools, one in a bourgeois neighbourhood for the girls from good families and one in the old quarter of Havana, where her pupils come from the Afro-Cuban section of the population. Together with them she searches for ways to combine the music of Stravinsky — the title of the book refers to one of his best known pieces — with bodily expression. Despite many problems and a great deal of opposition, they succeed in putting on a ballet performance to launch this "new style".

Thanks to her work Vera is financially independent of Enrique, who in the meantime has begun an affair with his wealthy cousin Teresa, a woman of loose morals and the only member of the family with mixed blood. When after a number of years Vera discovers her husband's relationship with the "mulatto" of the family, she and Enrique separate. The reconciliation does not take place until Enrique makes a complete break with Teresa, who flees to the United States out of fear for the revolution. Husband and wife meet again just as the counter-revolutionaries invade the Playa Giron, and Fidel Castro proclaims that Cuba is a socialist state with a "democratic and socialist revolution of, by and for the common man" (Carpentier 1978:575).

Thus the mulatto girl also appears in the novels which portray Havana after 1959, although she is no longer the same. Gone are the opportunism and financial dependence on men; however, her eroticism and servitude, as seen through the eyes of the male characters, are still emphasized. In this respect it is noteworthy that in spite of the — by Caribbean standards — excellent working conditions which they enjoy in Cuba, no women writers have chosen to highlight this theme, and to present it from the woman's point of view. In the literature we have discussed up to now the only woman character who refuses to accept the situation is a foreigner, a woman who lived for many years in the Paris of the thirties.

Caribbean Women Writers with European Experience

It appears that women writers of the Caribbean need this European perspective in order to view the social and cultural situation of their native land with a critical eye, and to be able to present the position of women there. At about the same time Villaverde was writing, the Cuban author Gertrudis Gómez de Avellaneda (1814-73) published the first abolitionist novel *Sab* (1841) in Madrid. She was born in Cuba, in Camagüey, which is also the setting of her novel, but she left Cuba at an early age and went to Spain, where she became one of the most emancipated middle-class women of her day.

Gertrudis wrote plays, poetry and novels, in which she focused attention on the problems facing women. In her novel *Sab*, her only book which is set in her native country, the plot centres on the love of the slave Sab for Carlotta, the daughter of the planter. His noble character contrasts sharply with that of Enrique Otway, the calculating merchant's son whom Carlotta hopes to marry. He is interested primarily in the size of her dowry, which he plans to use to promote his business interests. His plan succeeds, but not without the help of Sab, who magnanimously mediates between the two parties, and secretly donates the money he has won in a lottery to Carlotta's dowry. On the day of the wedding he dies of a broken heart and it is not until many years later, when Carlotta has discovered her husband's true nature, that she realizes what Sab's feeling for her were.

Although Gertrudis's novel is strongly romanticized — Sab is the son of an African princess and a wealthy creole landowner — its anti-slavery message is so loud and clear that it was immediately banned in Cuba for its subversive contents. This in contrast to the first part of *Cecilia Valdés* by Cirilo Villaverde. Though Villaverde wrote about the injustice of the social conditions of his day, he resigned himself to the situation, and ultimately sided with the creole slaveowners and planters, against the "free" or enslaved population of African origin. Gertrudis, however, shifts the setting from the city, where the slavery of the plantations is a taboo, to the rural areas where it is a daily fact of life.

The best known Caribbean woman writer of this century, Jean Rhys, also chose a provincial setting for her heroines. Rhys was born in 1890 in Dominica, a tiny island between Guadeloupe and Martinique which was then an English colony and has only recently become independent. She left the island in 1907 and until her death in 1979 she never returned to Dominica. Although she spent the greater part of her life in various European countries (England, the Netherlands, Austria, France), those childhood memories were influential in determining the course of her life, as she relates in her unfinished autobiography *Smile Please* (1979). She came from a family of impoverished planters, plunged into financial difficulties after the abolition of slavery. The tension between people like her own family and the local population, the former slaves, made a deep impression on her. She sensed the gulf which existed between them and which she was at a loss to deal with. This gulf is reflected in the relationship with her former nanny Meta, an older woman from Martinique and a practitioner of the obeah cult. Rhys calls her the "terror of my life". At home Meta is an outcast, and in Europe she is a refugee, accustomed to a warmer climate and a different kind of people.

In all her published stories and short novels there is invariably a woman from a Caribbean country living in Europe, and this cultural conflict plays a steadily more important role until, in her most famous work, the novel, *Wide Sargasso Sea* (1966), it is the central theme. This book is Rhys's answer to Charlotte Bronte's novel *Jane Eyre*, which was published in 1847 and was regarded at the time as an example to the women's movement. Jane Eyre is an ugly but capable girl who earns her living as governess in well-to-do families. She falls in love with the father of her pupil but cannot marry him because he is already married. His wife Antoinette Mason, a dangerous madwoman, is kept locked up on the top floor of the Rochester house. Little is said of the woman except that she is a Jamaican and comes from a "mentally unstable" family, a fact which was unknown to Mr Rochester when he married her (for her money). Now she is an obstacle to the lovers' happiness, and they are not free to marry until the woman dies in a fire.

In her novel Jean Rhys reconstructs Antoinette Mason's early life and the initial years of her marriage to Mr Rochester in Spanish Town, Jamaica and on the decaying family estate on Dominica. Antoinette spends her childhood there with her mother and a mentally retarded brother, surrounded by a neglected estate. After the father's death there is almost no contact with the "white" world, until the widow decides to remarry. She is motivated mainly by fear that otherwise her daughter will go through life as a "white nigger". Her marriage provides her with enough money to send Antoinette to a convent school in Jamaica. There the girl is conscious of the hostility of the rich daughters from the area around Jamaica (especially those from Venezuela), on account of her strange manner and appearance.

Antoinette's family arranges a marriage with an Englishman who is interested in her dowry. This man, Mr Rochester, is completely alien to her, as indeed she is to him: "Creole of pure English descent she may be, but they are not English or European either" (p. 56). During their honeymoon, on the way to the family estate on Dominica, Rochester is struck by the hostility of the local people towards Antoinette and her family, and gradually he distances himself from his bride. In despair she turns to her faithful old nanny Christophine from Martinique. She advises Antoinette to go away for a while, somewhere where she can think calmly about her own feelings and those of her husband. But Antoinette is adamant and refuses to leave. She begs Christophine to bring Mr

Rochester back to her bed by using her knowledge of obeah practices. Christophine, an independent black woman, feels the pull of solidarity: "All women, all colours, nothing but fools" (p. 91), but the relationship between the two women remains ambivalent. Though Christophine is her only refuge Antoinette still disregards her wise words because in her heart she considers her an ignorant old woman. The obeah experiment is a disaster and causes a definitive rupture between Antoinette and her husband. Antoinette never fully recovers; she remains distracted and mentally preoccupied. Christophine suffers as well, when Mr Rochester informs the police of her "crime".

In her first novel, the much younger black author Simone Schwarz-Bart from Guadeloupe also studies the female *béké* (the wife of a landowner of European origin). But her perspective is new, for she concentrates mainly on the rural background of this type of "authentic" black woman. In *Pluie et vent sur Télumée Miracle* (1972), the main character Télumée is employed for a short time as maid to one of the women *békés*. Her employer does not understand black people and her arrogance is all too evident. Schwarz-Bart depicts the life of the parents and grandparents of Télumée, who lives with her grandmother in Fond Zombi, the village of the living dead (i.e. the souls of the dead, her ancestors). The villagers live out their lives on the edge of the "white" urban society, and there is little or no contact between them. The blacks consider it humiliating to work for white people and only do so when there is absolutely no other way to earn a living.

The narrow world of Fond Zombi is gradually confronted with more and more problems from outside. The land around the village is being taken over by big companies and Télumée's first husband, Elie, loses his job as woodcutter. He takes out his frustration on her, brings a girlfriend into their house and finally sends his wife away. Her second marriage is shortlived; her husband Amboise is killed during a strike. In the monologues of the narrator and her conversations with the grandmother, Schwarz-Bart sketches the history of blacks and the position of black women in this type of society. She describes a way of life which is still very close to nature and which still places credence in the wisdom of one's ancestors. After a life of toil and hardship the now aged Télumée is resigned to her fate. She bears Elie no grudge and blames the break-up of their marriage on "circumstances".

The life of just such a black man and his attitude to women is the subject of Simone Schwarz-Bart's next novel *Ti Jean L'horizon* (1979). The main character is Ti Jean, a "child of nature" from Fond Zombi. At first he is happy and contented with his childhood sweetheart Egée, until one day she mysteriously disappears and at the same time the island is quite unaccountably cut off from the outside world. Ti Jean goes off to try to find the solution to these problems. His search takes him back in time to the Africa of the past, and leads by way of France to the Guadeloupe of the eighteenth century, when slavery still existed. During his travels he meets many women; in all of them he looks for his Egée, but in vain. Not until the end of the book, when the sun returns to his island and contact with the outside world has been restored, does he meet a girl "like she was, a black girl without airs or pretence, a pure nature in all her simplicity" (1979:285).

Simone Schwarz-Bart obviously sets great store by the background of her characters, the story of their ancestors and their ties with Africa. She distances herself from the "modern" period, as represented by urban society, and one may assume that she does so deliberately, as she writes all her books in Paris, where she has lived for many years. She is married to the well known French author André Schwarz-Bart, whose interest in history and in the Caribbean stimulated her to start writing. Her first work was written in collaboration with her husband, but she has since developed her own style, which is clearly evident in the two novels discussed above.

Her compatriot Maryse Condé has also lived in the French

capital for many years. After an unsuccessful marriage to an African and a stay of several years in Africa, she returned to Paris and is now employed at the university. Condé's novels, unlike those of Schwarz-Bart, are set very much in a contemporary context. She makes use of her own experiences during her student days in Paris, as well as her stay in Africa where, as in the Caribbean, people are still grappling with the political consequences of decolonization.

Maryse Condé's heroine in *Hérémakhonon* (1976) is Véronique, who lives in West Africa and teaches philosophy at the Institut National. Véronique was born in Guadeloupe, studied in Paris, and came to Africa in order to compare her idealized concept with the reality of Africa. Her choice of a lover, however, places her in the same sort of isolation as before, when she was forced to leave Guadeloupe for bringing disgrace upon her black "bourgeois" family. Her friend then was a member of the wealthy mulatto middle class, who refused to marry her when the two of them were "caught in the act". In Paris Véronique lived for a time with a Frenchman, Jean Michel, which elicited the fury of her militant Caribbean compatriots. And now in Africa she is again in disfavour, not because of a difference in skin colour but because she has a relationship with a minister, who comes from an influential family. Her students resent this because they consider themselves progressive and "critical", and are against corruption and favouritism. Intuitively Véronique agrees with them, but there is little she can do and she is fond of her lover. Her "Negro with ancestors" has a typical African marriage: his wife lives elsewhere with the children and in his official residence Hérémakhonon, he is free to receive his mistress. The name of his villa, which means "wait for happiness", does not apply to Véronique. As the political situation escalates she feels that there is nothing positive that she can do in this land and she returns to Paris.

In the course of events her recollections of her family in Guadeloupe and the years she spent in Paris all influence the way in which the heroine undergoes the reality of Africa. This is equally true in Maryse Condé's second novel. The Marie Hélène of *Une saison à Rihata* (1981) also comes from Guadeloupe and also studied in France, where she met her husband. For seventeen years she has lived in Africa and after all that time she is still considered *celle qui vient d'ailleurs,* a stranger. She has not been able to adjust to the way of life of the African women around her. They are obedient, never contradict their husbands and consider unfaithfulness on the part of the wife a "crime". In the eyes of her mother-in-law Marie Hélène is guilty of many a misdemeanour, and her marriage is not a happy one. And yet there are positive sides to her life in Rihata, such as her husband's sense of responsibility towards all those he considers his family. Daily life is dominated by political intrigue and there are several tragic deaths in the family. But in spite of everything the book ends on a positive note. After six daughters Marie Hélène finally has a son, whom she calls Elikia, which in the language of the country means *hope*. This suggests that there is a better future somewhere, in a still distant future.

In the works of these writers from Guadeloupe the present situation on the island is of little or no importance. Schwarz-Bart isolates her characters, both from urban society and from contemporary political events, preferring to link them with the past. Maryse Condé's heroines have mainly negative memories of the cramped atmosphere of their childhood in the land of their birth. They look for the consequences of political decolonization in Africa rather than "at home", where such developments have not yet made themselves felt.

The only woman writer to go into this point in detail is Astrid Roemer of Surinam. She alone breaks out of the isolation of skin colour and cultural background which still imprisons the heroines of the other writers. Her Noenka in *Over de gekte van een vrouw* (About a woman's madness, 1982) is the "pretty missy" from Parimaribo who breaks just about every rule in the book. When she leaves her Antillian husband Louis after nine days of marriage, she is sacked by the Protestant school where she teaches because of the disgrace. Her next job takes her to the Nickerie area of Surinam, where she begins an affair with the florist Ramses, a relationship which ends in tragedy. Noenka is carrying Ramses's child and when she has an abortion, he commits suicide. Noenka seeks comfort from Gabrielle, who is married with two mentally retarded children. Gabrielle, who has a very difficult relationship with her husband, cannot accept the bond which officially still exists between Louis and Noenka. She seduces him and then kills him.

The most significant aspect of the novel is Noenka's search for herself in the relationship with others. Her name means "not again" and this characterizes her rebellion against all that *was*, like the life of her mother who was never able to express herself in her marriage. For Noenka the meaning of her own existence as a woman and as a black is an unknown quantity:

> Born of two contradictions, a woman and a man who even break into my dreams. I am a woman, though I do not know where being a woman begins and where it ends, and in the eyes of others I am black, and each time I wait to see just what that means (p. 207).

The tension between past and present is maintained through her recollections of herself, her parents and her friends, but they only come into play when some past experience of Noenka's lends them significance. Thus at different points Indians, Hindustani, Javanese, Chinese, Antillians, Para negroes, Arowak Indians, Dutchmen, the inhabitants of French Guiana and Jewish people all play a role in Noenka's existence. However, her contact with other people is never based on initial "outward" impressions, but develops via an emotional process.

In Astrid Roemer's second novel *Nergens ergens* (Nowhere, somewhere, 1983), the Surinamese Benito comes to Holland. He wants to study economics in Leiden but his previous schooling is insufficient, and he is forced to earn a living at a variety of jobs. In Surinam Benito had an unhappy love affair with Tamara, which made him decide to leave the country. In Holland he is in need of warmth and security, which he looks for in many women and finally finds in Bessie. Theirs is not a "normal" relationship, for both have numerous other lovers. Bessie is a prostitute and on cocaine, while Benito even marries someone else. There is a fine line separating Benito from those people on the fringe of Dutch society. He refuses to become an "assimilated" Surinamese; this would isolate him from the Surinamese community, and he needs the sense of security which being with "his people" gives him. All of them lead very irregular lives, and are becoming more and more obsessed with the political upheaval taking place in Surinam after the coup in December 1982. Surinam is becoming a country full of uncertainty but it continues to play a significant role in all their lives.

The goal of Benito's exodus from "nowhere" to "somewhere" is not clearly defined in the book. He follows the crowd, joining the mass exodus out of Surinam — from "somewhere" to "nowhere" — and at the end of the book, on the way to the plane, he is carried along in a stream of humanity without knowing where he is going or why (p. 123, 191).

A Caribbean Image of Women

Is it possible to compare these writers from Cuba, Dominica, Guadeloupe and Surinam, who have lived for many years in Europe, with the stereotype of women in the Cuban novel, against the backdrop of the capital?

We began by placing this literary development against the background of political decolonization in the Caribbean, and by focusing on the problems of social and cultural polarization as a factor common to all the countries of the region. This produced a female stereotype which, in the cities in particular, manifested itself as a Caribbean stereotype, reflected most clearly in the Cuban novel set in Havana. In this, the largest city of the Caribbean which has seen extreme political and social changes over the past two hundred years, the mulatto girl has come to symbolize Cuban society before 1959. She is at once an erotic object and a deeply tragic character. There is almost no parallel to be found in the cities of the other islands for the crucial role which the mulatto plays in the literature about Havana, although she does occasionally appear in the more recent works. The character of Dinah from Kingston (Jamaica) in Orlando Patterson's *The Children of Sisyphus* (1964) displays the same traits, as does the senator's girlfriend from San Juan (Puerto Rico) in *La Guaracha del macho camacho* (1976) by Luis Rafael Sánchez.

We have seen how the tragic dimension of the mulatto disappears in socialist Havana, although her role as seductress remains intact. Some authors, especially Alejo Carpentier and Miguel Barnet, imply that as a result of social changes which have taken place stereotyping of women is now inconceivable. It is noteworthy that there are no examples in present-day Cuban literature of women authors reacting to these images in their work. This does not mean that there are no women writers. Many women now take part in literary workshops throughout the country, and publish their work in provincial newspapers. Nancy Morejón's poetry is devoted mainly to the position of black women and Dora Alonso writes about farm women and the history of the land in her novels and children's books. Two women writers have left Cuba because of the revolution, and write about their experiences in Havana from abroad. Lydia Cabrera's essays concentrate on Afro-Cuban culture, while Hilda Perera Soto highlights the position of women from bourgeois urban backgrounds, touching only indirectly upon the population structure peculiar to the Caribbean. Not one woman author has made this the theme of a novel, which is surprising when one considers the interest which male writers have shown in the subject. Machismo is also a popular theme in contemporary

Cuban films and it is the male directors and screen writers who give it precedence. The most popular film about women is *Retrato de Teresa*. The screen play was written by Ambrosio Fornet, who was formerly engaged in literary research. At the moment he is working on the script of a film called *Habanera*, in which the heroine is a black woman psychologist. The only woman director, Sara Gómez, has died. Her film *De Cierta Manera* was produced in 1975 (Schumann 1980). These films all depict the problems facing black working women on their own, who are presented not in their Caribbean — historically determined — world, but are seen in brief flashes depicting the Cuba of today.

Up to now the sole written testimony in which the mulatto girl herself speaks is to be found in scientific literature. In *Four Women* (1977) the North American anthropologist Oscar Lewis reconstructs the life of Pilar López González of Havana in fourteen thematic interviews. Lewis talked to Pilar in 1970 when she was 28. She tells of her childhood in the old neighbourhood, her parents' troubled marriage, her own two unsuccessful marriages, the reasons she turned to prostitution, her relations with men in general and her experience of the revolution. Poverty and ignorance brought her to the brothel, and she despised her occupation. So she jumped at the chance offered her in 1959 to follow a course of training, and she is now a medical analyst, with plans for a new course of study. But Pilar is not ashamed of her past and she is critical of anyone who condemns her for it. She speaks frankly of sexual relations, and the number of abortions which she — and her mother — have to their name is astounding. Pilar's relationship with her own mother was difficult, but she is very proud of her two daughters, one of whom is a *mulatica* like herself. The three of them live alone, and Pilar considers herself too old (!) to marry again. She does, however, have very concrete ideas about the kind of relationship she wants with a man. She considers a good sexual rapport — not for money —

just as vital to such a relationship as her own financial independence.

> I'm certain of one thing — I will never give up my study or my work. Nothing can compare with working for something and getting it. Sit around waiting for someone to bring me what I need? Not on your life!

Pilar is self-assured and strident and since 1959 she has learned to see herself and her situation in a new — social — perspective, something which her sisters in other Caribbean islands will not be able to do until the political and social situation in their country changes. But, as we have seen in the case of Cuba, that does not automatically mean that women writers will immediately present themselves and proceed to describe Caribbean relationships from a female perspective, as is happening in other parts of the region. For it is women writers with *European experience* who stress the "typically Caribbean" problems of men and women in their native country. No matter where the fictitious characters have chosen to live, there is always a bond with their country of origin. Moreover, women authors never present stereotypes but make an effort to enter into the emotional lives of their characters, which are dominated primarily by individual and not by collective feelings.

This was the method employed by Gertrudis Gómez de Avellaneda in the last century when she wrote the first abolitionist novel. Her book showed a higher regard for the human aspects of the social situation than an "objective" approach ever could have done. Jean Rhys meshed her childhood memories with her protest against that image of the "mad creole" in England who stood in the way of the eman- cipated young governess's happiness. Both authors stress the difficulties facing white women in their country. Without a dowry their marriage prospects were minimal, and for them there was no escape from the rigid social codes of the day. In the life and work of Gertrudis and Rhys, however, there is as yet no sense of responsibility for a "national" process. They never return to their native country, and they use their pen to settle up with the traumatic experiences of their youth.

This attitude is not shared by present-day women writers of the Caribbean. They do feel personally bound up with developments in their country, and they make this clear in a number of ways. Phyllis Shand Allfrey of Dominica, for example, is younger than Jean Rhys. After living for many years in the United States and England, she returned to Dominica in the early fifties and is now politically active in word and deed. In her only novel *The Orchid House* (1953) she chooses the same type of theme as her older colleague. The relationship which she sketches between the nanny Lally and her three creole pupils is not overly involved, and the emphasis is more on the way of life and the emotional world of the old black woman than is the case in the work of Jean Rhys. It is clear from the foreword that Rhys and Shand Allfrey had corresponded and that Jean was considering the idea of visiting Dominica. By renewing the acquaintance with her native land she hoped to be able to see her past experiences in a new perspective. However, Rhys's death put an end to these plans.

The women writers from Guadeloupe and Surinam whom we have mentioned are active in the discussion on the position of Caribbean women. In her work Simone Schwarz-Bart gives the "strong black woman" and her "faithless black husband" a link with the past. She regularly returns home and in interviews she stresses that her radio readings produce enthusiastic reactions. People write to say that they recognize their own grandmothers in the life and the ideas of Télumée. Maryse Condé's novels are a protest against the subordinate position of women in those areas of Africa which, like the land of her birth, are faced with the aftermath of the decolonization process. Condé regularly visits the Caribbean and her lectures on women and literature are extremely popular. In a book of essays entitled *La parole des femmes* (1979) she analyses the work of women writers from Haïti, Martinique and Guadeloupe, while the book also contains interviews with the authors. And yet it is above all Astrid Roemer who confronts her characters with the realities of daily life, in her case Surinam and the Netherlands. She passes over all the "normal" patterns of conduct and prejudices, and homes in on *individual experience*. The importance of her frank and direct literary dialogue has not yet been assessed at its real value in the Caribbean itself, because research into the subject is still in the initial stages.

At the end of this comparative study of the work of Cuban authors and of women writers who bring their European experience to bear on Caribbean conflicts, we can conclude that the main themes chosen by these women are racism and sexism. In their novels they *internationalize* their opposition to these evils by situating them within a broad historical and geographical framework. The bond with their native land has always been an important factor, but it is now emerging more clearly into the foreground. Unlike the Cuban writers, they find that this still offers little or no perspective for the social situation. But it is becoming clear that without their contribution to the development of a literature which must grow from Caribbean roots, the existing stereotypes of women (and men) will never be destroyed and, moreover, that this is a problem which is of topical interest in many other corners of the globe.

REFERENCES

Allfrey, Phyllis Shand, 1953, *The Orchid House*, London, Constable.
Barnet, Miguel, 1969, *Canción de Rachel*, Havana, Instituto Cubano del Libro.
Barnet, Miguel, 1981, *El Gallego*, Madrid, Alfaguara.

Brontë, Charlotte, 1847, *Jane Eyre*, London.

Cabrera Infante, Guillermo, 1971[2], *Tres tristes tigres*, Barcelona, Ed. Seix Barral. Trans. 1971, *Three Trapped Tigers*, New York, Harper & Row; 1980, London, Picador.

Cabrera Infante, Guillermo, 1979, *La Habana para un infante difunto*, Barcelona, Seix Barral.

Carpentier, Alejo, 1978, *La Consagración de la Primavera*, Mexico, Siglo XXI.

Clarke, Edith, 1966, *My Mother Who Fathered Me*, London, Allen & Unwin.

Cohen Stuart, Bertie A., 1979, *Women in the Caribbean*, Bibliography, Leiden, Department of Caribbean Studies.

Condé, Maryse, 1979, *La parole des femmes*, Paris, L'Harmattan.

Condé, Maryse, 1976, *Hérémakhonon*, Paris, Union Générale d'Editions; transl. 1983, Washington D.C., Three Continents Press.

Condé, Maryse, 1981, *Une saison à Rihata*, Paris, Robert Laffont.

Davis, Angela, 1982, *Women, Race and Class*, London, Women's Press.

Desnoes, Edmundo, 1946[2], *No hay problema*, Havana, Ed. R.

Desnoes, Edmundo, 1965, *El Cataclismo*, Havana, Ed. R.

Duin, Lieke van, and Anke van Haastrecht, 1983, *Theatre in Cuba and the Revolution* (in Dutch), Rotterdam, Ordeman.

Fanon, Frantz, 1961, *Les damnés de la terre (The Wretched of the Earth)*, Paris, Maspéro.

Fernàndez, F., 1975, "Los negros catedráticos", play, in: Rine Leal (ed.), *Teatro bufo Siglo XIX*, vol. 1, Havana, pp. 131-209.

Gómez de Avellaneda, Gertrudis, 1963, *Sab*, Havana, Instituto Cubano del Libro.

Guillén, Nicolás, 1974, *Obra poetica 1920-1958*, Havana, Unión.

Henriqúes, Fernando, 1976, *Family and Colour in Jamaica*, Jamaica, Sangster's Book Stores Ltd.

Leal, Rine (ed.), 1975, *Teatro bufo Siglo XIX*, Havana.

Leal, Rine, 1980, *Breve historia del teatro cubano*, Havana, Letras Cubanas.

Lewis, Oscar (ed.), 1977, *Living the Revolution: An Oral History of Contemporary Cuba*, vol. 2, *Four Women*, Illinois.

Ministerio de Justicia, 1975, *Código de Familia*, Havana.

Ministerio de Justicia, 1977, *La mujer en Cuba socialista*, Havana.

Nettleford, Rex M., 1978, *Caribbean Cultural Identity*, Kingston, Institute of Jamaica.

Patterson, Orlando, (1964) 1982, *The Children of Sisyphus*, London, Longman.

Pereira, Manuel, 1980, *El Ruso*, Havana, Letras Cubanas.

Phaf, Ineke, 1982, Interview with Miguel Barnet, in *Hervormd Nederland*, 5 juni.

Phaf, Ineke, 1983, "Havanna, ein karibisches Zentrum?", Berlin, Lateinamerika-Institut der FU, pp. 243-65.

Randall, Margaret, 1972, *Mujeres en la Revolución*, Mexico.

Rhys, Jean, 1966, *Wide Sargasso Sea*, London, Deutsch; 1970, Penguin.

Rhys, Jean, 1982, *Smile, Please: An Unfinished Autobiography*, New York, Penguin Books.

Roemer, Astrid, 1982[2], *Over de gekte van een vrouw* (About a Woman's Madness), Haarlem, In de Knipscheer.

Roemer, Astrid, 1983, *Nergens, ergens* (Nowhere, somewhere), nowhere, Haarlem, In de Knipscheer.

Sanchez-Albornoz, Nicolás, 1977, *La población de América Latina*, Madrid, Alianza Universal.

Sánchez, Luis Rafael, 1976, *La Guaracha del Macho Camacho*, Buenos Aires, Ed. de la Flor.

Sandner, Gerhard, 1980, "Antillen — Westindien — Karibischer Raum, Begriffe. Abgrenzungen. Inhaltliche Definition", in *Der Karibische Raum, Selbstbestimmung und Assenabhängigkeit*, Hamburg, Institut für Iberoamerika-kunde.

Sarduy, Severo, 1963, *Gestos*, Barcelona, Seix Barral.

Sarduy, Severo, (1967) 1980, *De dónde son los cantantes*, Barcelona, Seix Barral; trans. 1972 by S. J. Levine and H. D. Taylor, *From Cuba with a Song*, in *Triple Cross: Three short novels*, New York, Dutton.

Schroeder, Susan, 1982, *A Handbook of Historical Statistics: Cuba*, Boston.

Schumann, Peter, B., 1980, *Kino in Cuba 1959-1979*, Frankfurt, Klaus Vervuert.

Schwarz-Bart, Simone, 1972, *Pluie et vent sur Télumée Miracle*, Paris, Seuil; trans. 1975 by Barbara Bray, *The Bridge of Beyond*, London, Gollancz.

Schwarz-Bart, Simone, 1979, *Ti Jean l'Horizon*, Paris, Seuil.

Séjourné, Laurette, 1980, *La mujer cubana en El Quehacer de la historia*, Mexico.

Villaverde, Cirilo, (1882) trans. 1971, *Cecilia Valdés*, New York, Anaya Book Co.

INTERVIEW WITH ASTRID ROEMER
(SURINAM)

INEKE PHAF

Astrid Roemer was born in 1947 in Parimaribo. She trained as a teacher ("My family insisted that I should have a profession"), but up to now she has done mainly journalistic work. From 1966 to 1975 she travelled back and forth between Surinam and the Netherlands, but she now lives in The Hague. Her published works include *Sasa*, poetry (1970); *Neem mij terug, Suriname*, novel (Take me back, Surinam, 1974); *De wereld heeft gezicht verloren*, expressionist essay (The world has lost face, 1975); *Over de gekte van een vrouw*, novel (About a woman's madness, 1982); *Negrens, ergens*, novel (Nowhere, somewhere, 1983); *Parimaribo, Parimaribo*, musical drama; *Waaram zou je huilen, mijn lieve lieve*, short novel (Why should you cry, my darling darling, 1976).

Astrid, in a recent magazine article, you wrote about the difficulty Surinamese writers have in getting their books published. Is this particularly true of women?

The situation is much more difficult for women, although I have received the most encouragement from men. Generally speaking you need money and connections if you want to publish, and men have both. You can't do anything without them, and usually they see literature in a political context. As a woman you don't have much chance if your writing is innovative and doesn't fit a particular political line. Even the printer refuses to print your work if he doesn't agree with the contents. I financed the publication of my first novel myself. I took those one thousand copies to the five bookstores in Parimaribo, the only ones there are — and they were willing to sell the book, even though they don't specialize in literature. Literary works don't sell well, and there is no literary criticism anyway! In 1974 a second edition appeared, five thousand copies published by a publishing house we set up ourselves in the Netherlands. In Surinam there aren't any literary publishers. Women writers in the Netherlands are luckier. They don't need men to smooth the way for them. Writers work directly with publishers, who are used to women operating on their own, and don't consider it a personal favour when they publish your work.

Does most of the response to your work come from Surinam or the Netherlands?

That's hard to say. You really can't compare the two. In Surinam my first novel was put on the secondary-school reading list. And the same thing happened with my last novel, *Nergens, ergens* (Nowhere, somewhere), which is an adaptation of that book. But now that I live in Holland the people I hear from are mainly Dutch people or Surinamese living in Holland, and their reactions are quite varied. Some refer to my work as "invigorating" and "revolutionary"; others call it "pornography" or "rather complex". *Over de gekte van een vrouw* (About a women's madness) made quite an impact on a lot of women. They said it was the first time they actually recognized themselves in a book. They didn't see themselves in the works of my compatriot Albert Helman, who only writes about white women or slaves. And Edgar Cairo's women almost always live in compounds and thus constitute a very special group. My characters are contemporary, the women they are or would like to be. Dutch people — women *and* men — come up to me and tell me that they found something of the Netherlands, something of themselves in my books, which surprised and pleased them. Newspaper reviews stress the form and the themes of my work. In general reviewers are academically oriented. You just about have to have a degree in Dutch literature to be able to write, and I consider that unfair. I've read a lot on that level and I know where to find my information. Besides, the "strange things" of life are usually discovered or invented "by accident". My writing is a search for beauty which is inspired by the banality of life, answers to questions that my inward self asks. As far as technique is concerned, my writing is an intuitive process. I don't like repetition. At the very least I want to continue what has been written before, recreate, or better yet "create". That's why a remark about *De gekte van een vrouw* not being well thought out is so supremely arrogant. It's all right for literary criticism to be academically oriented, but here, too, critics ought to approach a work impartially. I spent four years working on that book, searching for the right images, the best wording, to make things as clear as I could, but at the same time as personal and as liberating as possible. But no matter — in this case the sales figures were my consolation!

What do you read yourself, mainly male or female authors?

I guess you could say I find my positive inspiration in literature by women, while I get my aggressiveness from works by men. They stimulate me to take the things that they don't see and to make them even more explicit in my own work. Besides that, I read just about everything that interests me — French, English, Dutch, German and North American literature.

Of course I read all Surinamese and Antillian books, but I can't situate my work within a national, literary history because it has not yet been written. I read *Hérémakhonon* by Maryse Condé, but it didn't really get to me. I feel closer to the Dutch than to the Africans. I don't know Africa yet. Indoctrination? Maybe. But I don't see that as a pathological conflict. I'm an integrated person who happens to have more rapport with Dutch people than with Africans. And yet Africans, black Africans, have something that never fails to move me, that brings me to my knees. Through literature I'm trying little by little to reach the continent of my ancestors.

Naturally I'm very interested in the work of women writers, the Dutch writers too. Although in some cases I wonder why some of them get such unreservedly good reviews. I don't get that feeling with Buchi Emecheta. Her work reads like romanticized history, which enriches my black consciousness. The difference is that Erica Jong and Toni Morrison also help me to handle my own intuition. Of course I have a great affinity for Surinamese writers in the Netherlands, Edgar Cairo, for instance. I admire what he's doing and the fact that he's such a professional. He's lifting Surinamese literature out of its stereotyped isolation. He deserves a lot of credit for that. But I have some objections to his work too. He wants to write about the history of black people, and describe their feelings, but in my view there's too little actual liberation in his work. The themes he chooses are often still too colonial, and that's not the way to bring black people out of their isolation. And yet this literature too will prove itself! However, I do not agree with his narrow view of other Surinamese writers. I don't think everyone has to start writing in one of the Surinamese languages in order to be credible, or has to advocate some kind of "homeland cult". To me every writer has the right to express personal experience in prose and poetry. That can only enrich our literature. The people of Surinam are like a crystal in the sun.

Do you consider yourself, like Edgar Cairo, a "professional" writer?

Not altogether. The other things, personal relationships and my fight against negrophobia, are just as important to me. I'm not interested only in earning a living by writing. I work two days a week for the government and I can get by on that. I see my love of literature as part of the struggle to present my people, my sex and myself, to make them recognizable and understandable. That is always uppermost in my mind. Two years ago I started teaching workshops for women who want to write. All sorts of women came, some motivated by political reasons, others more interested in the artistic side. I don't lay down any rules. Together we try to express in words and images what we consider important. People are ashamed of their fantasies, even though they're what keeps us standing tall and/or represses us. I try to explain how we can control these fantasies by writing. This sometimes produces really unusual results. But I talk about racism and sexism too, and — a different paradigm — violence. For a while we had black women in the group too. But they told me they couldn't feel free with so many white women there.

Now groups of black women (and one or two men) want me to form all-black groups. Years ago I was in favour of this kind of "apartheid", out of hatred for the arrogance of the whites. But my workshops and lectures are meant to promote meaningful communication, which is why they are open to "friend and enemy". Integration leads to understanding! Understanding leads to love and love is regeneration!

I'm happy to say that I lead a busy private life, that often takes precedence over my writing. The only thing that I do professionally is to fight negrophobia and racism in general. I've been at it so long — eighteen years now, rooting it out and bringing it to light — that it's almost contaminated me. This is more important to me than publishing literary works. I still haven't found a way to mesh together my struggle and my writing. My work against racism takes up so much of my time and energy on other fronts.

Whenever I write about Caribbean literature I always have trouble with the difference between black and white. I associate black writers with an African past which is clearly evident in their work. But I call writers of Indian parentage Hindustani and Chinese writers Chinese. Should I be calling them light brown or yellow?

The question of terminology is interesting, especially when you're talking about Caribbean people in Europe. In the Caribbean itself the oriental migrants (Hindustani, Javanese, Chinese) are proud of their biological ethnicity. They are of course "white" and everything that isn't white and doesn't come from the east is negroid. In Europe, in particular in the Netherlands, everything that isn't "Aryan" automatically belongs to the other race, with all the negative consequences which that implies. Fortunately in this way all the non-whites are thrown together, which increases their solidarity. Black and white have become political terms, and don't necessarily indicate a specific ethnic background. The same sort of thing is developing in the United States, as witness Jesse Jackson's "rainbow coalition".

And yet in my writings I use the term white in order to free the white man from his "whiteness". Whiteness has only negative connotations for me, just like the word "Negro". Black represents my attempt to free the African carried off as a slave from his "Negro-ness". I feel comfortable with this terminology, but of course everyone must make his own choice.

The difference between black and white is extremely important in the book Women, Race and Class *(1981) by Angela Davis, about the political role of black women in the history of the United States. She is often extremely hostile to white women.*

Yes, but the book was edited by Toni Morrison, who is said to have a deep-rooted aversion to whites who use their skin colour against blacks. And that's often the case in politics, women are no exception, too. You constantly sense the arrogant racist attitude in the discussion. Just because you belong to an oppressed group doesn't mean solidarity with all other oppressed people, not even within the same society. Do you know of any militant white organization in this society that has a "reappraisal of the black man" high on its list of priorities? The solidarity of white women did help black women in the first instance. But what we need in order to become truly emancipated is love and respect from the rest of mankind. I can't shout: "Proletarians of the world, unite!" But

I have been shouting for years, "Peoples of the world, respect and reassess black people" (in this case the so-called negroid people). Many, many blacks are suffering under racism, negrophobia and self-hatred, and this stands in the way of solidarity.

Anyway, Angela Davis and Toni Morrison are right: the more involved I get with racism, the more the "racist" in me rears its ugly head, even if in our case it's more a question of "desperation". I don't hate white people. I do adore black people, and perhaps the two are mutually exclusive!

I don't want party politics to be the main theme in my work. I am very involved with my country, but what is Surinam and what is Surinamese consciousness? I'm an individual, not a nation. I love Surinam and I love Holland, and I express both in my writing.

Speaking of racism and sexism in the Netherlands, I find both of these in the Spanish-language literature of the Caribbean as well. There you have the stereotype of the mulatto girl, erotic, high-spirited and of easy virtue!

I recognize that mulatto girl. She has always been a "threat" to black women, and the seductress of the black man and the white man. In *Parimaribo, Parimaribo*, my musical drama, the mulatto says "I'm pretty enough not to have to bow to the stereotype of the Third World." Well, I have recently come to see her as the incarnation of peace between two hostile races. The mulatto used to bother me. She had to keep proving to me that she was really black. But now I see her mixed race as something positive. In 1975 there was a demand for migrant workers in the Nickerie area of Surinam. This attracted many Venezuelan women who crossed the border and took up prostitution there. The Surinamese women despised them because they thought the Venezuelans were out to seduce their men. The fear was so strong that these women were forced into isolation. They were considered a threat and the political background of their presence was not understood.

Surinam has its internal racism too, based mainly on skin colour and type of hair. You could say it's an offshoot of negrophobia. It's been fairly widespread since colonial times. And Surinam has its sexism too — there are enough examples to fill quite a few novels. Sexism and racism play an important role in our politics.

Do people in the Netherlands see you mainly as Surinamese or as a black writer? And how do you see yourself?

The themes I use in my work are actually very universal. I write about love, death, sexuality and about the struggle of individuals, very often black people, to be happy. I also use the mother/daughter(son) relationship in my work, because I see that as the most important relationship in life. Any objections? World literature is full of the father-son(daughter) relationship and no one raises an eyebrow. About twice a month I give lectures for women, and the hall is usually packed. Dutch, Surinamese, South Moluccan, Moroccan women.

It wouldn't be true to say I work exclusively for women, or that I write and work specifically as a black woman. Where do you draw the line? If I give a lecture in a high-fashion suit, am I "white"? Am I truly black with dreadlocks in my hair? In things like this I try to rely as much as possible on my own instincts. Everyone is welcome to be a bit "white" or "black" or whatever. Be my guest! I don't want to put people in categories. This sometimes creates awkward situations for me as a writer. And the language I use is too racy for some people. My themes aren't the classic clichés of the familiar Third World problems. I seem to have risen above the stereotype of the Third World figure who thinks like a victim. I don't mind doing that either, but then with the strength and conviction of the *individual*. I try to individualize black people and not to portray them in such a way that people say, "Of course, that's how I always thought they were!'' I want to free my people from this collective image. We all know that averages only exist on charts. My characters exist only in my imagination. I don't want to typecast people in my writing. And I don't want to be typecast myself, although as a writer I try to be above all that. You won't catch me being discriminated against, as a black or as a woman. Few people have power over me for very long. I belong to myself. But then that's the only kind of isolation I want.

You've also written for the theatre. What was that like?

At the moment the government's theatre policy is not favourable. But there is the growing awareness that Holland has become a multi-racial society. I'm getting more and more commissions for plays. Sometimes I am given a theme, more often not. An unusual aspect of these commissions is that I always stipulate that no white actors are to appear as blackfaces in my plays. Blacks must be played by blacks. When they're played by European actors they present the wrong image, because they aren't familiar with a black man's world of ideas and they unconsciously reproduce their own prejudices. When I made that condition I was also thinking of a complaint voiced by non-European actors that they aren't given a chance in the professional theatre here.

Are you going to do more theatre now, and what are your plans for the future?

I place my writing in the service of the struggle and my life. If novels do more good I'll write novels, and if TV writing is more effective then I'll do that. My genres are not fixed. But any genre must serve my needs or those of others, often those who commission my work. I've written radio plays and songs, some for children. The drama group Menes, for instance, caters to young people from 15 to 20, because kids in this age group don't read but they do like plays. So I work with this group to create musical drama. I want to communicate, so I look for the channels of communication where I can reach the greatest number of people.

And I'll be leaving the Netherlands shortly — temporarily. I haven't seen all I want to of Europe, but as a writer I feel that I need to "recharge my batteries", and look for new inspiration elsewhere. So I want to go to South America, the hinterland of Surinam, filled with historical lines that run through our country too. That's what I'll be looking for!

V. LATIN AMERICA

PROVERBS

1. Women — long hair, short ideas. (Colombia)
2. The woman who bears sons has no worries. (Colombia)
3. Beautiful baby: flowers for a boy, garlic for a girl. (Colombia)
4. A woman with a moustache is greeted from far off. (Columbia)
5. To a chaste woman, her husband is enough. (Colombia)
6. Man with whoever he wants, woman with whoever she can. (Colombia)
7. A woman with freckles is a tasty morsel. (Colombia)
8. No woman at all is better than someone else's. (Colombia)
9. No mother dies with a full belly. (Colombia)
10. A woman who knows Latin will neither find a husband nor come to a good end. (Argentina)
11. Bitter tea and an ugly woman, only if you have no choice. (Argentina)
12. A woman is like a guitar: the more you play it, the better it sounds. (Chile)
13. A good wife repairs what her husband damages. (Chile)
14. Women hold up the other half of the sky. (Chile)
15. A good woman is priceless, but if she's bad, no stick is good enough to beat her. (Uruguay)
16. Like the scorpion woman is a relative of the devil: when she sees a poor wretch, she wiggles her behind and moves away. (Uruguay)
17. Woman is like a hen — she always chooses the best rooster. (Uruguay)
18. The woman who says no means yes; the woman who says nothing doesn't know what's going on. (Uruguay)
19. Some men are admired as demi-gods, but no woman is admired as a demi-virgin. (Uruguay)
20. No peasant revolution unless women take part. (Peru)
21. For the priest's housekeeper there is no hell. (Mexico)
22. Keep a woman and a gun loaded in a corner [i.e. ready for use]. (Mexico)
23. A crazy woman prefers her bread from the baker who touches her. (Mexico)

212

24. Women and motorways: the more curves, the more danger. (Mexico)
25. Women and wine improve with age. (Mexico)
26. Women and seagulls, the older the crazier. (Mexico)
27. Donkeys, women, mules — if they don't kick, they buck. (Panama)
28. A virtuous woman and a broken leg belong at home. (Panama)
29. Woman's honour is like a pane of glass: it fogs up at a single breath. (Panama)
30. Woman's advice is short, and whoever rejects it, a fool. (Panama)

ACKNOWLEDGEMENTS

Psiche Hughes, England, heard 1 and 2 from *Julieta Rubio*, 3 from la Gorda Wilches of Colombia and 10 from *Delia Rodriguez* of Argentina; *Hermien Gaikhorst*, Holland (4-9), selected from Luis Alberto Acuna, *Refranero colombiano*, Colombia (1947, 1951), and 24-6 from Shirley L. Arora, *Proverbial comparisons and related expressions in Spanish*, Los Angeles, Univ. of California Press, Folklore Studies 29, 1977; *Anna M. G. Perquin*, Holland (11, 13 and 27-30), selected from Carlos Villafuerte, *Refranero de Catamarca*, Buenos Aires, 1972; Agustín Cannobio, *Refranos Chilenos*, Santiago de Chile, 1901; Luisita Aguilera P., *Refranero Panemeno*, *Contribución a la paremiología hispanoamericana*, Santiago de Chile, 1955; *Ankie Peypers* assisted in obtaining 11, 13 and 27-30; *Angelica Dorfman*, Chile (12); *Ineke Phaf* assisted in obtaining 14 and 20-3, from *Juan Riquelme*, Chile (14), *Teresa Valiente*, Peru (20), *Miguel Velazco Valdés*, Mexico (21), *Manuel E. Condo*, Mexico (22 and 23); *Clara Piriz*, Uruguay (15 and 17), which she heard from *Nene Rebagliatti*, Uruguay, and 16, 18 and 19, which she recalled having heard.

WOMEN AND LITERATURE IN LATIN AMERICA

PSICHE HUGHES

To talk of literature in Latin America is to talk of the writers of approximately twenty countries. Any attempt to survey and analyse the situation of Latin American women in their different literatures would develop into an extremely lengthy and complex study which is well beyond the scope of this article. Arbitrary though this may seem, I therefore intend to limit my observations to some of the women writers from five countries — Argentina, Chile, Mexico, El Salvador and Uruguay — whose working life covers the last sixty or seventy years.

First, it may be relevant to explain the reason for the historical dearth of women writers in Latin America up to the first half of the present century. Illiteracy, rampant in the whole of the Latin American continent, has always been higher among women; this can be verified by looking at the following statistics of the percentage of illiterates per population in some Latin American countries chosen at random:

Country	Year of census/survey	Percentage of Illiterates	
		Male	Female
Bolivia	1976	24.8	49.0
Colombia	1973	18.0	20.2
El Salvador	1975	34.5	41.1
Mexico	1980	16.7	21.2
Peru	1972	16.7	39.2

Moreover, the traditional role of women, universally accepted in Latin American societies, has, if not excluded, certainly considerably limited their presence within the spheres of intellectual and creative pursuits. In the last century a female author would feel the necessity to forsake her private life, as did Juana Manuela, the wife of Manuel Isidoro Belzú, Bolivia's first popular President. Driven by an intense desire to write, she decided to give up her position and leave her husband, in order to be able to fulfil her ambition. Those women who ventured into writing did so remaining within the patterns set and established by their male colleagues. An example of this is the Cuban Gertrudis Gómez de Avellanada (1814-1873), who spent many years of her life in Spain. Her lyrics follow the neo-classic tradition in which she was educated, while her novel *Sab*, centred on the theme of slavery, portrays Cuban society of the time as illustrated by her contemporaries. Another example is the Peruvian Clorinda Matto de Turner (1854-1909), author of *"novelas indigenistas"* such as *Aves sin nido*, which describes life in Amerindian communities, and the struggle of the indigenous population of America, in a society dominated and exploited by the "white" landowners.

Gabriela Mistral (1889-1957)

This century has seen the progress of the suffragette movement. The Chilean poetess Gabriela Mistral joined the movement which achieved its aim throughout the Latin American continent between the years 1929-61. This she did not so much in the spirit of feminine revolt, but rather in defence of human rights, that women be included in the political life of their countries. It is interesting to compare Gabriela Mistral with other Latin American women who wrote during and after her time. Proud of her Indian origin, she declared her love for her country and celebrated the life and the cults of her people. Her concern with humanist values led her to accept the Mexican government's invitation to collaborate with the educationist and philosopher José Vasconcelos in organizing the education system in rural areas. This experience reinforced her awareness of the moral and social duties that confront any educated person in an underdeveloped continent. Commissioned by the Mexican government, she then travelled to Europe where she followed both a diplomatic and an academic career during which she only returned to Chile on visits. Despite the variety of contacts which she made during her travels and their enlightening influence, her vision of womanhood and of the female role does not succeed in liberating itself from accepted literary stereotypes. This is clear in her writings whether she speaks of love "If you look at me I become beautiful like the grass under the dew. . . ." (*Desolación*, 181) — or addresses herself to other women as in her *Lecturas para mujeres*. When she widens the scope of her vision, she exalts the eternal basic values of her land and people: she sings of maternity in the fields, of the peasants struggling in the mountains and in the deserts of Chile, of the ever-renewing energy of the indigenous race. The modernist tradition that informs her poetry finds in these themes a new inspiration and an energy which contrast with the precious imagery into which its followers degenerated.

As a result of her intellectual stature and her moral stand, Gabriela Mistral was admired and even worshipped but from afar. She felt isolated, she laments, into "the frozen niche in which men placed you" (p. 89). Her attempts to break out of this isolation are reflected in the anguished expressions of her frustrated maternity: "A son, a son, a son! I wanted a son from you. . . . In my days . . . bitterness drops with slow salty and cold tears" (p. 108).

Victoria Ocampo (1893-1979)

Victoria Ocampo, the Argentinian high priestess of culture who outlived Gabriela Mistral by some twenty years, had many contacts with the Chilean poetess and both loved her as a person and admired her poetry. She did, however, express reservation about Mistral's attitude towards the plight of women in Latin American society. Though aware of their situation and of the cultural problems this involved, Mistral was not prepared to denounce the tyranny of men. Intellec-

217

tually, Victoria Ocampo seems to think, she was not a feminist.

Victoria Ocampo has a specific position in the context of women writers of the later generation. Aristocratic and highly cultured, she represented for decades the axis around which many writers moved, both Latin American and otherwise. She was a friend of Virginia Woolf, mingled with well known authors like Tagore, Ortega y Gasset and Valéry. *Sur*, the literary review she founded in 1931, though attacked by Neruda for its bourgeois mentality, listed among its contributors the most eminent names in Latin America at the time. Nevertheless Neruda did, years later in 1960, praise its achievements at a PEN Club meeting in New York.

Described as "*machona*" in the 1920s, for driving a Packard, Ocampo began her feminist career by befriending the Spanish teacher Maria de Maetzu, who, inspired by Krause's educational reform theories, advocated a liberal and lay education for boys and girls alike. Ocampo's feminism manifested itself throughout her life: having always lamented that women still lived too much in the shadow of men, in 1975 she refused to attend the Argentinian Women's Conference because, she explained, "to argue about progressive legislation when '*patria potestas*' is still in existence is an absurdity" (from a letter published in *La Opinon*, September 1975). With a similar attitude, in 1945 she had declared herself against Peron in spite of his call for female suffrage, because she suspected a political trap behind the dictator's move. Her main concern, however, was for the cultural aspects of feminism. She aspired to see women not only expressing their ideas and emotions with the freedom that men had always enjoyed, but also establishing a position in the artistic world on an equal basis with men, asserting their individual identity, as independent from that of men. Women's talents, she argued, have always been unexplored and unrealized because "it is evident that the quantity of innate talent that a person possesses depends for its realization and expression upon the outlets it encounters for its development". The emancipation of woman did not mean her separation from man but to "bring her closer to him in the most complete . . . conscious way". (*Testimonios,* Vol. II, p. 251 and ff.) A woman writer must be able to find this outlet for her own intellectual development, which means that she must neither conform to expressing herself in the terms traditionally expected of her as a woman, nor speak "with a man's voice". She must find her own language and her own way to write "like a woman", in order to explain herself and all the members of her sex to the other half of humanity. Ocampo talks of "a blind spot" at the back of our heads which distinguishes men's way of envisaging reality from women's: "Each sex must assume the responsibility of describing that spot for the benefit of the other." Men have done it for thousands of years. She adds, "We must now repay it." ("Carta a Virginia Woolf", *Testimonios*, Vol. I, pp. 11-12.)

I therefore propose now to examine the work of some women writers whose creative output was mainly realized during the course of this century. Though many might smile with a certain irony and condescension at the mention of the name of Victoria Ocampo, because she is associated with a cultural establishment which they may oppose, in evaluating the work of authors of a younger and more radical generation, I shall avail myself of her criteria. I would like to establish to what extent they write "like a woman", which are the traditions they adopt or disown, how they break away from the stereotyped images of women which have so far been presented by men and, finally, what new facets of a woman's identity they reveal — that blind spot referred to by Ocampo — in the process of expressing and realizing their own intellectual talents.

Women, as Seen by Latin American Male Writers

First, we ought to review briefly how male writers from Latin America have presented women in the context of their society. To simplify the task, I need to make certain classifications and must be forgiven if these inevitably appear to be generic and arbitrary. Jane S. Jaquette in her article "Literary archetypes and female role alternatives" (in Pescatello 1973) analysing the presentation of female characters in the work of Latin American authors, distinguishes between symbols, stereotypes and archetypes. I, too, have arrived at a similar conclusion. Glancing through the major novels and poetry, I find that we can make this distinction; on one hand, the female stereotype is presented in a "realistic" setting, which changes with the period and social class to which she belongs; on the other hand, woman is viewed in her symbolic role as an extension of man's experience. As such either she represents the source of his inspiration and creates the ideal conditions in which he can realize his artistic and intellectual pursuits, or she offers him a literary image by which to interpret his destiny, that of his continent and race and consequently find his position in the historical moment in which he lives.

Stereotypes

Seen traditionally as the object of man's sexual desire, women often figure in the works of writers such as the Argentinian Roberto Arlt and the Uruguayan Onetti, as the measure, if not the cause, of his intellectual disintegration and downfall. They act with the blind drive of a life force bent on securing the ideal situation in which they can safely procreate: marriage.

This is the theme of *El amor brujo,* a novel by Arlt. In it the author, while giving the most detailed and elaborate description of the tortuous reasoning with which the male protagonist talks himself into and out of marriage, confines the analysis of the heroine's ordeal to her basic instinctive needs; whatever mental process might occur within her remains totally opaque. Marriage also looms bleakly in many of Onetti's writings, creating a condition of alienation and annihilation. Woman is only desirable and a source of joy at her youngest and virginal state; as her body corrupts, she corrupts the body and the mind of her companion.

The range of stereotypes in whose form women are presented is as vast as it is varied: in a story by Borges, which well reflects the mentality of the Argentinian male for whom friendship with members of his sex overrides any other relationship, she is "The Intruder". Representing preoccupation with sex and its momentary satisfaction, she comes between two brothers who, though rivals for a brief period of time, are so attached to each other as to eliminate the woman who has succeeded in dividing them. At the other end of the social scale, in the works of the Peruvian Vargas Llosa and Bryce-Echenique, woman is often presented as the mother of a rich family, impeccably performing her domestic and social duties, unaware however of the intimate problems of her children and totally blind to the political unrest that troubles the society in which she lives.

These are the stereotypes; whether using their femininity to control man or victims of his aggressive lust, these women do not appear to exist on the same individual level as he does, no more than they integrate within the society in which he thinks and acts. Moreover, within man's world, they perform a further role. In some of the novels of Vargas Llosa, for example, dealing with the moral and political corruption of the nation, women's moral weakness and ambiguous promiscuity are often a sign of the decayed society and the object on which man vents his perverted emotions.

Symbols

Removed from the more realistic contexts, woman assumes a symbolic role in the literary vision of many Latin American writers. Here, once again, we are confronted with a wide variety of images which, needless to say, repeat and interconnect in the multiple texts. We see the figure of Doña Barbara, in the novel of that name by the Venezuelan Romulo Gallego, who represents the primitive force of an untamed people, "*el alma de la raza*" opposed to the softening and corrupting influence of civilization. Alongside her, the warm and beautiful Camila, in *El Señor Presidente* by Miguel Angel Asturias, personifies the life-giving strength of a nation which fights for its freedom, against the sterility and destruction of dictatorship.

Moving from prose to poetry, the symbolic role of woman becomes even more evident. To Neruda, for instance, the female body is rich with connotations which have multiple allusive qualities: caressing it, he compares its anatomy to the geography of the beloved South American continent. Calm and silent, woman is the harbour in which he seeks protection from the storm. Like many other Latin American writers, Neruda feels the spiritual need to assess and accept his position as a man of different races, resulting from the conquest of his land by the Spaniards. This is the most important moment in the history of the continent, a moment which goes on recurring in the poet's mind. Woman and her conventional role offer the specific symbolic elements to relive the historic episode and exorcize its trauma. Cuba, and by synecdoche the whole continent, is seen as a virgin raped by the Conqueror: "Cuba, my beloved, they drew open your legs of pale gold, they tore your sex of pomegranate . . . they divided you, they burnt you" (*Canto General*, Book III, Sect. II). We see how the female figure serves to illustrate the poet's emotions and how the passive beauty of the victim contrasts with the sadistic details of the sexual aggression to create a passionate image which rings with deep patriotic sentiments.

For the Mexican Octavio Paz the female sex stands as symbol of the reality whose mystery man seeks to describe: to speak and to copulate are the two primordial activities, both aiming at the expression and liberation of the inner man: "falo el pensar y vulva la palabra" (the thought is the phallus and the word the vagina). To penetrate a woman is equal to penetrating reality for she is "made in the image of the world". The emotion of poetry rests on the space between one word and another, this is the cleft *"la hendidura"*, in other words, the female sex.

Paz is also concerned with the hybrid nature of Latin American people as a result of the conquest. The language we speak and in which we write is the language of the conqueror with the rules he has imposed upon it. Conversant with the thought of George Bataille and Jacques Lacan, that language is "the desired mother" where "father" represents the law that forbids the contact, Paz sees writing as an act of sexual rebellion, which shatters the property of the Conqueror. Hence both historic and literary aspects of writing are piled with sexual connotations. Present-day Mexico exists, in fact, as the result of a woman's action. This is La Malinche who, violated by Cortez, helped him into her land, acted as go-between with her people and gave him a son, the first mestizo, the first Mexican. Since then, all Mexicans are "Hijos de la Chingada", sons of a whore.

It might be interesting at this point to remember how Victoria Ocampo viewed the same episode. La Malinche, who broke out of the traditional patterns of the female role, is one of those women who, "because they happen not to be men, live on the border of the territory that would otherwise be theirs". Endowed with the ambition for power and command, conventionally attributed to man, "she struggled against the customs, only obliquely" and established her position by tactics and manipulation. It is regrettable, Ocampo adds, that La Malinche was forgotten in the Women's Year and that only a volcano is named after her. But, she ironically concludes, it is traditional in our society to give female names to the major disturbances of nature (*Testimonios*, X, pp. 39-46).

Archetypes

Moving from woman's symbolic function to the traditional archetypal roles she has assumed in the work of men writers, I should like once again to avail myself of Jaquette's classification; these roles are for her that of the Mother, the Wife/Mistress and the Witch.

The heroine of Alejo Carpentier's novel *Los pasos perdidos*, the warm generous Rosario (who is also symbol of the American race in so far as in her are combined the traits of the white, the Indian and the black people inhabiting the continent), represents both the mother and mistress archetypes. In her lap the narrator not only finds deep sexual pleasure but also seeks refuge and comfort from the dangers that assail him during his journey. Moreover, Rosario offers him an escape and a salutary contrast from the automated life and the emotional aridity of the mechanized culture of North America, from which he comes, personified by his wife, Ruth, and by Mouche, his mistress.

Another maternal wife is the practical, all-capable and all-knowing grandmother in García Márquez's *One Hundred Years of Solitude* who is always ready, though scornfully at times, to attend to her husband's plans and creative dreams, while sturdily struggling to keep the house together, give the family a sense of stability and bring up four generations of Buendías. It is evident in both cases how these two women, though perfectly fitting within the context and the scheme of the books, are not real human characters. Just as they answer to the needs of the men who depend upon them, they perform a role within the artistic vision of the writer. These women are little more than an extension of nature, comparable to the earthly female figures of the *"novelas indigenistas"*. To quote an example of these, Jaquette reminds us of an episode from the beginning of *El mundo es ancho y ajeno* by Ciro Alegría. Old Rosendo, the leader of a small Indian community, thinks of himself and his wife, both moving towards their death and compares her to the ever renewing earth: "Is the earth better than woman? . . . he liked and loved the earth very much."

One of the characteristics of the Mother archetype is that sexual manifestations are confined to the sacred area of marriage or projected on the level of "a meaningful relationship". Both for Rosario and Ursula, sex is the expression of their devoted love. While the male Buendías are characterized by an unusually strong sex drive, of Ursula we know that she acquiesces to her husband's love-making, despite her better reasoning which would advise her not to procreate for the danger of conceiving a baby with a pig tail, as had been prophesied. But what do we know of her dreams and longings outside the fulfilment of her marital role? As for Rosario, her healthy response to the advances of her man are in character with her being young and "a child of nature". The reader is left in no doubt, however, as to there being no traces of promiscuity or sexual ambiguity in her, such as seem to contaminate the behaviour of the other two women in the life of the main character.

Another characteristic of the earthly woman is her instinctive wisdom which involves no learning nor intellectual pursuits. On the contrary, Ursula looks askance at her husband's experiments and inventions, seeing no reason for his mental curiosity. Rosario is actually shown reading a cheap romantic novelette, and her simplicity is contrasted with the intellectual affectations of Mouche (a symbolic name?). She has her own sense of beauty, but no artistic ambitions such as have the narrator himself, who is a musicologist, and his wife, a theatrical actress. Of course one is aware of the allegoric character of this book, whose plot marks the stages of a man's attempt to find his ancestral roots and his lost innocence away from the corruption of modern society; all the same, there is no doubt that Rosario remains a totally literary figure, expressly created to establish features relevant in the personality of the male character and his development, and so are Ruth and Mouche, the other two women in the novel.

The final archetypal role of women, to complete Jaquette's classification, is that of the Witch. Spiritually, if not physically isolated from her surroundings, endowed with an understanding which verges on the supernatural, woman exerts a power over man which changes his life, brings him awareness of his more secret identity and helps him realize his most hidden dreams. This is the case of many of Carlos Fuentes's female characters. I am thinking of the blind Hortensia, in *La region más trasparent*, who offers Federico Robles — the rich banker of Amerindian origin living totally alienated from the society into which his success and ambition have placed him — the chance to clarify his position and find again his natural role; or of the old Ludivinia in *La muerte de Artemio Cruz* who, living behind the closed shutters of her crumbling mansion, knows of the changes which have occurred within her society, senses the blood ties which bind her to the mulatto boy playing in the yard outside and rejoices in the prospect of her family being reborn in him. The most witch-like of all Fuentes's characters is the heroine of *Aura*, who entices a young journalist into her house to write the biography of her long-dead husband and bring him back to life. In all these cases woman is the enchantress, under whose spell man shapes his life. Her function is to prophesy and help realize man's destiny; her identity and destiny are of no concern to the author.

The heroine of Cortázar's best known and most controversial novel, *Rayuela*, is aptly referred to as La Maga. She is both a witch-like figure enveloped in mystery and the symbol of the man's life search. The book, in fact, starts with Oliveira, the main character, asking himself whether he will ever find La Maga, and develops as an enquiry into the nature of the new novel. The literary aspects of the work run parallel to the hero's quest, both dominated by the ever-elusive image of the woman. While anguish and humour make Oliveira a totally human and lovable character, La Maga remains an unknown identity. Her psychology (she loses both her baby and the man she loves, and suggests that she may contemplate suicide) is never investigated.

To endow a female character with a metaphysical function or to surround her with a halo of mystery is the ultimate way of denying her identity. We see therefore how, whether stereotypes, symbols or archetypes, Latin American women have suffered from a highly reduced fictional reality in a literary world dominated by male writers.

Sor Juana Inés de la Cruz (1648-95)

Over a century after La Malinche acted as interpreter between her people and the Conquistadores, there lived in Mexico another woman who distinguished herself not only for her achievements but also for asserting women's rights to study, think and express their ideas: Sor Juana. Sor Juana came from a noble family. In order to avoid marriage (a status which did not appeal to her independent nature) she opted for the convent (the only other door then open to a woman). From the cloisters she wrote poems and plays both religious and secular. These works were greatly admired at the Mexican court. What is of interest in the present context, however, rather than the baroque quality of her verse, which conforms with the literary traditions of writers like Góngora and Calderón, or the allegoric beauty of her "autos de fé" and the supple dialogue of her plays, is her intellectual attitude. Endowed with a very alert mind, she would analyse questions and discuss any event or statement which confronted her. True to her nature, on one occasion she wrote a letter commenting on and arguing some of the theological points made in a sermon on the nature of Christ's love delivered some forty years earlier by a Jesuit preacher. This letter was published by the Bishop of Puebla together with his own missive written under the pseudonym of Sor Filotea, in which he rebuked the nun for daring to address herself to subjects well out of her province. At the same time, the Bishop advised her to confine her readings to the Gospel and not to stray out into secular matters. In her "Respuesta a Sor Filotea", a letter which is almost an autobiographic essay, Sor Juana declares her unquenchable thirst for knowledge, the need she feels to verify all accepted truths by experiments and reasoning, and her right to satisfy her investigative mind.

Sor Juana's attitude reflects the intellectual atmosphere of the end of the seventeenth century, fermenting with belief in the power of reason (this is the time when Descartes's *Discours de la méthode* was first being read) and anticipating the enlightened doctrines of the following century. In line with the eclectic mentality which was beginning to spread from Europe, Sor Juana claims the right, indeed the need, to study sciences and art as well as theology, for they are all complementary in the understanding of nature. She seeks the logical explanation for all phenomena which she does not attribute to an unquestionable scheme of the Divine Mind, but considers yielding to logical investigation. For her the world is no longer the place where humanity seeks its spiritual redemption but a challenge to its reasoning power. Why must anyone be excluded from this privilege? And why think that these pursuits are unsuitable or excessive in a woman? Even in the kitchen, when she has dedicated herself to menial tasks in order to conform with the spirit of the Order, she has found intellectual stimulus and handy means to experiment, test and prove many of the natural laws. And why must she abandon her books? When she once tried to do so for a period of three months, she found that, though not reading, she was still watching all the things which went on around her, trying to work out from their behaviour the movements of the universal machinery.

The bishop's letter had contained a quotation from the Gospel: *"Taceant mulieres"* (let women be silent). Sor Juana brilliantly finds an answer also for this: yes, let them be silent because, in order to learn, they have to watch and listen. So that they will, in their turn, be able to teach others. In her criticism of the Jesuit's sermon, Sor Juana once again takes the stand of a woman's right to express her opinion, argue and disagree, if she thinks it necessary, with other people's statements. If a man is free to disagree with her, is she not as free as he? Towards the end of her "Respuesta", Sor Juana strengthens her case by confronting her adversary with a list of many illustrious woman cited through history and concludes ironically: "To think that women are considered inept whilst men, just by virtue of being so, are considered wise!"

Such militant feminism appears remarkable certainly, all the more so in a seventeenth century nun. But Sor Juana's voice did not go unheard.

Rosario Castellanos (1925-74)

In 1973 (if I may jump three centuries) another Mexican woman, Rosario Castellanos, published a booklet entitled *Mujer que sabe latin . . .*, the first words of a well known proverb which continues: *ni tiene marido, ni tiene buen fin* (a woman who knows Latin neither gets married, nor comes to a good end). In it she also upholds the intellectual equality of women and their right to pursue a career of learning, without having to feel that their lives are compromised, as the proverb referred to in the title suggests. It is interesting that, following the example of Sor Juana, to whom she refers, Castellanos also strengthens her arguments with portraits of women whose life and achievements are evidence of that very equality. The list includes, among others, Virginia Woolf, Simone de Beauvoir, Doris Lessing, Betty Friedan, Penelope Gilliat and Mary McCarthy.

Rosario Castellanos, who died tragically not many years ago in Israel, is also the author of poems, two novels, which can be classified as close to the intention of the *"novela indigenitsa"* and several collections of short stories. Many are the facets of society represented in her work, but the one dominant aspect is her portrayal of female characters and of their situation. Whatever the social level to which they belong, their life constitutes a denunciation of a system which thwarts their nature and victimizes them.

The life of "Modesta Gomez" is one of the many stories of poverty and exploitation which recur in the narrative of Latin American authors. Sent to serve in a rich family at an early age (so young that her legs, as yet unformed, are bowed by the strain of carrying the young master), raped and pregnant, she is thrown out of the house after many years of service. Now a widow, with three children to feed, she remembers with a certain nostalgia the husband who often beat her, yet loved her enough to make her a "señora" and give a name to her illegitimate child. It is a well known plot but for the climax and conclusion of the story, which add a novel aspect to this kind of narrative. Modesta Gomez increases her meagre earnings as a shop assistant by working as an "atajadora". This is an established "profession" which consists of going out early in the morning, meeting the Indians who come down to the towns to sell their few products in the markets, and "attacking" them (hence the name "atajadora") in order to steal from them whatever they can. The fatalism with which the Indians regularly face these encounters and the behaviour of the women rolling on the ground and fighting tooth and nail for a jug or a sweater are the signs of the despair and the animal aggression which extreme poverty and injustice create. Having fought for nothing — since another "atajadora" gets the shawl she was after — Modesta nevertheless looks with satisfaction at her nails encrusted with the blood of her victim, a young woman, in fact. Such is the distortion of human values and the elimination of compassion that society operates on its members! Far from seeing in the Indian girl an image of her own predicament, Modesta rejoices at the pain she has inflicted on her. In the scale of social misery it is comforting to know that there is always someone who suffers more than you.

Others of Castellanos's stories, such as those from *Convidados de agosto*, depict a different social setting, yet their insight into the mentality and situation of its female characters is equally striking. On the one hand, the pathetic picture of loneliness and frustration of those women who, in order to maintain that distance and those standards which man-dominated society demands of them, are unable to break out of the environment in which they are caged and remain unfulfilled like "faded petals"; on the other, satirical sketches sharply portraying the literary poses and the rivalries of pseudo-intellectual women and the hypocrisy of their excuses for not being able to live outright what they theoretically profess.

The stories of a later collection, *Album de familia*, are equally characterized by a subtle insight into the feminine mind and by a style of writing whose feminist intent overrides any other connotation. The first story, "Lección de cocina", satirically alludes to the line of conduct a woman has to establish between herself and her husband and to what extent she will have to sacrifice her dignity and the truth in order to live peacefully with him. A newly married woman has burnt the joint and elaborates on her future line of conduct. How to present the case? Pretend that nothing has happened or exaggerate her grief? Beg forgiveness or stand by her own version of the incident?

Another story, "Domingo", also about a married woman, deals with the split within her life as an individual and as the centre of the domestic environment. It is Sunday, all the family is around, guests visit the home, various social topics are superficially discussed; with an amiable smile on her lips she watches, supervises, participates, while her mind is intent on the prospect of Monday when her own personal life starts again.

Considerably more argumentative are the essays of the book I have already mentioned: *Mujer que sabe Latin. . . .* Many of them are centred on the myths of women; the myths that men have created about them. The aura of mystery surrounding a woman, her reputed unpredictability and contradictions which enable man to place her outside the range of his understanding, and so despise her and enslave her when he no longer desires her. The myth of female purity which she must guard as repository of man's honour, which forces the woman into a position of *"espera"*, waiting for man to make the first move in love, and depending on him to arrive at a full awareness of her sexuality. The taboos which surround her feminine functions relating to conception and maternity once again emphasize the unknown element of her nature and increase the gap which separates her from man. Thus she is pushed into a position of subjugation and into the necessity of having to use devious methods in order to achieve her ends for "hypocrisy is the answer of the oppressed" (p. 25).

Still on the theme of oppression, Rosario Castellanos addresses herself to the question of the language spoken in most of Latin America: Spanish, the tool of the masters and symbol of the privileges they enjoyed, originally used either to give commands or to communicate with one's equals. For centuries the "Americans" made little use of it, the Indians because of their ignorance, the Mestizos because of their timidity. For too long they have been silent, unable to express and assert themselves and *"larga costumbre de callar . . . entorpece la lengua"* (long habit of being quiet thickens the tongue, p. 177). Now the silence is broken and *"la palabra anda . . . como moneda para cambiar ideas"* (words go around like coins to exchange ideas, p. 179), but, like all coins, they have to be constantly polished to restore their pristine purity. And this is achieved by the use of exact terminology, by finding the expression that perfectly fits the experience, like "the arrow that hits the target", without in any sense betraying the reality which is being described.

We see then how, as well as being aware of the necessity of renovating Spanish, making it the Latin American language, Rosario Castellanos reveals also this aspect of the problem: how to transform a symbol of tyranny into the manifestation of identity and freedom. An experience not unlike that of the women who first ventured into writing adopting the language of men, to establish their position and assert their point of view.

Marta Brunet (1897-1967)

A generation older than Rosario Castellanos, the Chilean Marta Brunet already had attempted to break with the literary traditions which bound women writers and denounce the social conventions which enslaved her sex. Her novels and short stories, depicting the life of her people, are free from the detailed descriptions of places and situations traditionally expected within that type of narrative, and concentrate instead on the psychological realization of the characters, mainly women, who retain their intrinsic identity through their independence at the cost of becoming social misfits. Marta Brunet's language, a pure Castillian inherited from her Spanish mother, presented her readers with a style both rigorous, strong and logical, such as "only men could equal". What, however, mostly caught the attention of her critics was the audacity of her stories and the frankness of their erotic details.

Among the many characters of her fictional world recurs that of young Marisol, "Solita", the daughter of a middle-class family, who cannot reconcile herself to living within the conventional environment of her family and complying with the standards expected of her. Her mother, a beautiful, gentle and totally spineless creature, lives in a world of adorable distractions (*Obras completas*, 172); her father, strict and authoritarian, insists on his daughter not having an alarm clock, "for the subconscious must remind her of her waking hour, so as to extend his discipline even to the realm of sleep" (p. 181). Solita rebels against the tedium of her embroidery lessons and of games with the doll's house of her little friend Berta who "concentrated on this little world at her reach, reflection of the domestic one, which she cannot but accept . . .in the fulfilment of her feminine nature which will force through the years until it accomplishes the irrefutable destiny of all women" (p. 174). Against all this, Solita takes refuge in a world of her own, the world of her imagination, the only realizable escape for a girl of her age.

233

María Lopez, the heroine of the novel *María Nadie*, is another rebel against the family structure in which she has grown up and against the values it stands for. Being already an adult, she breaks away from it and chooses to live alone and work for her living. But she has to pay a heavy price for her independence; the loneliness she has chosen "is a mould tightly enveloping her body until it suffocates it" (ibid.:774). This is why she becomes "María Nadie", a nobody, while the people of the town where she has come to live, resentful and suspicious of her aloofness, turn against her, and call her "Mala Pajara" (evil bird). Love seems to come to her rescue in the form of an attractive, pleasure-seeking extroverted man with whom María knows moments of bliss, but also the agony of uncertitude, for he refuses to commit himself to any arrangemens which will limit his freedom. After a tormented pregnancy which ends in miscarriage, she realizes that it is ultimately better to live alone, than to be condemned to the "Servidumbre de un amor" (slavery of love).

Loneliness is the keynote in the life of Marta Brunet's characters, as the names and titles often imply. The protagonist of "Soledad de la sangre" (a story from *Aquas abajo*, 1949) is 36 years old, half of which time she has lived with her parents and the other half as a married woman. Industrious and economic, she is appreciated by her husband for being "hardworking as women should be". After so many years of work and devotion, she is allowed to spend some of the money she earns to buy a gramophone and a record which she has the luxury of playing once a week, after her husband has gone to sleep. Then music fills the core of her intimate world, awakening a vision of momentary happiness and glimpses of a past dream which, *"mirada verde para dulzor de su angre"* (memory of green eyes to sweeten her blood) fills the loneliness of her life. When the music ends she returns once again to being alone, "with nobody for her tenderness, to gaze at her and to light within her that burning which before had run through her blood and made her mouth quiver under the

234

trembling touch of her fingers." Alone, her sensuality and passion are once more frustrated. When her gramphone and disc are shattered (she would never allow them to be defiled at the hands of her husband's guest), she can only think of running away. But what awaits her outside is death and death means renouncing for ever the images of her memory. So she returns to her house to her loneliness "loaded with memories".

The spirit of independence of Marta Brunet's heroines, the revelation of the existence of a private world within the feminine mind, of an untapped well of sensuality, excluding the investigation and control of man, coupled with the classical form of her writing and the forceful directness of her style, which permitted no accusation of womanly sentimentality, proved a considerable challenge, unbearable at times, to her reading public. This reaction saddened the author and embittered her relationship with her own people. Breaking out of the literary moulds to which women's writings were expected to conform and exploring the secrets of the female mind, Marta Brunet can be said to have pioneered the movement of contemporary female authors in Latin America.

Like the Mexican Rosario Castellanos and the Chilean Marta Brunet, women writers all over the Latin American continent in the course of the last century have felt the need to speak out against the restrictions imposed on their language, to break the taboos which bound feminine behaviour, and denounce the tyranny of a male-dominated society.

Alfonsina Storni (1892-1938)

Such is the case of the Argentian Alfonsina Storni, one of the many illustrious contributors to Victoria Ocampo's review *Sur*, who began publishing her poems in 1916. Starting from the lyrical imagery of the "Ultraista" movement, she soon found a motif of inspiration in themes relating to the situation of women, the social and psychological stigmas which apply to them living in a *"patriarcado"*. Her comedy *El amo del mundo* (1927) is based on the theme that man, in spite of the flattery and courtship with which he surrounds woman, is her enemy, *"el enemigo dulce"*, and looks upon her as morally inferior: "Being man he thinks himself master of the world. Woman in relation to him can be the object of his whims, a distraction or even a moment of madness. But never another being of equal moral integrity". Already defiance of the conventions which for thousands of years have hampered women's emotional expression and prevented them from revealing their sensuousness and the passion of their desire, had found expression in her poetry. Let me quote from two poems from *Irremediablemente* published in 1919: *"Para decirte, amor, que to deseo,/Sin los rubores falsos del instinto,/ Estuve atada como Prometeo,/Pero una tarde me salí del cinto./San veinte siglos que movió mi mano . . ."* (p. 156) and: *"Pudiera ser que todo lo que en verso he sentido/No fuera mas que aquello que nunca pudo ser/No fuera mas que algo vedado y reprimido/De familia en familia, de mujer en mujer"* (p. 188) [To tell you, love, that I desire you, without the blushes which betray one's instinct, I was tied up like Prometheus; but one day I freed myself. My hand has shaken up twenty centuries . . . and: It might be that all I have felt in my verse was no more than what was not allowed to be, was no more than what had been forbidden and repressed from family to family, from woman to woman].

From *Ocre,* a later collection whose mood oscillates between tenderness and irony, come these provocative lines of "Saludo al hombre", whose sarcasm declares that the battle of the sexes has not yet reached its end: *"Con mayuscula èscriba tu nombre y te saludo/Hombre, mientra depongo mi feminino escudo/En sencilla y valiente confesión de derrota. Omnivoro nasciste para llevar la cota . . ."* (p. 270). [I write your name with a capital letter, and I greet you, Man, as I lay down my feminine shield, simply and bravely acknowledging my defeat. You were made to be omnivorous, in order to carry your superiority. . . .] Imagine how outrageous Alfonsina Storni's attitude must have appeared, particularly since her challenging words were strengthened by her action: she had a child out of wedlock. Her later work, however, overcomes the resentfulness and defiance whose objective had been the demythification of man so often quoted "el hombre pequeñito," — poor little man.

In 1934 Storni published *Mundo de siete pozos,* in which her poetry assumes an allegoric thoughtful character, as she centres her vision on cosmic themes. The tone moves from lyrical or satirical to epic; the style acquires a baroque richness which comes from the author's preoccupation with language and her desire to explore its symbols and possibilities (probably the influence of James Joyce's *Ulysses*, also felt by other Latin American writers). The quality of Alfonsina Storni's writing and the reputation which she finally gained formed the first step towards including women at the same level as men in the history of Argentinian literature. Storni moved from "poetess to poet", as Rachel Phillips ironically says in the title of her study. Recalling one of the things which Victoria Ocampo had stated, that "a woman cannot really write like a woman . . . until she no longer feels obliged to respond to attacks and defend her intellectual freedom and equality", one realizes the inevitable presence of a transitional stage during which she cannot as yet write with the sole purpose of "translating her thoughts, feelings and vision" ("Carta a Virginia Woolf", I, 15). Only then, no longer concerned with defending her position, will she be able to turn her mind to the tasks which confront every writer within the literary and historical context in which she lives.

It is difficult to separate the image of women writers from that of a militant feminist movement, just as it is difficult to destroy the assumption that the movement deprived women of their feminine qualities. This has been the impression of many, including even the more liberal and radically orientated thinkers.

In Latin America the feminist movement has been not only

misinterpreted and slandered but also exploited for political purposes, as we have already seen in the case of the Argentinian president Peron. A similar attitude was assumed by Rafael Trujillo, President of the Dominican Republic, who in 1940 proclaimed women's equal rights and called for the feminine vote (which was granted two years later). This he did in order to gain the alliance of one half of the population, and, more important, to appear a liberal-minded, benevolent dictator and whitewash his image after the uproar which the massacre of 15,000 Haïtians, ordered by him in 1937, had caused throughout the world.

Though political leaders have occasionally appeared to help the cause of women in order to manipulate them for their own ends, the social and economic situation in Latin America has been considerably responsible for the slower process of women's liberation. The cult of male dominance is in fact, partly at least, the result of poverty and underdevelopment. Men who are unable to maintain their self-respect by earning a reasonable living take it out on those weaker and more vulnerable than themselves. It could even be, paradoxically, that women encourage and expect aggressive behaviour in men, since only the strong and brutal are likely to prosper, or even survive, in the political environment of their nations.

This situation has compelled some women writers to leave their countries, both to escape political persecution and in order to be able to realize their creative project, away from the compulsions and restrictions which bound them at home and thwarted their freedom of expression. Among the non-intellectual and the working classes, however, women may have felt less the need for feminine emancipation, for where the system undermines basic human freedoms, the first fight is to secure the right to live.

Domitila Barrios de Chungara (1937-)

As long as this is threatened, men and women share and fight for a common cause. This is at least the view of Domitila, the wife of a Bolivian tin miner, who, though not a writer by profession, is nevertheless the author of a book called *Let me speak*. In its she describes the life and struggle against poverty and oppression which she and her people have suffered from time immemorial. Morally strong and physically brave — far more so than her husband — she has led the tin miners of Bolivia through over a decade of rebellion and, facing imprisonment and torture, has succeeded in uniting the women and involving them in the workers' strikes. One of the last episodes of her book, however, describes how when she was invited in 1975 to Mexico City for the Women's Year Conference she found that many of the topics discussed there did not relate to the needs of most Bolivian women, still fighting for the survival of their people, and she concluded: "It's not that I accept machismo, no. But I think that machismo is a weapon of imperialism, just like feminism is."

There is in the process of oppression and violence a system of hierarchy, as I have already mentioned. This is an aspect of what the Uruguayan Eduardo Galeano calls *"la violencia invisible"*, the undocumented acts of violence, which one, living in a constant state of fear, perpetrates against a weaker person: the husband, bullied all day at work, comes back home and takes it out on his wife. Living conditions can be such as to brutalize anyone's behaviour: the poor peasant, crippled in the war, who violates his young daughter (as narrated in a brief but highly dramatic account by the Mexican writer Judith Ortega Martinez) is an example of the perpetuation of violence.

Claribel Alegría (1924-)

Claribel Alegría's report on the condition of women in El Salvador offers a detailed and highly informative picture of the phenomenon to which I have referred: how, where poverty and injustice reign, women are the most victimized. Girls sent to make a living in the city where, seduced at an early age, they have no alternative but to become prostitutes, daughters deprived by their fathers of an education which might enable them to become economically independent, until the day they get married, passing from one system of patriarchy to another, are both the product of the process of oppression which generates more oppression. It is the same social situation which is exemplified by the last episode of Rosario Castellanos's story "Modesta Gomez". At the lowest level of this system of hierarchy is the mother who repeats the centuries-old rite of clitoridectomy on her baby daughter so that she will be less likely to go off with a man at an early age and will, instead, be prepared "to work harder". Thus, woman perpetuates the tradition of female victimization.

Claribel Alegría, whose commitment to the cause of women is clearly revealed in her report, is also a poetess and prose writer. In her book *El detén,* published in 1977, figure three women; a nun, Sor Mary Ann, Natalia, a divorcee sexually infatuated with Mark, and Karen, her 15-year-old daughter. Karen is studying in a convent where she has been sent by her father so that her education can be carried out without overburdening his responsibilities and, at the same time, away from the dangerous influence of Mark. It is through the perspective of the adolescent's feverish imagination that we are acquainted with the events which take place around her. "There can be many realities; besides the one we touch there is also the one we dream and the one we invent," (p. 50) states Karen.

The girl's mischievous manipulation of the people around her and her insight into the multiple levels at which they exist create a disturbingly lucid portrayal of the psychology of adults and of their relationships. We see how Mark takes advantage of Natalia's passionate attachment to him and revels in being cruel and in tantalizing her by his attentions to Karen, whose budding womanhood stimulates his sexual appetites; and how the tight-lipped nun, to whose special care Karen has schemingly entrusted herself, is both shocked and excited by the episodes which the girl narrates with apparent candour: "What did you feel when Mark touched you?" she morbidly asks. "Men are like animals . . ." (p. 42).

At the end of the book, both Natalia and the nun have reached a state of moral disintegration: Natalia utterly subjugated by her lover, the nun totally corrupted by the desire which the recounting of the girl's experiences has awoken. While a fleeting vision of the adolescent's future reveals the traumatic and warping effects of her early exposure to Mark's corrupting influence; Mark, on the other hand, appears to survive unscathed.

Claribel Alegría, though born in Nicaragua, was brought up in El Salvador, with which she feels closer emotional links. Now resident in Mallorca, she has returned to her country of adoption and become involved in its people's struggle for justice and freedom, as shown by her report on women. The oppression of the government and the exploitation and persecution of the peasants on behalf of the military now trained and supported by the US Army are the themes of some of her later poems. "La mujer del rio Sumpul", for example, describes at length the ordeal of a peasant woman who, having lost husband and sons in the battle, escapes from the guards and hides herself and her two youngest children by the water of the river Sumpul; her wounds are bleeding, her babies on the verge of crying and alerting the soldiers, while vultures fly low over their heads. The poetic language flows easily, like the waters of the river, like the language of the people sharing the fight of the guerrilla movement, whose life (as the history of all mesoamerican nations) blends with myths. A mythology of fierce gods and of angry volcanoes, a history of aggression and rebellious resistance which like pouring lava silently invades the "pueblo incandescente" (the aroused people) (cf. *Poesia Rebelde*).

Elsewhere, we read a brief poem, "Por las noches", in which Claribel Alegría evokes in her sleep the images of dead friends and wonders upon awakening whether they also have dreamt of her. Again, as in *El detén*, we find the allusion to realities beyond our perception; but the barrier between living and dead is broken, for the dead awake and share the dreams and aspirations of the living.

Elena Garro (1920-)

History, mythology and the unsuspected dimensions of reality are also the basis of Elena Garro's vision of Mexico. In 1963 she published a novel, *Los recuerdos del porvenir*, set during the presidency of Calles (1924-8) which illustrates episodes of political tyranny of that period. Among these, the most fierce was the persecution of members of the Church, which developed into a war known as *"la Guerra cristera"*.

Ixtepec, the town in which the action of the novel takes place, is occupied by a group of military under the command of General Francisco Rosa, the archetypal Latin American dictator. (It is interesting, incidentally, to observe how his characterization anticipates the many novels on dictatorship written at the end of the sixties and during the seventies throughout Latin America; for example, *Conversación en la catedral* (1969) by M. Vargas Llosa; *El secuestro del general* (1973) by Aguilera Malta; *Yo el supremo* (1974) by Roa Bastos; *El recurso del método* (1974) by A. Carpentier; *El otoño del patriarca* (1975) by G. García Márquez.)

Many are the people, generally Amerindians, who are imprisoned and executed on the orders of Francisco Rosa. Each morning the town awakens to the spectacle of new corpses hanging from the trees. Their death is the manifestation of the state of mind of the general, who is desperately in love with a girl he has stolen from another town and brought along with him. She, Julia, is very beautiful, magically so; her beauty radiates all over the people around her, but she does not respond to the love of Francisco Rosa who nightly vents his frustration and unhappiness upon his victims.

The macabre figure of the despot, aloof and remote in his cruelty, symbol of death and extermination, bears some of the mythical connotations of the dictator in *El Señor Presidente* by

Miguel Angel Asturias. But many other elements concur to form the material of this book. The magic is not limited to Julia's appearance (she is silently watched strolling at sunset in her satin dress on the arm of the general, looking pale and sad) but also contaminates other characters and their perception of reality. Living in a state of tyranny, when there is no hope for the future, time loses its progressive rhythm. In the house of the Moncadas (one of the most eminent families of the town) the clock is stopped every night at 9.00; its inhabitants then enter a new time, *"nuevo y melancólico"*, whose images break the barrier between the past and the future: "Martin remembered his death. He saw it . . . already accomplished in the past . . ." (p. 83). With the children, fantasy compensates for their dissatisfied aspirations and dreams: "The whole house travelled through the sky, entered the milky way and then fell noiselessly back in its own place . . ." (p.33). To describe the condition of violence and terror in which the people live, the author resorts to surrealistic images which blossom into poetic vision and humorous situations. Felipe Hurtado, Julia's ex-lover who has followed her here, personifies at once the spirit of rebellion and the triumph against tyranny; his eyes are described as *"hondos con rios y con ovejas que bailaban tristes adentro de ellos"* — deep with streams and sheep that sadly danced within them (p. 39). One night he and Julia manage to flee away on his horse. Julia's laughter is heard then for the first and last time; she is never to be seen again, except as a fleeting image in some other town.

Juan Cariño, who runs a brothel, is the owner of a large number of dictionaries. By these he hopes to keep down the number of atrocities which are continuously occurring in the town for "Words were dangerous because they existed on their own; to prohibit dictionaries would avoid unimaginable catastrophes" (p.59). So every day he chases the cruel words which have escaped the dictionaries, in order to put them back in the books and avoid a repetition of last night's murders.

Contrasting with Julia who fades away from the narrative, Isabel, the third of the Moncadas children, strikes the reader by the wilfulness and determination of her character. She looks upon the prospect of a conventional marriage with boredom and a sense of humiliation. The figure of Francisco Rosa, instead, fills her with excitement and the prospect of becoming his mistress becomes her living passion. And so determined is she that he eventually invites her to replace Julia in his bed. Once there, however, he is disconcerted by how dominant her presence is in the room — "and the room filled with lianas and fleshy leaves. There was no more room for him" (p. 247).

The end of the novel sees the death of the three Moncada children; dreams are destroyed by tyranny: *"Aqui la ilusion se paga con la vida"* — "Here one pays for one's illusions with life" (p. 264), as Felipe Hurtado has said. But the tyrant also is destroyed by the open hostility of Ixtepec which has by now closed its ranks against him: "He was pursued by mouthless screams . . . he advanced through endless valleys and only reached the insult of a tree and the threat of a roof" (p. 182).

The study of the Indian mentality and the ambiguous relationship between the indigenous population of Mexico, with its legends and beliefs, and the incredulous *"criollos"*, with their fictitious sense of reality and personal superiority, form the theme of a story by Elena Garro entitled "El arbol". Marta and the Indian Luisita are its two characters. The first looks on the other with contempt: "Many of her relatives and friends thought that the Indians were much closer to animals than to man and they were right". In fact, as it turns out, the Indian woman is much more familiar with the tools of civilization (showers and telephone) than Marta thinks. Yet the *"criolla"* still believes that it is easy to manage the Indian by making use of superstitions: "It was enough to name the devil." Only later, too late, does Marta realize that what she considers to be Luisita's silly beliefs is a concrete awareness of evil which the more sophisticated mind has lost, that the childish voice and apparently naive ways of the Indian woman disguise a cruelty and a wisdom a thousand years old.

It is then that the magic evoked by Luisita begins to invade Marta's household: "El arbol seco", the tree on which the Indian woman had unloaded her secret sins and which dried out afterwards, "entered the room; the whole night was drying within the walls and the dried-out curtains". And with it enters the concept of the sacrifice which must be performed, for Marta too has heard Luisa's confession and she too will have to die, like the tree.

Latin American reality — so vast and varied, steeped in the legendary, living through historic events which can only be referred to in epic terms — presents a formidable challenge to those authors who aim at describing the traditions and the life of their people. It is a reality whose dimensions are bigger than life, that combines opposed elements and therefore commands in its literary image the unorthodox juxtaposition of different categories. Accordingly, each author seeks those literary devices which she considers most appropriate for the recreation of her artistic vision.

Armonía Somers (1920-)

The stories of the Uruguayan Armonía Somers present traits which range from the humorous to the macabre. To describe a situation which she considers to stretch beyond credibility, she too resorts to the use of surrealistic images which, combined with a kind of black humour create effects of unique quality. I am thinking, for instance, of her collection *Mis hombres flacos* and of the story "Las mulas", in which a man figures who, literally unable to keep his food down, is in fact a skeleton. Imagine the sensation he creates walking into shops, sitting in a café, approaching a prostitute, catching a bus. This is balanced by the revulsion he feels for normal human beings: " '*Gusanos gusanos' los apostrofó. . . . Así los vería también Diós desde arriba, enfrascados en su pretensión de larvas*

245

eternas.'' (*Todos los cuentos*, 13) (Worms, worms, he addressed them. . . . God would also see them like this, enwrapped in their pretension of eternal larvae.)

Suffering from unbearable pains in his guts, he dashes for a pharmacy against the fast oncoming traffic, defying a motorcyclist, one of those young men whom he detested because ''they would ride with their eyes open, towards the abyss, or would live all their lives with no reason, as if they had an instinct on the tip of their noses which protected them from all danger'' (p. 16). In order to avoid him, the motorcyclist swerves and crashes into a lorry. All that is left of him is a hand emerging from under the metal: ''A hand still alive, full of tenderness, its potential life denied for ever''. A hand which declares all the vulnerability and pathos of being young and human, helpless in the face of hatred.

In ''La calle del viento norte'', coarse realism blends with elements of the supernatural, represented by the north wind under whose tyranny live the inhabitants of a poor and desolate village. Only one man can keep check of the north wind, a man who in his youth was knocked unconscious by it and consequently lost his wits. Only he is capable of restoring the peace of mind of the villagers. Living alone in a hovel by the church, when the wind starts he gets up from his ragged couch and, dragging his filthy boots on, goes to close the gate through which it enters: ''Of course, it gets into the bars and screams like a prisoner. But that is only his breath. The actual body remains struggling outside,'' (p. 66) says the halfwitted man, and night after night the sound of his boots dragging to close the gate restores the calm in the village. But one day he is killed: a tribunal is installed in the filthy hovel whose stench is enough to disqualify some of the attendants who, being too *''maricas''* to bear it, would have never been able to commit the murder. As the possible suspects are eliminated one by one, the actual criminal is left to remove those filthy boots from the dead man and take over from him, nightly repeating the ceremony which will allow the people to feel once again protected from the wind.

In "Muerte por alacrán", the macabre moves into a totally different sphere: the luxurious holiday house of some very rich people where, in the middle of the hottest summer afternoon, fire logs are being delivered "so that they might not be overtaken by anyone, not even by the first rain" (p. 97), as sarcastically comments one of the two lorry drivers.

There is a scorpion among the logs and the butler of the house is told of this after the delivery, just as the lorry drives off. This announcement totally breaks down the composure of the man just described as having "the expression of a lock, one of those made with a chisel for a period-coffer" (p. 98). He starts a frantic search (for scorpion poison is deadly in tropical lands) and, understandably enough, he can see scorpion tails everywhere: in "the ceiling beams which happened to be varnished scorpion-colour" (p. 101), in the twisted corner of the cover of a diary. As he turns the contents of the bedrooms upside down, the secret life of his employers is revealed to him: the sexual fantasies of the teenage daughter, the sordid business deals of the master who caused the bankruptcy and suicide of a colleague, and the amorous intrigues of the mistress who "was a carrier of unmade beds as others are of typhus" (p. 106).

At the moment when the masters return to confront the ransacked house and the totally dishevelled butler, the scorpion, still in the lorry, in a little crevice behind the seats of the drivers, emerges from his hide-out following "his last hallucinatory scheme" and begins "to hesitate at the sight of the two necks . . . which emerged above the seats" (p. 107).

There is an impressionistic and at the same time incisive quality in Somers's diction, a disturbing ability to allude to evil which make her writings totally unique. Here and elsewhere in her stories the reader finds herself oscillating between laughter and shivers, asking herself whether she is confronted with a "cautionary" tale, a social satire or a tantalizing joke and is thus kept in a constant state of expectation and wonder.

Commitment to the social cause in general and in particular to the position of women in society; breaking down the moral and sexual taboos which have bound and limited women's freedom of expression over the centuries; asserting the same rights as men to follow all intellectual pursuits; and finally exploring the possibilities which language offers in order to create one's own form of writing other than the passive imitation of already established patterns; these have been the aims of Latin American women writers during the last half century. As these aims are progressively being achieved, there seems to be among the younger generation a sense of liberation and an eagerness to enter new fields of self-expression, as we have seen in the case of Somers.

Cristina Peri Rossi (1941-)

Another Uruguayan, Cristina Peri Rossi (1941), living in exile in Spain since 1972, has undergone during the course of her writing career, which began in the early sixties, a rapid process of emancipation from the apparently derivative forms of some of her first works, and a development which has culminated in the creation of a new and personal style.

In 1969 she published *Los museos abandonados*. In it is a long story, "Los estraños objetos voladores", which presents the realistic and humorous picture of an old couple in the rural setting of Uruguay, against the surrealistic presence of a strange flying object in the sky, whose malevolent influence disrupts the personality of the main character, Lautaro. Already one is struck by the image association and the verbal richness of the writing. Feeling persecuted and distraught by the disappearance of half his face (no doubt "they" had taken it away from him) and by the fear that with only half a mouth left his intake of air might no longer be sufficient, for he was

248

getting old and "it was no longer the case of skimping on air for his lungs" (p. 35), Lautaro examines the interior of his house to see if anything else had disappeared. Here too, he meets with an unfriendly atmosphere: "in the dining-room the furniture had the same mocking and ambiguous look of everyday" (p. 42).

"They", the unknown responsible, as unknown as the object flying overhead, identify in Lautaro's mind with those who rule and are arbitrarily in charge of the life of people like him — in other words, the government, of whose activities he feels both ignorant and suspicious: "As for the government, he had only seen it once when it came to give a talk on the sacrifices that they must do so that the country got back on its feet" (p.37).

Holding on to his trousers (for fear that they also might be stolen) he goes to the doctor, a bitter man bored with having to prescribe analgesics and sedatives, who tries to lighten the burden of his boredom by sporadically sleeping with his nurse. She resignedly accepts the situation — "with that somewhat obscene plasticity of women who accept a situation they can't easily change" (p. 55), hoping that one day he will marry her.

When Lautaro returns home he is surprised to see how empty the landscape is all around him: "The road was peeling like a dry fruit" (p. 73). Finally, as he can't even find his house, he looks up to the flying object and sees that it has also disappeared. "They" have taken it away, too, is the bitter, though resigned conclusion of the old peasant.

Lautaro's wife, María, is the sort of woman who has always waited for her husband at home, whenever he has gone to the town to do "business" and discuss events with other people. In the house she performs her duties, and upon his return listens rather sceptically to his enthusiastic descriptions of all the wonderful things available in the big markets. Depending on her innate common sense, she wonders why people need to use gadgets and machines, and are not satisfied with their hands which, apart from not needing constant attention and not running the risk of breaking up, are also capable of absolutely everything: they can "seize, gather, sow, shine, pile, paint, caress, recognise, touch hot and cold, sew, nail, defrost the grass, take the lice off the chickens, hold the hoe, nurse the trees, cook, water the plants, embroider, mend socks, take stones out of wells, dig, erect walls, milk, plant nails, cross oneself, touch the holy water, greet, take one's hat off, thread needles, shell beans, command, take feathers off birds, hang out the washing, sweep, and most of them even know how to write" (p. 29).

Such a virtuous display of vocabulary illustrates Peri Rossi's concern and preoccupation with language; that sense of its inadequacy felt by many authors, but perhaps more strongly in Latin America where the language in use, originating from another continent, is not only insufficient to express a reality infinitely richer, but also bears the mark of the dominion of which it has been instrument over several centuries (as Rosario Castellanos said in *Mujer que sabe Latin . . .*). Hence, the author feels that writing not only involves a constant fight between her creative force and the restriction which language imposes, a concept which we have already considered in relation to Octavio Paz, but also an endless attempt to liberate oneself from these restrictions, renew the language and impress upon it the identity of the new continent. This condition forms the inspiration of several of Cristina Peri Rossi's poems, some of which appear in *Diáspora*. If only speech were allowed to flow unhampered by rules! *"Amabas a las niñas/porque su lenguaje/volaba libre/ . . . desconociendo las leyes fundamentales . . ."* (p. 58) (you loved children because their language flies freely, ignoring the fundamental laws . . .). If it could be as instinctive and spontaneous as the manifestations of our emotions *"Si el lenguaje . . . fuera el modo/de hacer el amor. . ./de meterme entro tu pelo"* (p. 20) (if only language were the way of making love, wrapping myself in your hair). The frustrations which language entails and the desire to rebel against its laws, are often manifested in Peri Rossi by outbursts of poetry within prose narrative. This has been frequently the case in her earlier work, of which the story "Los trapecistas" is an example. In it the love theme is dramatically entwined with that of political persecution and leads to the tragic conclusion: Maria Teresa is denounced, though the identity of the denouncer is deliberately left ambiguous; "The list, Maria Teresa, was already so long without your name, that I could easily not have resigned myself to adding yours . . ."

It is a story in which images of sensuality and cruelty combine, where love becomes synonymous with persecution: ". . . Y las noches eran venereas/Noches de balsamo y vigilia,/de dicha y sentinela/de vértigo y de celo" (Nights belonged to Venus/balmy wakeful nights/of happiness and alarm/vertigo and passion), reflecting the spiritual and political atmosphere of Uruguay (it was written in 1970 before Peri Rossi left the country). Only the rhythm and images of poetry can project the mounting tension and the growing elements of fear and doom leading to the final sacrifice: "Sustituir el circo y el león con el cristiano adentro/por cualquier calle el ejercito y uno de nosotros al centro bailando" (To substitute the circus, the lion and the Christian inside/with any street, the soldiers and one of us dancing in the middle).

When finally the loved one is betrayed — "María Teresa I did not intend to make them such a gift" — the search, the arrest and the following guilt and pain are, once again, expressed in poetic metaphors: "Nuestra casa, revuelta y revisada,/niña desvestida . . . este tiempo duro/como un pan muy viejo que me niego a masticar/va envolviendome con su humo" (Our house searched and turned upside-down like a girl undressed(. . .) time as hard/as the stale bread which I refuse to chew is enwrapping me with its smoke), and so is the fear that goes on, that no sacrifice can appease: "Fear, Maria Teresa, of the circus."

The stories from Peri Rossi's latest collection, *El museo de los*

251

esfuerzos inútiles, reveal a newly found control of language and the ability to handle a variety of themes with directness and clarity without losing the power of images nor stopping the flow of a poetic vision. The author challenges sexual conventions and the traditional distinction of roles; a startling statement like: "We have the sex they impose on us — at most we accept it" (p. 173), appears in the middle of a story, and opens up a totally ambiguous set of meanings adding new facets to the situation described. Men's and women's inability to break up a deteriorated amorous situation, the destructive parasitical function of those who "give themselves for life" demanding at the same time a life in return, these are some of the myths of love which she attacks with caustic sarcasm and convincingly destroys without the hint of a polemic accent or the use of rhetoric images.

Highly evocative and verging on the metaphysical is the story "El corredor tropieza", which reads as a metaphor of the author's aspirations of her need to break out of the expected patterns and, ultimately, of the subversive function of the writer. It is the story of a long-distance runner near to breaking the all-time speed record. Proud of his steady pace, he is disturbed by the recent theory that light does not move at a constant speed, as has so far been believed. This announcement, which breaks the assumed pattern of cosmic order, while at first filling him with a sense of personal pride for being able to hold a rhythm of movement more exact than that of light, suggests that he too can break out of the expected pattern of action which his trainer and the public demand. While still racing, he begins to think in terms totally alienated from the ambitions of a runner: of stopping and lying on the grass verges by the side of the track, looking up at the trees and at the patterns which the branches and the flying birds make against the blue sky. For him, too, as for the light, "his speed was constant but got a strong desire to stop" (p.36). The story suddenly ends with a sentence brief yet tense with meaning and poetic expectation: *"Y elevó los ojos hacia el cielo"* (and he lifted his eyes to the sky).

With this final note, I should like to end my observations on women in Latin American literature which, if by no means comprehensive, should prove sufficiently panoramic to give the reader an idea of the ordeals which the women have come through, of the changes they have managed to bring about and of the development they have achieved both on an individual and on a general basis, as members of a class of people considerably undervalued and repressed within the stratification of their society. I hope to have shown how, having fought against the conventions which bound them and having established the equality of their intellectual rights, women are emerging as authors of strong individual identity, each one seeking a personal answer to the literary problems which confront her and a long-term solution to the political situation in which her country labours and suffers.

REFERENCES

Alegría, Claribel, 1977, *El detén*, Barcelona, Lumen.
Brunet, Marta, 1963, *Obras completas*, Santiago de Chile, Zig-Zag.
Domitila (with Noema Viezzer), 1978, *Let Me Speak*, London, Monthly Review Press.
Castellanos, Rosario, 1964, *Convidados de agosto*, Mexico.
Castellanos, Rosario, 1971, *Album de familia*, Mexico, Juan Mortiz.
Castellanos, Rosario, 1973, *Mujer que sabe Latin. . . .*, Mexico, Secretaria de Educación Publica.
de la Cruz, Juana Inés, 1959[10], *Obras escogidas*, Mexico, Austral.
Garro, Elena, 1963, *Los recuerdos del porvenir*, Mexico, Joaquin Mortiz.
Lavrin, Asunción, 1978, *Latin American Women: Historic Perspectives*, Westport, Conn./London.
Macía, Anna, 1972, *Against all Odds*, Connecticut, Greenwood Press.
Meyer, Doris, 1979, *Victoria Ocampo*, New York, George Braziller.
Miller, Yvette E., & Charles M. Tatum, 1977, *Latin American Women*

Writers: Yesterday and Today, Pittsburgh, Latin American Literary Review.

Mistral, Gabriela, 1961, *Lecturas para mujeres,* San Salvador, Ministerio de Educación.

Mistral, Gabriela, 1962, *Obras completas,* Madrid, Aguilar.

Mistral, Gabriela, (1922) 1969, *Desolación,* Madrid, Espasa-Calpe.

Ocampo, Victoria, 1935, *Testimonios,* Vol. I, Madrid, Revista de Occidente.

Ocampo, Victoria, 1941, *Testimonios,* Vol. II, Buenos Aires, Sur.

Peri Rossi, Cristina, 1969, *Los museos abandonados,* Montevideo, Bolsilibros, Arca.

Peri Rossi, Cristina, 1976, *Diáspora,* Barcelona, Lumen.

Peri Rossi, Cristina, 1983, *El museo de los esfuerzos inútiles,* Barcelona, Seix Barral.

Pescatello, Ann, 1973, *Female and Male in Latin America,* Pittsburgh.

Phillips, Rachel, 1975, *Alfonsina Storni, From Poetess to Poet,* London, Thamesis.

Poesia Rebelde, 1982, published by El Salvador Solidarity Campaign, London.

Randall, Margaret, 1981, *Sandino's Daughters,* London, Zed Press.

Rosenbaum, Sidonia, 1945, *Modern Women Poets of Spanish America,* New York.

Somers, Armonia, 1967, *Todos los cuentos,* Montevideo, Arca.

Storni, Alfonsina, 1919, *Irremediablemente,* Buenos Aires, Soc. Coop. Ed. Ltd.

INTERVIEW WITH CRISTINA PERI ROSSI
(URUGUAY)

PSICHE HUGHES

Cristina Peri Rossi was born in Montevideo in 1941. Since 1972 she has been living as an exile in Barcelona. She is the author of several volumes of poetry: *Evohe* (1971), *Descripción de un naufragio* (1974), *Diáspora* (1976) and *Linguistica general* (1979). She has also published collections of short stories: *Viviendo* (1963), *Los museos abandonados* (1969), *Indicios Pánicos* (1970), *La tarde del dinosaurio* (1976), *La rebelión de los niños* (1980) and *El museo de los esfuerzos inútiles* (1983). In addition she has written two novels: *El libro de mis primos* (1969) and *La nave de los locos* (1984).

Cristina Peri Rossi is at present correspondent of the Spanish newspaper *El País*.

This interview took place in the spring of 1984.

Why do you think there are so few women writers in Latin America in comparison with the number of male writers of international reputation?

One of the reasons why there are less women writers than men in Latin America is the enforcement of the traditional female role which still occurs in our countries, especially in the least developed ones whose social customs are still those of the last century. In many cases, the Latin American woman is still limited to the domestic and family world with a specific set of duties. As such, she is the victim of circumstances which have prevented her from developing a personal cultural life and a specific space around herself, what Virginia Woolf called a "room of her own".

Do you know whether women writers active now in Latin America are writing more prose, drama or poetry?

I believe that the general tendency so far has been for women

255

to write more poetry than prose. In Mexico and Argentina, for example, there have been and there are many women who have written poetry of high quality. The reasons for this are many and complex. The principal one is that poetry, whilst it is a rigorous and exacting discipline as far as expression and language use are concerned, needs less time and less space than a long term project like a novel. Also, traditionally, lyrical poetry (and I mainly refer myself to the poetry which has been written by Latin American women) deals principally with emotions, sensitiveness and affection, all of which have been traditionally the private lot of women, attributed to women. The world for men, emotions for women. . . . To write a novel, on the other hand, almost always implies a worldly vision and a rich vital experience of life, neither of them generally within the reach of the Latin American woman.

Do women writers in Latin America form an intellectual élite or do they integrate with the rest of the population, try to communicate with them and interpret their desires and amibition?

It is difficult to generalize and see the Latin American countries at the same level of economic, political and social development. In fact, Latin America is a series of countries of different races, different origin and in many cases with a different history. I am not happy talking of Latin American writers in general when their countries are so different, without distinguishing between the one who lives in a large industrial town in Brazil or in Buenos Aires and the one from a village in Peru or in Ecuador.

My personal experience is very limited because I only know Uruguay, and Argentina a little. I do not know the rest of Latin America, even though I know the work of many of its women. Up to say 1950, there was a series of women writers, particularly Argentinian writers, belonging to a class which may be described as an intellectual élite. But from 1950 onwards, during the period of great economic and social crisis in Latin America, I believe that women writers have been as politically committed as their male colleagues and have reflected the great conflict of our countries as much as men have done.

In general, the work of women in Latin America has great difficulty in crossing national frontiers. There are some Mexican women writers, for example, who are very much in touch with the questions of their country and yet they are only known in Mexico. It is very hard for a writer who has not travelled and has always lived in her own country to have her works known outside the geographical context in which she lives. In Latin America the frontiers are real barriers against communication among the various nations, in spite of their common language. Also, publishing houses in Latin America are on such tight budget that that in itself prevents books from being known outside their countries of origin.

How are Latin American women writers received by the society to which they belong? Are they admired, criticized, or ignored? Are they treated with the same respect with which men writers are treated?

The very existence of the word "poetess" which has a pejorative connotation, reflects the fact that society does not treat a man and a woman writing poetry the same way. In general, female poets (and I use this term to avoid the word "poetess") are considered capable of writing poetry within the terms of what I would call "official literature", a decorative literature. Certain Central American politicians, for instance, considered it to be a matter of good taste to have wives who could write occasional verse, at public occasions. As a toast, during a banquet, it was not uncommon for the wife of a particular minister to get up and recite four or five lines of homage to the national flag or to the dictator in power. Within what is considered "official literature" in Latin America, the attitude towards women has been ambiguous:

on the one hand it is considered proper for them to write decorative, incidental (and accidental) poetry; on the other hand we see how the very application of the word "poetess" carries slighting connotations.

With regard to what is not "official literature", that is real literature, the attitude towards women cannot be generalized. In some cases, and I am thinking particularly of the biography of the Latin American woman poet *par excellence* the Brazilian Clarice Lispector, we see the struggle she had in order to write within the social context in which she operated, in order to write. In other cases, there has been admiration but it has been ambivalent. I know of instances of people praising the beauty of a woman writer, who deserves to be praised for her work. Elsewhere, they criticize women when they no longer accomplish the traditional feminine literary role and instead compose literature of a more liberated or ambiguous kind. There is no doubt that the attitude towards women writers in Latin America is permanently ambivalent and that at the same time it reflects the uneasiness of men in the face of a woman who performs an activity which until then has been the exclusive purview of the male sex.

In Latin America who writes radio serials, the text of soap operas, the novelettes and short stories of magazines? Is it men or is it women? And, as far as you know, does this kind of writing reflect the influence of the European and or North American culture or is it based on the Latin American scene?

I confess that I am not in a good position to answer this question. First, I have been away from Latin America for twelve years. Secondly, my disregard of commercial literature has made me not pay too much attention to its manifestations. In order to answer you I must say this. I believe that the commercial literature on the radio, television and magazines has been created by both men and women but destined principally for feminine public. It seems to me that the writer is of less interest than the public at which the work is aimed. The programmes, both on radio and television, have been for several years even in countries of a higher cultural level like Uruguay and Argentina, the daily nourishment, a permanent form of escapism and alienation for women of all social classes.

As for the world which these programmes and this kind of commercial literature reflect, I believe it is a fictitious world, specially created to compensate for the poverty of reality, the conflicts of reality. The problems they present are generally of a sentimental nature. Hardly ever of a social or political one. Moreover they reflect a universal model. There is no difference in the style and content of North or South American serials and there is not much difference between those made by men and women for the daily consumption of housewives of any social class. In all cases it seems to me that this kind of art accentuates the most trivial, the most banal aspects of life and in general deforms the expression of sentiments and emotions and creates a sort of sentimental mystification of life totally removed from the real conflicts of existence.

Do you think that Latin American writers of today intend to break the moral and sexual taboos which have been imposed on women and society for thousands of years? If so, do you believe this is done more by women than by men?

Once again, one cannot generalize because men and women writers of different Latin American countries obviously reflect different realities. Your question can only be answered by analysing one by one the case of each individual writer. On the whole, I do not know whether most writers have been consciously aiming at breaking social and sexual taboos. One must not forget that many of them have lived during the 1970s, through a process of great political and social conflicts. The exacerbation of these conflicts in the face of the great dictatorships of the Southern Cone for example, has produced some specific consequences for literature causing it to give priority to social and political problems. Therefore, all the revolutionary and subversive intents of the writers have been directed towards certain fields, neglecting others. All the same, I think that there are some instances, mine among them, of authors who have realized that it is not only a matter of denouncing political problems, but also of denouncing the fixed roles and all the forms of social oppressions which still apply in Latin America.

Among Latin American intellectuals what is the general opinion about feminism and what attitude do critics assume faced with a feminist writer?

Feminism has been problematic in Latin American countries. First, for the reason I gave in my previous answer: the priority writers have given to the political struggle, justified by political tyrannies and by the economic crisis which the continent has suffered and is still suffering. This has pushed other struggles, equally justified, in the background.

Feminism has appeared only very recently in Latin America and in a very tentative form. All the same it has created great problems and embarrassment for men, generally quite satisfied and complacent when watching women accomplish the role allotted to them. This embarrassment has manifested itself in attitudes of great ambiguity among intellectuals faced with women writers who assume a positively feminist attitude. In some cases what has happened is that men have superficially accepted the revindication of feminism. This is a false and dangerous way of adopting feminist ideas. What I mean is that men continue being *"machistas"* and only consider it necessary to change some gestures and some forms of behaviour towards women. I think this is what has happened with many male writers and intellectuals in Latin America who have realized that they could not go on with the traditional manifestations of machismo. All they have done is to change for the time being some of their attitudes, but in the daily contact with their wives or sweethearts, I do not think their sexual and social behaviour has changed at all. These changes of course cannot occur suddenly. Machismo is a form of alienation, I'm sure of this. The process of integration is slow and needs a lot of deep thought.

My personal experience tells me that, faced with a feminist writer or even just a woman writer who does not play her habitual role, that is, for example, the poetess who writes occasional verse for toasts and ceremonies, male writers feel uncomfortable. They feel confronted with a person out of her natural place. A person who calls into question their own position, who makes them feel unhappy by just being there. This is of course a permanent source of a dialectic process of conflict. I believe that a feminist woman writer, even though she is not necessarily so in a militant way, creates a kind of bad conscience in men and therefore their relationship with this kind of woman is generally awkward.

As for the critics, I believe that they can be similarly classified. Although it is easier to analyse a text without having to refer to the author, I have observed that when the text breaks with a traditional scheme both in its content and in its form, it creates a very embarrassing situation for the critic who would of course prefer that the author of this text were either already dead or someone with no apparent sex. Someone who is just a mind and an abstraction.

Is there any difference in the form of criticism which men and women write in Latin America?

Only recently have women had access to critical activities in Latin America. Principally because these activities require a formation which women did not have. Also because the language, the apparatus necessary to exercise criticism, had already been chosen by men. One had to learn it as one learns any other form of knowledge. This explains the fact that there are less women than men involved in critical work in Latin America. The few women critics in existence, however, have shown deep sensitivity and a perception which in my opinion reflect a richer, deeper and more flexible understanding of literature.

What do you think and what do Latin American women writers think of European women and of their position in relation to men and to their society?

I am glad you have asked me this question because it is a subject on which I have reflected a lot. Having lived both in Latin America and in Europe, I have been able to observe the curious and different relationships established between women writers of the two continents. I would say there is a phenomenon of reciprocal admiration and at times, of course, also of reciprocal interests. Admiration because the conditions in which Latin American and European female writers work are different. For a European a Mexican woman writer, for example, is the object of great admiration because, in order to publish a poem or a book of poems, she has had to fight against a quantity of hostile factors which in Europe have already been overcome. She has had to break with her traditional role and make a place for herself in the intellectual world exclusive to men. All this requires great courage and energy and provokes the admiration of European women who have lived and succeeded in another context.

On the other hand, Latin American women writers in contact with their European colleagues have realized to what extent it is easier in Europe for women to write and to create. Women here have already been accepted. This has caused a deeper awareness of our situation in Latin America. It has made us understand that it is not only a matter of improving the economic and political conditions of our countries but also of effecting a social revolution. Personally, I have felt as much at home with European women writers as with Latin

American. From them I have understood that the personal effort I had made in order to be able to write and publish, and free myself of the myths and taboos involved in my feminine role, is something that they had already done. This put me on a level of sisterhood with all European writers whatever language they used.

Do many Latin American women writers leave their countries and, if so, why?

The case of Latin American women writers living outside their country or even in other Latin American countries is not frequent. The insecurity of the social and material position in which women find themselves in Latin America, their dependence on their social role and in many cases their economic dependence on men prevent them from leaving their homes. On the other hand, of course, they all share the dream of travelling to Europe, of knowing Europe. But this does not mean wanting to establish themselves there. There are writers in exile, of course, a much more dramatic condition in which some Latin American intellectuals and artists have lived in the last ten years, but, as you know, they are a minority.

The greater majority of women have preferred to remain in their countries, even if this limits their chance of writing and being published because their work might be forbidden there, rather than facing that option. They have decided against having to start life afresh in another country and having to find an opening in other societies which, as well as proving protective towards them, might exact a higher level of intellectual performance. Therefore there are very few women writers in exile and very few artists by profession who at present live in Europe.

I would now like to ask you some questions concerning your own work. I have noticed that, in spite of the inevitable changes and developments, there are some recurring constants. As with many Latin American writers I think that you feel a strong preoccupation with language and are urged by the necessity to renovate it. This is noticeable in the use you make of syntax, punctuation, images, word-associations, neologisms and "genres". The position of the writer vis-à-vis the language she uses and her continuous frustration is something which you express in many of your poems. I am thinking of some poems from Diáspora. *May I quote? "If only language were the way of making love, of wrapping myself in your hair . . ." or: "You loved children because their language flies freely, ignoring the fundamental laws. . . ." And elsewhere: "You stopped talking out of sheer prudence, then out of annoyance, finally to punish the words." Would you like to comment on this, please?*

It is a complex question which involves a certain amount of clarification. My work has been constant, preoccupied with language not only in the poems but also in the stories. I refer in particular to the book *The Rebellion of the Children*, in which I often refer to language as a manifestation of social oppression, being institutionalized and posing a permanent dialectic relationship between its official and personal usage.

Many Latin American writers who have contemplated a literary revolution, as well as social and political, have believed that to change a society implies also a free and more creative use of language. Accordingly they have set out to make frequent breaks with the traditional linguistic structures and, above all, with literary genres and these have undertaken a total transformation in contemporary literatures. Novels in our countries are much less formal, much less along the patterns of nineteenth century novels than they were at the beginning of the century. In the same way, short stories, which are in great supply in Latin America, have broken the conventional rules and often been converted some into aphorisms, others into a kind of prose poem or into a vignette. There is a tendency not to accept the conventional patterns of "genres" as a symbolic way of breaking with the limitations of reality.

I too have felt the same necessity of forcing literary forms, of utilizing a quantity of personally imaginative and creative techniques to establish my own identity outside the norm. Any kind of norm. I think this has been the great contribution of contemporary Latin American literature: the freedom that it has achieved. I imagine that literature has been the only territory of real freedom that we Latin Americans have had for a long time. We, especially the exiled, who have been able to publish all we have written. Personally, I consider myself a rebel against all laws. Literature has been the space which has permitted any transgression. I think this is the key word which explains most of the work of Latin American writers: transgression, the desire to break with norms and create a proper time and space.

Latin American reality is so complex and so rich in landscapes which change rapidly from one place to another in the same country that it has been too difficult to enclose it in forms. In spite of the wealth of language, we still lack the words to name the enormous number of nuances and shades of this reality, accounting for the fact that the imaginary is also a form of it. These poems of mine from which you quote are no more than a way of expressing exactly the poverty of traditional inherited language in the face of this multiple, complex, contradictory reality. I believe that almost all Latin American writers have felt on the edge of the genesis. Neruda's poetry, for example, is a way of giving a permanent name to this multiplicity of Latin America. The task, of course, is almost impossible. We have to be like gods to be able to name all that exists. In the poems which you mentioned I reduced this challenge to circumstances purely personal.

Museums feature in your first collection of stories of 1969 and also in the last collection of 1983, and these museums are always old, deserted, abandoned, and have succumbed to dust and disorder. Am

I correct in attributing to them a symbolic function? Do they constitute a reflection of the society in which we live?

I am aware that the title of my last book in relation to my second one creates a certain confusion. But this confusion does not bother me. I have deliberately played with it. In actual fact your interpretation is correct. Both in poems and in prose I have used museums as allegory, more than as a symbol, because they are a complex symbol. Museum is an image which I have tried to enrich as it returns in a dialectic form in the various books I have written. It constitutes for me an allegory of the culture, society and world in which we live. The content of this allegory is multiple and only with an analysis of the term in relation to the context in which it appears can one visualize exactly what it means. I don't think it is difficult. Museums are in the first case a symbol of an old society which retains old values, principally aesthetic ones, and enters into contradictions with modern ideas and with life and death.

In other cases museums are a symbol of exactly the opposite. They indicate the dream of crystallizing time and space. What attracts us when we enter a museum is exactly the fact that we are confronted by the most positive aspect of humanity: its creativity. In fact a picture always fixes a time and a space and at the same time it eliminates the anxiety which arises in man when in conflict with time, which means death, and with space. The crystallization involved in a work of art, a painting or a poem is a way of comforting, of protecting us from the essential anguish which is created by the sense that all is transitory, all is ephemeral. It has been very important to me to emphasize this element of museums. Because I believe that the fundamental drama of life, of personal existence, is the struggle against the ephemeral; we die but also die all the things around us. They are changing. The permanent process of life and death is a source of the anguish which, it would seem, the work of art manages to suppress by presenting us at the same time with something which is permanent. Be it in the words of a writing, the colours and shapes of a picture, or the sounds of a piece of music. The great merit of art is, banal though it sounds, that it triumphs over time, and finally over death.

In many of your stories one notices traces of cruelty and in those landscapes of surrealistic nightmares which you describe one senses a feeling of alienation, anxiety and persecution. Is this the reflection of your particular position, or is it also an expression of the predominant political situation in Latin America?

El museo de los esfuerzos inútiles, my last book of 1983, begins with a series of quotations among which there is one by the German poet Gottfried Benn which goes: "The category in which the universe manifests itself is that of hallucination." I was very happy to find this sentence, which expresses something I have felt during most of my life: hallucination, the paranoiac hallucination of persecution is a way of interpreting and understanding the world.

Your observations are very accurate. For me literature is a vision, a creation of symbols to interpret and understand reality. This reality is nightmarish not only for those political elements to which you refer and which exist in Latin America. Not only because, for instance, in Argentina thirty thousand people have disappeared and one out of five Uruguayans have suffered cruel torture and persecution, but also because when it is not the military, the totalitarian regime in power, who persecute us, there often remain our internal phantoms, our own hallucinations.

My literature is one of a disturbing and paranoic nature. I believe that paranoia is one of the most real ways of understanding the world. I remember an anecdote, which I will tell you. I have a friend in Uruguay who is a psychoanalyst. Once, when she was attending a paranoiac patient trying to convince him that life was not persecuting

267

him as much as he thought, six soldiers armed with machine-guns broke into her clinic to inspect her files. They lined up against the wall and handcuffed her patients and held her captive for various hours.

Paranoia is not just a fantasy. It often reflects the tension and the struggle of life. On the other hand my literature is generally symbolic. Therefore I often start by writing my own nocturnal nightmares. I believe that there are a few writers (and Kafka is one of them) who have succeeded to give literary form to their internal visions and fantasies, to that nightmarish world where all is symbol. I often start writing from my dreams knowing perfectly well that dreams are symbolic constructions whose task is to interpret reality. If the writer is a creator of symbols, man in his dreams is also one.

Psychoanalysis — for which I feel great respect — and literature are similar in this: both work with language trying to discover the meanings contained in language. I am well aware that these dreams, which are often a source of inspiration for a writer, are not the property of the individual. By this I mean that a large number of our nightmares are part of a collective unconscious. We dream what others have already dreamt years and centuries ago and we dream with the same fears that men have had, faced by a reality which pursues them. The theme of my stories is in fact fear. Fear of all forms of exterior life, fear of freedom, as well as the fear which produces in us the daily acts of aggression of the world. Be they spiritual or concrete. I think that this fear exists in all of us in different forms. At times it takes the appearance of euphoria, at other times it is simply the horror of death. Finally, it is fear of the rest of the humanity which appears to consist of potential aggressors and persecutors.

You have been away from Uruguay a long time, some twelve years. Do you miss it and do you miss your own people?

Exile is always a form of tearing oneself away, a loss, a

breakage. In this sense I think it is the final experience in which one's whole identity crashes. When I arrived in Barcelona in '72 I was 30, had published five books in Uruguay and so was relatively known in my country. Besides I had a career, I was professor of literature, had a circle of friends and ample contacts within the context in which I lived. The change was a violent uprooting and therefore had consequences which I could not foresee. I was living in Barcelona but of course I was merely existing there.

What we must realize when talking of exile is that we have to start living afresh, being in a place where nobody can name us, in a place where nobody knows us. Identity is to have a name in relation to others. To exist for the rest of the people, to see that their look reflects us, recognizes us. Exile is to lose this context, this look which others give us, and therefore exile sets a challenge. We have to be reborn in a place where nobody knows us yet and can share our past. All those things which until then had been part of our identity. I believe that this challenge puts in question the whole of our personality.

The first years of exile are the most dramatic. One's heart and emotion are elsewhere. One becomes a ghost. One has stopped existing for one's country and for the people with whom one was living and one is still not in the place to which one has arrived. This ghost-like existence of being in exile makes us less real even in front of ourselves. The city we left appears in our dreams, in our nightmares, yet we still do not know the city to which we have come. All this causes anguish, but also makes for deep reflection. I believe that all those who have lived in exile can talk of the grief, terror and separation of their experience.

At the same time, one can talk of the stimulus, painful though it may be, created by having to live suddenly at the age of 30-35 in a place where we have no past, only a present (because often we don't even have a future). For me Montevideo has become a city remote in time and space. I am completely aware that the Montevideo I knew and where I lived the first thirty years of my life no longer exists. The present Montevideo is another. Twelve years have elapsed during which I have not been there and in which the city did not exist except as a memory for me. My main fear, in fact, is to feel a stranger the day when I return to Montevideo, even if it is only for a visit. I prefer to feel a stranger in a country where I know I am a stranger because I know I was not born there.

I believe that the exile is victim of certain fantasies. One is that of time: the exile lives in an unreal time which is static. It is the time in which she left her country. This staticness, immobility of time, is like a delirium. It is also a delirium of space. The exile mentally lives in a geographic space which is not the city to which she has come to live but the one in which she has lived her fundamental experience, the one which she has left behind. These two deliriums of time and space provoke that permanent sensation of unreality, of floating, which the exile feels.

I have understood in a very dramatic way that exile is something more than leaving one's country, being torn away from the place of one's birth. It is a great metaphor of the human condition. We have been exiled from almost everything. We have lost childhood, innocence, friends, loves. Above all for me to be exiled symbolizes that space in which writers, those who interest me anyway, write. The writer is the person who looks on from a certain distance (which of course does not at all imply lack of emotion), the distance which is the one of the person who observes and judges. In other words I mean that the writer is the person who entirely complies with the sentiments of Adamow, who said that the duty of the writer is to describe the horror of the time in which he has had to live. I think that this defines perfectly the condition of the writer. She is an exile because not only she "suffers" the time in which she has to live, but also because she has to create a space, a distance which will allow her to reflect the time in which she has to live.

In your work there are many allusions to sex and to love but they are almost always of a rather bitter nature. I am thinking for instance of how you describe the deterioration of a love relationship when the two lovers are incapable of ending it, and also of the destructive element present in a situation in which two people are compelled to be together for life. A character of one of your stories says: "We have the sex that they impose upon us; at the most we accept it." Do you think that your attitude is in part a consequence of the sexual conventions and of the stereotypes which society forces upon us?

First of all I would like to say that there certainly are many references to love in my books and in particular in my poems. I don't, however, think that in most cases the destructive aggressive element of love is what I have emphasized, on the contrary.

There is a book which you will of course not know, a book which I published in Uruguay in 1971 and which is now out of print and forbidden. It is a book of poems called *Evohe. Evohe*, as you might know, is a Greek word transferred into Spanish. It is a call of the Bacchantes during Dionysiac ceremonies. I was in fact writing a book which I would describe as dionysiac. It is a book about the pleasure of love, in which I celebrate the joy of the human body. It belongs to my youth, it is an erotic book, in fact its other title is *Erotic Poems*. In it I compare the pleasure of physical love to the sensual pleasure which the use of words gives to the writer and to the reader of poetry.

Erotic action and the action of writing hold for me something in common which is the ludic element. The element of play. In the same way in which a body has density, colour, light and shape, so words have texture, density, and there are bodies which I love and words which I love in the same way in which there are bodies and words which repel me. Eroticism is very similar to the creating activity.

This is however only one of the aspects of love. It is true that

271

in other texts (and you refer particularly to the story "Punto Final" in my last collection) I have accentuated the destructive element of love, because love is not only one thing. It is sensual pleasure, communication, but it is also a terrible struggle between two identities which lose their individualities and enter into conflict. The only way out of this situation is the survival of one of the two. This double-headed monster, as at times married couples have been described, implies the fight between two individuals in a state of osmosis and it implies also the predominance and the power of one or the other.

It is true also that our concepts of love are historic and therefore reflect the ideology of social and sexual classifications. In Latin America they have almost excessively caricatured the element of power in heterosexual couples.

Power relations are always ambivalent. This I wish to point out because between the master and the slave one finds multiple types of relationship where sometimes power is not total but partial. At times slavery possesses the expedients of power so that I would not want in any case to fall into the category which affirms that heterosexual relationships in Latin America are purely relations of power. It is true that these relationships are that of the master and the maid. But it is also certain that they are subject to all the contradictions which are proper of any struggle for power. In this sense I think that when I describe the destructive element of love, I refer fundamentally to the appearance. That is, in many cases, love relationships, so-called love relationships, enclose other elements which are not specifically of love. For example, envy; power provokes envy and envy leads in many cases to attitudes which are not just, which betray and therefore destroy. Love is not, or hardly ever is, Christian love based on compassion such as a whole tradition has assumed throughout the centuries. Love is often destruction, fight and triumph on one side and defeat on the other.

As for sex, I believe we do have the sex which is socially

imposed upon us, first by our parents and next by society. Sex for me is not the simple result of biological elements and of genetic characteristics. These genetic characteristics impose a social role (and this in Latin America is felt in very strong terms), a social role which is almost always an imposition on our sentiments and on our free behaviour. In this sense we don't have the sex we would like to have for in many cases this would be a multiple sex. And in this sense I am convinced that to limit this multiple sex to one sex only involves a limitation of our freedom. Of course I understand the social reasons for this limitation but I also believe that they are a source of neurosis and of pathological conditions. If only we could all have various sexes and use them at liberty without society feeling attacked and upheaved by this!

What do you think of the role of women? In your poems woman is described as "filling the world" but at the same time as "looking and destroying". Perhaps it is not fair to take sentences out of their context. What seems to be most relevant at this point is your poem which says: "You are here as the result of twenty centuries of predestination in which men of the past made you so in order to love you according to their needs and their rules, and this tradition, though injust and offensive, is not after all the least of your attractions." The end of this poem is for me very interesting because it turns an argument which could be feminist in a banal way into something much more thoughtful, complex and ambiguous.

Talking of women's role and also of men's role, I think that the problem is to have a specific role generally imposed on us by our education, tradition and by the people around us. What is terrible about roles is that they limit our freedom of choice and even our freedom to make mistakes, to misunderstand ourselves. Therefore I rebel against traditional roles both in my personal life and in my writing, which means that I have to break away from the conditioning of society which sets definite and predetermined ways both for men and women.

I believe that just as it would be better if we had various sexes during the course of our life and if we could enjoy them all, it would also be better for each of us to elect our role. This would not have to be predetermined and unchangeable and above all would not be a role imposed in social or historical terms by the functions which we have to perform in society.

It is true that I have played extensively in my poems with the role traditionally attributed to women particularly in the field of literature and art. It is a role full of ambiguities from the poetry of the troubadours to the portraits of the Renaissance. The way of presenting women has always been complex and contradictory. On one hand, woman has been turned into an object of veneration, into a myth. On the other hand she has been sold and prostituted. By tradition woman has played different and multiple parts. We all write by this tradition and base ourselves on the dialectical interplay with it.

Woman in my poems and in my books is made up of many, not just one. I often place myself in the position of those who look at her and watch her birth and are fascinated by the multiple aspects within one person. Ambiguity, which is for me a source of poetry, is also a source of love and therefore, perhaps, in some of my poems the image of woman is not only based on the aspects which previous poets have given her, but also undergoes a process of mythification, counterbalanced by a vision which is ironic up to a point and also critical of woman.

What I am sure of is that each woman must look for the role which corresponds to her in each individual stage of her life and must not yield to the conditioning to which society submits her because of tradition or because of man's needs. This role must at once be highly flexible and must be able to evolve constantly.

RECOMMENDED FURTHER READING

AFRICA

Barnett, Ursula A. 1983, *A Vision of Order, A Study of Black South African Literature in English (1914-1980)*, London, Sinclair Browne/University of Massachusetts Press, Amherst.

Bruner, Charlotte H. (ed.), 1983, *Unwinding Threads. Writing by Women in Africa* (short stories), London, Heinemann.

Cutrufelli, Maria Rosa, 1983, *Women in Africa. Roots of Oppression*, London, Zed Press.

Finnegan, Ruth, 1970, *Oral Literature in Africa*, Oxford, Clarendon Press.

Obiechina, Emmanuel, 1975, *Culture, Tradition and Society in the West African Novel*, Cambridge University Press.

Schild, Ulla (ed.), 1980, *The East African Experience. Essays on English and Swahili Literature*, Berlin, Dietrich Reimer Verlag.

Schipper, Mineke, 1982, *Theatre and Society in Africa*, Johannesburg, Ravan Press.

Taiwo, Oladele, *Female Novelists of Modern Africa*, London, Macmillan.

ARAB WORLD

Allen, Roger, 1982, *The Arabic Novel: an Historical and Critical Introduction*, University of Manchester Press.

Altona, S. J. *et al.* (eds)., 1982, *Arabic Literature in North Africa: Critical Essays and Annotated Bibliography*, Cambridge, Mass.

Brugman, J., 1984, *An Introduction to the History of Modern Arabic Literature in Egypt*, Leiden, Brill.

Déjeux, Jean, 1973, *Littérature maghrébine de langue française*, Ottawa, Naaman.

Fernea, Elisabeth W., and Basima Q. Bezirgan (eds.), 1977, *Middle Eastern Muslim Women Speak*, Austin/London, University of Texas Press.

Gaudio, Attilio, and René Pelletier, 1980, *Femmes d'Islam ou le sexe interdit*, Paris, Denoel.

Kamal, Boullata (ed. with transl.), 1978, *Women of the Fertile Crescent*, Washington D.C., Three Continents Press.

Kilpatrick, Hilary, 1974, *The Modern Egyptian Novel. A Study in Social Criticism*, London, St Antony's Middle East Monograph.

ASIA

Casper, Leonard, 1966, *New Writings from the Philippines. A Critique and Anthology*, Syracuse, N.Y., Syracuse University Press.

Farooki, Nasir Ahmad (ed.), 1955, *Pakistani Short Stories*, Karachi/Lahore/Peshawar.

Kripalani, Krishna, 1968, *Modern Indian Literature. A Panoramic Glimpse*, Bombay.

Li Cuan Siu, 1975, *An Introduction to the Promotion and Development of Modern Malay Literature (1942-1962)*, Yogyakarta, Yayasan Kanisius.

Narasimhaiah, C.D. (ed.), 1970, *Indian Literature of the Past Fifty Years*, Mysore, University of Mysore.

Obeyasekere, Ranjini, and Chitra Fernando (eds.), 1981, *An Anthology of Modern Writing from Sri Lanka*, University of Arizona Press.

Sahitya Akademi (ed.), 1982[3], *Contemporary Indian Short Stories*, I and II, New Delhi.

Teeuw, A., 1979, *Modern Indonesian Literature*, I and II, The Hague, Martinus Nijhof.

CARIBBEAN

Herdeck, D.E. *et al.*, 1983, *Caribbean Writers: A Bio-

Bibliographical Critical Encyclopedia, Washington D.C., Three Continents Press.

Ramchand, Kenneth, (1970) 1983, *The West Indian Novel and Its Background,* London, Heinemann.

Salkey, Andrew (ed.), 1977, *Writing in Cuba Since the Revolution,* London, Bogle L'Ouverture Publications.

Smart, Ian, 1984, *West Indian Writers from Central America,* Washington D.C., Three Continents Press.

Viajeras al Caribe (selected and introduced by Nara Araújo), Havana, Casa de las Américas.

Voorhoeve, Jan, and Ursy Lichtveld, 1975, *Creole Drum. An Anthology of Creole Literature,* with trans. by V.A. February, New Haven, Yale University Press.

Warner, Keith Q. (ed.), *Critical Perspectives on Caribbean Literature in French,* Washington D.C., Three Continents Press.

LATIN AMERICA

Bastide, Roger (ed.), 1974, *La femme de couleur en Amérique latine,* Paris, Editions Anthropos.

Lavrin, Asunción, 1978, *Latin American Women: Historic Perspectives,* Wesport/London.

Lindstrom, Naomi, 1984, *Woman's Voice in Latin American Literature,* Washington D.C., Three Continents Press.

Miller, Yvette E. and Charles M. Tatum, 1977, *Latin American Women Writers: Yesterday and Today,* Pittsburgh, Latin American Literary Review.

Pescatello, Ann, 1973, *Female and Male in Latin America,* Pittsburgh.

Rosenbaum, Sidonia, 1945, *Modern Women Poets of Spanish America,* New York.

Terry, Edward D. (ed.), 1969, *Artists and Writers in the Evolution of Latin America,* Alabama, University of Alabama Press.

Young, Ann, 1984, *The Image of Black Women in 20th-Century South American Literature,* Washington D.C., Three Continents Press.

ABOUT THE CONTRIBUTORS

Sanjukta Gupta studied Sanskrit at the University of Calcutta (M.A. 1952), and did research work at the Visvab-Harati University in Santiniketan, West Bengal, where she received her doctorate in Indian philosophy (1959). From 1960 on she taught Sanskrit at the Jadavput University in Calcutta and since 1967 she has been on the staff of the Institute for Oriental Languages and Cultures of the University of Utrecht, the Netherlands, as senior lecturer in Indian literature and religion. There she obtained a second doctorate in Indian religion. She has published several books on Indian philosophy and religious studies, among them *Laksmi Tantra: A Pancaratra Text* (Brill, Leiden, 1972) and *Hindu Tantra* (Series: Handbuch der Orientalistik; Brill, Leiden, 1979).

Tineke Hellwig was born in 1957 in Surabaja, Indonesia. She studied Indonesian language and literature at the University of Leiden, the Netherlands, as well as women's studies and cultural anthropology. In 1980 and 1981 she attended lectures at the Institut Keguruan dan Ilmu Pendidikan in Malang, Indonesia, where she collected material for her thesis on the woman writer Nh. Dini. Since 1983 she has taught Indonesian at the University of Utrecht, and she is preparing her Ph.D. on the image of women in modern Indonesian novels.

Flora van Houwelingen studied French language and literature and literary theory at the University of Amsterdam. She is involved in research which centres on the Francophone literature of the Maghreb, as seen from a female perspective. As an active member of lesbian organizations in the Netherlands and abroad, she collects and analyses data on the condition of lesbian women in North Africa. In addition, she teaches French conversation to young Moroccans in Amsterdam, is a member of the Project Group Feminist Studies (Greece), and is the Dutch contact of the Institute for Mediterranean Women's Studies (Kegme) in Athens.

Psiche Bertini Hughes studied classics at the Universitá di San Marco in Florence and later Italian, Spanish and Classics at the University of London, where she received her doctorate for a dissertation on Latin American literature. Having taught in secondary school for several years, she joined the City College of Literature in London as lecturer in Latin American and Spanish literature. Since 1981 she has also been teaching Latin American literature at the University of London (Extramural Department). She has published a number of articles on Latin American literature and is presently working on *A Dictionary of J.L. Borges*.

Hilary Kilpatrick read Arabic language and literature at Oxford and her 1971 dissertation was later published under the title *Social Criticism in the Modern Egyptian Novel* (Cambridge, 1974). She taught Arabic at the University of St Andrews, Scotland, wrote radio programmes for the Arabic Department of the BBC, and has lived in both Egypt and Lebanon. Since 1977 she has been senior lecturer in Arabic literature at the TCMO (Institute for Middle East Language and Culture) in Nijmegen, the Netherlands. Her English translation of Ghassan Kanafani's novel appeared under the title *Men in the Sun* (Arab Authors Series, Heinemann, London, 1978). She regularly publishes on modern and classic Arab literature.

Ineke Phaf was born in 1946. She studied Spanish and South American literature in Leiden and Berlin, and sociology at the University of Amsterdam. She has published a number of articles in the field of Caribbean and Latin American literature and recently received her doctorate from the Free University of Berlin; her dissertation is entitled *Havanna als Standort (Standortgebundenheit und städtische Perspektive im kubanischen*

Roman, 1959-1980). At present she is engaged in research on the sociology of the literature of Latin America at the Latin America Institute of the Free University of Berlin.

Mineke Schipper studied French language and literature in Amsterdam and literary theory in Utrecht. From 1964 to 1972 she taught at the Université Nationale du Zaïre and received her doctorate from the Free University of Amsterdam in 1973. Her dissertation was entitled *Le blanc et l'occident au miroir du roman négro-africain* (Amsterdam/Assen, 1973). She teaches literary theory and intercultural comparative literature at the Free University of Amsterdam. In the field of African literature she has published a number of books, among them *Le blanc vu d'Afrique* (Yaoundé, Editions CLE, 1973) and *Theâtre et société en Afrique* (Dakar, Nouvelles Editions Africaines, 1985).

Lourina de Voogd studied Arabic and Turkish at the universities of Leiden and Utrecht. She has written extensively on Moroccan literature and Arabic juvenile literature, and has translated works of Arabic authors. Her "Bibliography of Modern Moroccan Arabic Literature" appeared in the *Journal of Arabic Literature*, XIII. For many years she was involved in education programmes for women from other cultures. At the moment she is on the staff of the Dutch Centre for Public Libraries and Literature in The Hague, where she is involved in the preparation of foreign-language collections and the special training of librarians.

INDEX